SHEKHINAH/SPIRIT

Studies in
Judaism and Christianity

Exploration of Issues in the
Contemporary Dialogue Between
Christians and Jews

Editor in Chief for
Stimulus Books
Helga Croner

Editors
Lawrence Boadt, C.S.P.
Helga Croner
Leon Klenicki
John Koenig
Kevin A. Lynch, C.S.P.

 A STIMULUS BOOK

SHEKHINAH/SPIRIT

Divine Presence in
Jewish and Christian Religion

by
Michael E. Lodahl

A STIMULUS BOOK
PAULIST PRESS ◆ NEW YORK ◆ MAHWAH

3/93

Library of Congress Cataloging-in-Publication Data

Lodahl, Michael E., 1955–
    Shekhinah/spirit: divine presence in Jewish and Christian
religion/by Michael E. Lodahl.
        p.   cm.—(Studies in Judaism and Christianity) (Stimulus
book)
    Includes bibliographical references and index.
    ISBN 0-8091-3311-3
    1. Holy Spirit.   2. Presence of God.   3. Process theology.
4. Christianity and other religions—Judaism.   5. Judaism—
Relations—Christianity.   I. Title.   II. Series.
BT121.2.L63   1992
231′.3—dc20   92-5525
                                                                                        CIP

Published by Paulist Press
997 Macarthur Boulevard
Mahwah, N.J. 07430

Printed and bound in the United States of America

c.1

Contents

Introduction

It used to be the theological fashion for anyone writing on the doctrine of the Holy Spirit to begin by bemoaning the comparative lack of attention given to the subject. The fact that so many books and articles in the past two decades have begun with just such an observation already suggests that this silence is no longer the case. It simply is no longer true, or certainly less true than once it was, that pneumatology is a forgotten doctrine in Christian theology.

Why, then, another work on the Holy Spirit? There are three distinctive reasons for this particular pneumatology. *First,* it is a *process* pneumatology, i.e., an approach to understanding the doctrine of the Holy Spirit by way of the language and concepts of process philosophers and theologians, all of whom, in different ways and to varying degrees, gain inspiration from the writings of Alfred North Whitehead (1861–1947). While process theologians such as John Cobb, David Griffin, Will Beardslee, Norman Pittenger, Bernard Lee and Marjorie Suchocki, among others, have addressed and creatively reinterpreted many important Christian doctrines,[1] the work in process pneumatology yet remains rather scant. Pittenger, in his 1974 volume *The Holy Spirit,* has offered a brief and highly readable rendering of the doctrine of the Holy Spirit from the broadly processive perspective which characterizes all of his writings. But Pittinger's little book, two doctoral dissertations,[2] and an occasional essay or two[3] comprise the whole of the work done to date. Taken together, it is insufficient.

Further, it has been convincingly argued that within what is known generally as "process theology" two variant movements may be discerned, both with legitimate claims to Whiteheadian origin: (1) the "rationalist" movement, which hails especially from Whitehead's *Process and Reality,* is strained through his successor Charles Hartshorne's revival of the ontological argument for God's existence, and finds expression in the writings of, for example, Griffin, Cobb, Beardslee, Suchocki, Lewis Ford, Schubert Ogden and Delwin Brown; and (2) the "empirical" movement, which draws on Whitehead's empirical concerns and, reading him through William James and John Dewey, is represented in the writings of Henry Nelson Wieman, Bernard Loomer, Bernard Meland, Daniel Day Williams and, presently, of William Dean, Nancy Frankenberry, Bernard Lee and others.[4] Thus Hartshorne and Wieman, who were colleagues at the University of Chicago through the third and fourth decades of this century, are understood as successors of Whitehead who carried forth his thought on the divergent paths of rationalistic and radically empirical process theologies.

But there are undoubtedly many cross-paths. It would be misleading to suggest that there is some clear-cut line dividing these two streams, or that any one of these thinkers is purely rationalistic or empirical. There is plenty of overlap between the two groups and, as Cobb has written, "Every rationalist begins with experience, and every empiricist employs reason in his treatment of the empirical data."[5] Certainly in the following process pneumatology, I will happily give attention to process theologians of both sorts, particularly in my attempt to suggest the fundamental way in which God is experienced as "present" to the world, and to human beings especially. Nonetheless, my concern is to move within the tenor of the empirical theologians, with whom I feel a deep affinity. That tenor might best be adumbrated through the following characteristics suggested by Bernard Lee:

> . . . a keen sense of the limitations of both reason and language . . . less of a focus upon the sure and the certain, and more upon the probable and the ambiguous . . . an affinity for the temporal, perhaps even for the temporary . . . a strong sensitivity to the processes of resistance, to sin and evil . . . an abiding suspicion of abstraction whenever its derivation cannot be located somewhere in concrete experience . . . [and] the theme of relationality . . . far more to the fore than that of becoming.[6]

It should be clear that the sort of empiricism I am interested in is not a reductionistic approach to human experience. Rather, it involves a sense of wonder and mystery in the midst of life's vicissitudes, a felt conviction that lived human experience is "more than we can think" (Meland), a kind of "thinking with the body" (Moltmann). The notion of "spirit," whether used to point to the elusive mystery of God in the midst of human life, or to the depths of human experience, is, I believe, a helpful category for such a theological orientation. And it is arguable that it shares much with the "feel" of Hebraic thinking about God.

William Dean, whose book *American Religious Empiricism* is a sustained attempt to isolate and describe this empirical tenor in theology, and to argue its palatability with deconstructionists like Richard Rorty and Jacques Derrida, has offered an even briefer characterization of this approach: "history and its religious burden," issuing in the direction of an interpretive religious historicism.[7] Such an historicism understands religious faith to be composed of layer upon layer of communal interpretation (and continual reinterpretation) of historical events—which *become* "historical events" *for us*, in fact, only through becoming incorporated into the religious community's process of interpretation. The use of the word "process" here is not coincidental; I understand empirical process theology to be concerned primarily with the processes of interpretation by which human beings strive to create a meaningfully ordered world out of the potential chaos of an individual's or community's experiential flux. Suffice it to say that the sparse work done in process pneumatology to this point has drawn far more from the rationalist stream than from the empirical. I believe there is, therefore, an opportunity to break new ground in working empirically, and so essentially hermeneutically, from the notion of God as Spirit toward a new and constructive apprehension of Christian faith and practice.

Second, this is specifically a process *pneumatology,* an attempt primarily to understand God as Spirit, and *not* primarily an essay in trinitarian doctrine. Thus, we will approach pneumatology not as discourse about the "Third Person of the Holy Trinity," but rather as discourse about God in relatedness to the world. "Spirit," for me, does not signify primarily one of three distinct persons or hypostases in the Godhead, nor even a description of the divine nature or being, but *a way of talking about God as "near" or in active relation to creation, and especially to humanity.* I will suggest in what follows, in fact, that "Father," while differently nuanced, is, like "Spirit," a metaphor of relatedness which refers to the living God, and that "Son" is Christian faith's metaphoric description of the man Jesus in filial relationship and obedience to God. Thus, the sonship of Jesus will in what follows be understood first in historical and ethical, rather than metaphysical, categories.

In assuming this position, I have both theological foils and friends. My primary foils are Christian theologians who adopt the social analogy in their trinitarian deliberations and thereby verge upon, and at times fall into, tritheism.[8] In contrast, a best friend in this regard is Geoffrey Lampe, who in his 1977 publication *God as Spirit* argued convincingly that "Spirit" refers essentially to "God: God experienced as inspiring, motivating, empowering, vivifying, indwelling, and acting in many ways which are . . . recognized by faith as modes of the personal active presence of God."[9]

Certainly the implications of this understanding of God for the traditional doctrine of the Trinity are challenging, and while these merit a whole other book, I present at least some rudimentary reflections in these pages. Stated in traditional terms, to explore what has traditionally been called the "immanent" or "essential" trinity, i.e., to attempt to express the inner relations among Father. Son and Spirit, or the eternal logic of "threefoldness" within the Godhead, is not within my purview. To do so would, obviously, transgress the stated commitment to a broadly empirical methodology. Not the inner life of deity, but rather what can be said about God on the basis of what have been interpreted to be God's actions in history, will concern us.

Again in traditional terms: I favor the notion of an "economic" trinity—God as perceived in the history of salvation as Creator, Redeemer, and Sanctifier—as the only trinity there is. From the perspective of a religious historicism, it is particulars such as *ruach,* covenant, Israel and its living God, and a Jew named Jesus which are foundational for this attempt at pneumatological reconstruction; conversely, the abstract theologic of the "Blessed Trinity" or the inner relations of Father, Son and Holy Spirit are not.

Such considerations as these already reflect the *third,* and undoubtedly most critical, factor in this pneumatology: its *foundation in Jewish-Christian conversation.* Thus, the most decisive justification for what follows is that it is written from within the context of the lively Jewish-Christian conversation currently taking place in the larger conversation which theology is. It is my conviction that the encounter of Synagogue and Church is one of the most urgent items on the Christian theological agenda today. Most of the theological work in this area has, for good and obvious reasons, focused upon Christology. And while this book includes a rudimentary chapter on that subject, my overall orientation is to approach selected issues of Jewish-Christian conversation from the perspective and concerns of pneumatology.

The consonance of this third distinctive factor with the first two should be explained. First, in regard to the process-relational methodology of religious empiricism, Dean argues that this theological approach, while distinctively American, is rooted deeply in the Hebrew scriptures and in the historical process by which those scriptures emerged as authoritative for particular Jewish religious communities.[10] Hence, it follows that this theological orientation may well provide a way of interpreting Christian faith which will more readily uncover its Jewish roots. Second, in the present attempt to perceive God as Spirit, and in that context to suggest the outlines of a Spirit Christology, an important motive is my desire to cherish and to protect for Christian faith the Hebrew heritage of monotheism.

Beyond these considerations, the theologian who writes out of a Jewish-Christian conversational context recognizes that such reflection must occur at the precarious edge of the historical abyss called the Holocaust. Indeed, no sustained theological encounter occurs between serious Jews and Christians that does not, at some point, move to the issues and questions raised by the Holocaust. I believe, further, that *no* responsible Christian theologian can dismiss as irrelevant to theological inquiry the Nazis' sickeningly methodical destruction of nearly six million Jews in our own century. This nightmarish eruption of the twentieth century is even more compelling in the case of an empirical theology, in which attentiveness to historical events, and their possible religious interpretations, is primary.

It has become almost a truism of Jewish-Christian conversation that the Holocaust presents a monumental challenge to both Jewish and Christian theologians. Some of its questions they share in common, others address themselves uniquely to the theologians' respective traditions. Either way, those questions loom large, and we in the Christian tradition especially have barely begun the difficult task of constructing an adequate, intentionally post-Holocaust theology. J. B. Metz and David Tracy, among others, have argued that every Christian statement or doctrine must undergo revision after the Holocaust. Their challenge will be continually operative in the following work, which is offered as a contribution to this task, and specifically as a reconstruction of the doctrine of the Holy Spirit "after Auschwitz."

For example, Christians traditionally have spoken of the Spirit in terms of God's power and presence; but how, if at all, can divine power and presence be discerned in the camps, or in the "special actions" of the **Einsatzgruppen**? And what of the traditional responses to human suffering—whether Christian or Jewish, whether rabbinic or rationalist or mystical? Does the Holocaust render them all wholly inadequate and pathetic? Many process theologians have claimed that Whitehead's system provides key insights, if not a viable solution, for the problem of evil.[11] How well do those claims stand up at the edge of pits filled with bleeding or burning corpses? Indeed, can an empirical process pneumatology offer any reply to the question of radical evil, paradigmatically raised in our century by the Holocaust? When theology is risked at the edge of the abyss called Holocaust, one must allow many of its sentences to end with question marks. I would not pretend to offer comprehensive answers in the present work; I only hope to allow the questions to have their way in the text.

The questions, of course, become even more pointed and painful when one admits and assesses the complicity of Christianity in the horror. Roy Eckardt, Franklin Littell and Rosemary Radford Ruether, and among process thinkers Clark Williamson, have been pioneers in this regard. They have argued that, relatively early in the Church's history, the apostles' ambivalence concerning Judaism grew into a venerable **adversus Judaeos** tradition which was finally to help pave the way for the Nazis' secularized anti-Semitism. This has all been well rehearsed, and the calls have been many to reformulate Christian doctrine and preaching so as to undo anti-Judaism. Most of the attention to this point has been focused on Christology.[12] I intend to show in this work, however, that most traditional Christian pneumatology, closely connected as it is with Christology, has also shared in the anti-Judaic bias. One of the central arguments of this book, in fact, is that as long as the Holy Spirit is considered to be either (**1**) a function or result of the event of Jesus, rather than its ground and source, or (**2**) at work solely within the context of the Church, Christian triumphalism regarding Judaism and every other non-Christian people, culture, or religious faith will continue.

This, then, is a process pneumatology founded in Jewish-Christian conversation. The usual word is "dialogue." But I find the word "dialogue," however noble its connotations within a Buberian framework, to be overused to the point of wearing out. "Jewish-Christian dialogue," especially, is a stilted and tired cliché. It is used so often and so freely that it means almost anything and therefore virtually nothing; it generally conjures images of prescribed meetings where we amicably tell one another how much we have in common. In addition, because of its frequent usage in connection with Buber's I-Thou orientation, it suggests a "duologue" between two persons—an I and a Thou. On the other hand, the word "conversation" suggests to me an informal, open, verbal interaction in which anyone may join.[13] And where "dialogue" may lend a sense of two dialogic positions, e.g., "the Christian viewpoint and the Jewish viewpoint," "conversation" opens for me a greater recognition of the pluralism which lurks *within* any supposedly monolithic religious orientation. In the Jewish-Christian conversation out of which this book arises, the aim has been to keep the interaction as open as possible and to celebrate the plurality of voices, particularly Jewish voices, from whom I as a Christian theologian have learned: the many voices of the biblical authors; the tangled and sometimes confusing and convoluted paths of the rabbinic writings; the mystical commentaries of Moses de Leon and Isaac Luria; Buber's existential, neo-Hasidic philosophy of dialogue; the deconstructive readings of Derrida and Harold Bloom, which gain as much impetus from the kabbala as did Buber's thought; and the intentionally post-*tremendum* ruminations of Arthur Cohen and Emil Fackenheim. In this open conversation there is one item for which we should listen most closely: *how Jewish thinkers have spoken of the presence, or indeed the absence, of God in human history, particularly in the ruptures of history signaled by radical evil and senseless suffering.* One of the traditional terms for speaking of such a presence, particularly as a certain exiled presence, is "Shekhinah." My experience has been that such careful listening is invaluable in formulating a process-relational Christian doctrine of the Spirit.

To be sure, any attempt to write on pneumatology must be chastened by a deep sense of the unfathomable, uncontrollable mystery surrounding human intimations and interpretations of the Spirit. The Spirit, we read in John's gospel, is like the wind: one does not know whence it comes or whither it goes, and one would not know it was there if its effects were not seen and heard (3:8). It cannot be caught or boxed in. Yet its presence can be as horribly evident as the stormy gust which in its fury uproots trees and destroys homes—or it can be as quiet and subtle as the gentle caress of a spring breeze upon one's cheek. "The wind blows where it wishes," and so it is with the Spirit of God. Thus, what is true about all theology seems particularly true about pneumatology: nobody can write the definitive work. Certainly such a disclaimer holds true here. And with a healthy recognition of the elusiveness of divine presence, even what I do offer here is hardly more than a "thought experiment." The rabbis employed a very simple phrase in their writings, **k'b'yakhol,** meaning "as it were" or "so to speak," to remind themselves and their readers not to take literally, or even too seriously, their all-too-human words and ideas about God.

Christian theologians, too, need to learn to say "as it were," not only to keep themselves humble regarding the "fallible forms and symbols" (Meland) which they employ, but also to liberate themselves toward a deeper sense of risk and imagination in their God-talk. In this regard, I think it would not be inappropriate to characterize the present work as a **k'b'yak-hol** pneumatology.

This study in the doctrine of the Holy Spirit revolves around three interrelated problems, all approached from within the context of Jewish-Christian conversation: exclusivism, evil and eschatology. Hence, it is divided into Parts I, II and III, with each part containing two chapters.

In Chapter 1 I argue that the traditional Christian approach to pneumatology has participated in, and contributed to, the Church's exclusivist claim to be the sole community bearing the presence of God's Spirit. I try to show also how this claim has had particularly disastrous consequences for the people and faith of Israel. Chapter 2, then, represents a reply to the problem as outlined in Chapter 1, for it offers a way of taking seriously the history of Jewish interpretations of the divine Spirit as the proper context for formulating Christian pneumatology. A process-relational understanding of God and creation, which is assumed throughout, is in Chapter 2 specifically explicated as the basis for a reconstruction of the doctrine of the Holy Spirit. In many ways that chapter provides the key argument of the entire work.

In Chapter 3 I continue to appropriate Jewish insights into the mode and activity of God's presence in creation, looking specifically to the work of the medieval kabbalists Moses de Leon and Isaac Luria. I believe they are important because of the ways in which they incorporate a serious attention to evil into their ideas about God, creation and humanity's role in redemption. Their deliberations provide the foundation for Chapter 4, which is an attempt to write pneumatology as it comes into contact with, and is transformed by, the problem of evil. As mentioned earlier, I believe that both the quality and the quantity of extreme and senseless human suffering in the Holocaust have made it a paradigmatic evil of our century. Chapter 4 attempts to ask, then, whether and how God was present in the Holocaust. It cannot be considered an answer to Chapter 3 in the way that Chapter 2 is an answer to Chapter 1. For when it is the unimaginable suffering and senseless death of fellow human beings that is under theological consideration, it seems more appropriate to allow the questions to be raised in all their radicality than confidently to provide answers to them all. I have in Chapter 4 drawn upon the writings of Martin Buber,

Emil Fackenheim and Arthur Cohen to help me hear those questions more clearly.

In Chapter 5, through an imaginative reading of selected gospel narratives, I present the outlines of an intentionally post-Holocaust Spirit Christology. Because the problem of Part III is eschatology, Chapter 5 can also be characterized as a Christology which is in tension with traditional eschatological estimations of Jesus' significance. But a pneumatology which is responsive to the Christian tradition cannot ignore the eschatological framework which shaped not only the Church's doctrine of Christ, but also its doctrine of the Holy Spirit from the very beginning. Thus, Chapter 6 provides a reply in the form of a reinterpreted eschatology which takes seriously what I believe to be God's intentions in the divine activities of creation and covenant-making.

The three problems are not isolated. Parts I and III are related in that Christian exclusivism is based largely in the early Church's eschatological claims for Jesus, and for itself as the eschatological community of the Spirit. Hence, any attempt to engage the problem of Christian exclusivism must inevitably deal with traditional Christianity's eschatological assumptions. Parts I and II are related in that much of the evil and suffering in the world is inflicted by human communities—whose ideologies often have taught them that they are superior—upon other human communities who are considered inferior, inhuman or even satanic. This means that many of the concerns normally addressed in theodicy are more adequately handled when shifted to "anthropodicy." Of course, within the context of this study, the historical contribution of the Church's **adversus Judaeos** tradition to the Nazi ideology concerning Jews is a prime example. Parts II and III are related in that eschatological hopes have always functioned, at least in part, as a response to the problem of unjust human suffering and death. And even as eschatology is reinterpreted in Chapter 6, it still is intended to offer a provisional reply, even if not the most comforting, to the problem of evil.

Both biblical and rabbinic writings are used extensively in the study. The biblical quotations are from the *New American Standard Bible.* Quotations from sources considered apocryphal by Protestant standards are from *The New English Bible.* I have maintained capitalizations of pronouns referring to deity only in quotations from these and any other resources utilized. More importantly, in the effort to liberate myself and others from the language of "Old Testament"/"New Testament," which reinforces triumphal Christian attitudes of displacement of the Jews as

God's covenant people, I have consistently used instead the phrases "Hebrew scriptures" and "Christian Testament."

There are four people whom I have had the honor to consider my teachers, without whose instruction and inspiration this work would not have been begun, let alone accomplished. David Blumenthal of Emory University first introduced me to the wonders of Jewish religious experience and reflection in a doctoral seminar on the Hasidic rebbe Levi Yitzhak, and thereby gave me access to a new world. His colleague at Emory, the late Jack Boozer, first challenged me to think about Christian faith and practice in the light, or rather the darkness, of the Holocaust. In addition, their efforts made it possible for me to study the Holocaust at the Yad Vashem Institute in Jerusalem during the month of July 1986. That study trip whetted my appetite for more; I spent the following month of January in Jerusalem again, this time as a fellow in the Center for Contemporary Theology at the Shalom Hartman Institute. There I was privileged to learn from Rabbi David Hartman, whose ideas about covenantal relationship continue to stimulate and shape my thinking. But that month was most blessed in that I was privileged to study under Paul van Buren, who has become, par excellence, my teacher. To these four, I say thank you.

NOTES

1. Consult bibliography for representative works.

2. G. Palmer Pardington III, *Spirit Incarnate: The Doctrine of the Holy Spirit in Relation to Process Philosophy* (Berkeley: The Graduate Theological Union, 1972); and Eleanor Pratzon Rae, *The Holy Spirit in Whiteheadian Process Theologians* (New York: Fordham University, 1984).

3. See, for example, Griffin, "Holy Spirit: Compassion and Reverence for Being," and Pardington, "The Holy Ghost is Dead—The Holy Spirit Lives," both of which are included in *Religious Experience and Process Theology,* a useful collection of articles edited by Bernard Lee and Harry James Cargas (New York: Paulist Press, 1976).

4. For descriptions and comparisons of these variant modes of process thought, see Larry E. Axel, "Process and Religion: The History of a Tradition at Chicago" (*Process Studies* Vol. 8, No. 4, pp. 231–239); Dean, "An American Theology" (*PS* Vol. 12, No. 2, pp. 111–128), and "Deconstruction and Process Theology" (*Journal of Religion* Vol. 64, Jan. 84, pp. 1–19); and Lee, "The Two Process Theologies" (*Theological Studies* 45, pp. 307–319). The single best brief history of the empirical movement remains Bernard Meland's "Introduction: The

Empirical Tradition in Theology at Chicago" in the book which he edited. *The Future of Empirical Theology* (The University of Chicago Press, 1969).

5. John Cobb, "What is Alive and What is Dead in Empirical Theology?" in Meland, ed., *The Future of Empirical Theology*, p. 96.

6. Lee, "The Two Process Theologies," pp. 315, 316.

7. Dean, *American Religious Empiricism* (Albany: State University of New York Press, 1986), p. xi.

8. Leonard Hodgson, Jurgen Moltmann and Catholic process thinker Joseph Bracken come immediately to mind.

9. Lampe, *God as Spirit* (London: SCM Press Ltd., 1977), p. 42.

10. "For many Hebrews [of the biblical era], then, what is real in the deepest sense is nothing but a sequence of evolving interpretations. . . . Reality is not composed of something static, whether divine or human, which could be doctrinally set forth. . . . Instead, the Hebrew community lives with a changing God, who interprets the Hebrews differently in different times. And the Hebrew community itself is a changing community, which interprets its nature, its history, and its God differently in different times. The ancient Hebrew community and its God lived in a relation of mutual interpretation. They lived in history, nothing more. There was no escape. . . . The subsequent 'canonization,' the closure of the canonizing process and the freezing of interpretations, represented a change in this original attitude." *American Religious Empiricism*, pp. 3, 4.

11. Griffin's *God, Power and Evil: A Process Theodicy* (Philadelphia: The Westminster Press, 1976) is the primary and the most thorough, though not the only, argument for process theodicy. For a process argument with radically different conclusions, see Jim Garrison's *The Darkness of God: Theology after Hiroshima* (Grand Rapids: Wm. B. Eerdman's Pub. Co., 1982).

12. Ruether helped get the Christological ball rolling with her claim in *Faith and Fratricide* (Minneapolis: The Seabury Press, 1974) that anti-Semitism is the left hand of Christology. *Anti-Semitism and the Foundations of Christianity* (New York: Paulist Press, 1979), edited by Alan T. Davies, is an uneven but helpful collection of essays intended to answer directly Ruether's often passionate indictments of the historic Church, including its Christological formulations. Other specifically Christological works arising out of Jewish-Christian conversation include Michael McGarry's *Christology after Auschwitz* (New York: Paulist Press, 1977) and Eugene Borowitz's *Contemporary Christologies: A Jewish Response* (New York: Paulist Press, 1980). In my opinion, though, no other Christian theologian has done Christology in this context with either the breadth or the depth of Paul van Buren (consult bibliography for relevant texts).

13. For some insightful observations about the nature of conversation, see David Tracy, *Plurality and Ambiguity* (San Francisco: Harper & Row, Publishers, 1987), pp. 18–23.

I. THE SPIRIT OF GOD AND THE PROBLEM OF EXCLUSIVISM

A Christian thinker repenting of
supersessionism can surely think theologically
about Jews only with Jews—and seek
the Holy Spirit only between himself
and his Jewish partners in dialogue.

Emil Fackenheim, *To Mend the World*

1. Christian Pneumatologies and Anti-Judaism

> Where the Church is, there is also the Spirit of God and where the Spirit of God is, there are also the Church and all grace. And the Spirit is truth.
> —Irenaeus

It would not be an overstatement to say that, in the predominant traditions of its reflection, the Church has followed this formulation of one of its greatest fathers. The Church usually has thought of itself as that religious community in which God's Holy Spirit dwells and labors in a unique if not exclusive way, instilling faith and actualizing grace in the hearts of Christian believers. And since the Spirit is indeed the Spirit of truth (Jn 14:17), the Church has been confident, too, that the indwelling Spirit was able also to lead it into all truth, guarding its theologians from error. Accordingly, the Spirit's presence in the Church was interpreted to mean that the Church was the locus of divine grace, divine truth and divine presence. Eventually, in fact, the Spirit became not only restricted to, but virtually identified with, the Church—as was the case in Schleiermacher's pneumatology.

The implications of such exclusivist tendencies in the Church's doctrine of the Holy Spirit are readily discernible. For example, not long ago, I shared with a theological colleague my intention to undertake a process-relational interpretation of the doctrine of the Holy Spirit rooted firmly within the context of Jewish-Christian conversation. In essence, his reply was, "That seems like a good approach, since it's really there that the distinction between Judaism and Christianity is found." The implications, I sensed, were that God's presence as Holy Spirit was given distinctively to the Church, and that pneumatology was an exclusively Christian category and concern.

15

The surprising element in my friend's remark is that, from my perspective, it is belief in Jesus as the Christ that appears the more decisive point of difference between Christians and Jews. It is also apparent that traditional Christological formulations have served to heighten and accentuate that difference to an unnecessary degree. The controlling assumption of the present work, in fact, is that a pneumatological orientation might not only offer a way of affirming God's active presence among both Jews and Christians—and so by implication among peoples of other religions and cultures—but also provide the framework for a Christology that is less foreign both to Judaism and to contemporary thought in general.

Despite the predominant tradition of exclusivism in Christian pneumatology, the notion that the concept of the Holy Spirit could serve as a fruitful medium for Christianity's approach to other religions and cultures has been suggested by others in recent years. Henry van Dusen hinted at this possibility in his classic work *Spirit, Son and Father,* and it is obvious in Paul Tillich's readiness to intuit what he called "the Spiritual Presence" among diverse religious and cultural groups, peoples and concerns. How much more so, then, might pneumatology offer rich possibilities in reflecting upon Christianity's relationship to Judaism, since the Christian idea of the Holy Spirit is rooted in the Hebrew scriptures' notion of **ruach** and the eschatological expectation of an outpouring of God's Spirit upon all flesh (Jl 2:28–32; Acts 2:17–21)?

Nonetheless, my friend's response certainly was consonant with the tradition which has prevailed in the history of Christian thinking. And that tradition has had the gravest consequences in the matter of Christianity's understanding and estimation of Judaism; it has claimed that the Church is the possessor of God's Spirit, and that *the Jews in particular* have forfeited the blessings of God's presence because of their rejection of Jesus. Traditional Christian pneumatologies, then, have made their own unique contribution to the anti-Judaic bias which continues to infect Christian faith and practice. In this chapter, I intend first to trace this bias in the Christian doctrine of the Holy Spirit through a few representative passages of scripture, and then through the writings of two Christian theologians writing after the Holocaust. I want to show briefly, but clearly, how Christian notions about the gift of the Holy Spirit have often encouraged spiteful and even hateful attitudes toward Jews in the history of the Church, thereby contributing significantly to the genocidal consequences of our own century. This is an important preliminary step in attempting to overturn Christian triumphalism through a radical revisioning of the doctrine of the Spirit, the rudimentary form of which will be suggested in the final section of this chapter.

A. PNEUMATOLOGICAL ANTI-JUDAISM

1. In the Christian Testament

A particularly crucial passage with which to begin is 2 Corinthians 3:1–18. This is so for two reasons. First, it was written by the apostle Paul, whose vital importance for the Church's understanding of the people Israel not only has been, but continues to be, beyond question. Certainly Paul historically has occupied a central position in Christianity's formulation of its understanding of the gospel, and consequently also of its relationship to Israel and Torah. "Whether the church understood Paul," argues Paul van Buren, "is therefore a question central to the church's reconsideration of its relationship to the Jewish people."[1] Second, and beyond its Pauline origin, this passage has been formative historically with respect both to Christian pneumatology and to Christian anti-Judaic attitudes.

In this passage Paul contrasts his ministry of a "new covenant," which is "not of the letter, but of the Spirit" (3:6), with that of his unknown (to us) foes, who came to the Corinthian church with letters of commendation (v. 1) and accused Paul of preaching a "veiled" gospel (4:3). These foes traditionally are thought to have been "judaizers," infiltrating this Gentile church with the subversive message that obedience to the law of Moses was necessary to salvation. Thus the passage has been read as a Pauline juxtaposition of Moses and Torah, "the letter" of which "kills," over against the new covenant of the Spirit who "gives life" (v. 6).

Paul, referring to Exodus 34:29–35, freely admits that the giving of Torah, a "ministry of death" with its "letters engraved on stones," came with a glory of its own, a glory which shone on Moses' face (v. 7). But the glory of the ministry of the Spirit is even greater, since it is written "not on tablets of stone, but on tablets of human hearts" (v. 3). Traditional Christian exegesis, then, even while conceding the glory in which the "old covenant" was given, has claimed that the Law given to Israel through Moses was merely external and indeed fading because of its temporary character (vv. 7, 11), just as the glory faded from the face of Moses. The surpassing glory of the "new covenant," on the other hand, is intimate and internal, a fulfillment of the eschatological hope pronounced by Jeremiah and Ezekiel. In the rhetorical words of nineteenth-century commentator Charles Hodge, "What was a bright cloud overhanging the cherubim, [compared] to the light of God's presence filling the soul?"[2]

Because of this greater glory, Paul speaks boldly and openly in contrast to Moses, who spoke through a veil "that the sons of Israel might not look intently at the end of what was fading away" (v. 13). Even the transient glory of the Mosaic law is more than "the sinful Israelites"[3] could be allowed to behold without interruption and concealment. And why was even this rather dull glory hidden from them? Because "their minds were hardened" (v. 14).

Paul proceeds to claim that the same veil which hid the glory on Moses' face is yet "unlifted," for "to this day whenever Moses is read, a veil lies over their heart" (vv. 14, 15). This veil is lifted only "in Christ," ostensibly "the Lord" to whom one must turn to have the veil removed (vv. 14, 16). When the veil is removed, then "we all"—as opposed to the old covenant in which Moses' face alone shone with the **shekhinah**— "with unveiled face beholding as in a mirror the glory of the Lord, are being transformed into the same image from glory to glory, just as from the Lord, the Spirit" (v. 18).

A traditional Christian reading of the passage, then, supports the claim that the Jews have tragically and blindly missed the inner meaning of the Mosaic covenant, which was fulfilled in Christ. It is only in Christ, under the inspiration of the Spirit, that the true intention of the "old covenant" is discerned. Meanwhile, the Jews continue to wander in the darkness of a veiled heart, tragically unable to comprehend their own scriptures. To quote Christian theologian George Hendry,

> The crux of the matter for the first Christian generation, confronted with unbelieving Judaism, was the interpretation of the Old Testament. In other words, they were concerned, not so much with how the Old Testament was written, as with how it was read, and it was in the reading of the Old Testament, which found in it testimony to Christ, that they saw especially the work of the Holy Spirit.[4]

In other words, to use Paul's phrase, "where the Spirit of the Lord is, there is liberty" (v. 17)—liberty perhaps not only from the Law, but correspondingly liberty in the Spirit also to read the Hebrew scriptures in a new way: as testifying to Jesus Christ, and as finding their fulfillment in him. And so one of the primary ministries of the Spirit in Christian theology has been to enlighten believers to read the scriptures Christocentrically—

a hermeneutical privilege forfeited by "unbelieving" Jews, with their hardened and veiled hearts.

One may readily conclude that such an interpretation of the passage, whether or not true to Paul's intentions, has contributed to the history of a highly spiritualized reading of the Hebrew scriptures by Christians. In this reading, the sense of an historical God in authentic interaction with the people Israel—the "external" and "temporary"—is displaced by a preferably static, timeless truth fulfilled in an ahistorical (because pre-existent) Christ through the inspiration of an atemporal Spirit—the "internal" and "eternal." Such a reading, of course, readily complements the Christian terminology of "Old Testament" and "New Testament," which indeed can be lifted directly from the passage (vv. 6, 14), with the implication that the old covenant is preliminary and incomplete apart from Christ, through whom the new covenant has arrived.

It is impossible to know for certain whether Paul would be wholly pleased with such developments. But in the freedom of a text in the history of interpretations, this spiritualized Christian reading has become a dominant way of reading him. There is, however, at least one alternative. We might call what Paul has offered here a Christic midrash of Exodus 34 in a typically rabbinic style. That is, he creatively and imaginatively reinterprets the scripture in the light of new historical developments—for him, the death and resurrection of Jesus, and so the expectation of the dawning of the eschatological age—and pressing contemporary questions. In an attempt to combat Jewish-Christian missionaries (11:22–23) who are urging the Gentile converts to add Torah observance to their faith in Christ, Paul turns the glory of the Mosaic covenant on its head for the sake of his argument. Yet it is more than that. He is arguing for a place, indeed a prominent place, for a Christian reinterpretation of the Hebrew scriptures in the freedom of the Spirit. And even more than that, he is arguing that this reading is *the* proper reading, for it is so read with unveiled hearts and faces; apparently the ambiguities of text and history are removed with the veil.

But this midrashic approach must now turn Paul upside down. Paul had this confidence (cf. v. 4) in the Christocentric reading as *the* proper one because of his deep conviction that the death and resurrection of Jesus marked the beginning of the end, the eschatological age of "the Spirit of the living God" (v. 3; cf. Ez 11:19; 36:26). When Paul wrote in Romans 11 of the fullness of the Gentiles coming in, and the pursuant salvation of all Israel, it appears that this was for him an eschatological finale which he expected in the very near future. One of the critical historical developments for Christians to consider is that, obviously, it did not happen. I have argued elsewhere that since Paul, by every indication, was mistaken about his eschatological expectation, it is incumbent upon the Church to begin hard and renewed reflection upon its faith in Jesus as the Christ in the context of the ambiguities of subsequent history, as Paul himself undoubtedly would.[5] It can be argued that Paul's exclusivist understanding of Jesus was tied to his belief that the eschatological age had dawned in him. With the passing of centuries of unredeemed history, Jews have every right to ask whether such exclusivist claims do indeed exhaust God's activity. Meanwhile, faithful Jews have continued to walk and to worship in accordance with Torah, in covenant with the God whose gifts and calling, according to Paul himself, are irrevocable (Rom 11:29).

John Koenig, in his book *Jews and Christians in Dialogue*, applies the same argument further to the problematic passage of 2 Corinthians 3. Koenig points out that Paul refrains from offering any concrete examples of this dawning splendor of the new covenant. "His argument is logical rather than empirical; in fact, it depends largely on his eschatological assumptions."[6] This is a strong claim, but Koenig buttresses it with an examination of the verb tenses in two crucial verses: Paul writes in verse 9 that "the dispensation of righteousness must [literally "*will*"—future tense] far exceed it in splendor," and in verse 11 that "if what faded away [literally, "what *is fading* away"—present tense] came with splendor, what is permanent must have much more splendor."[7] Koenig then presents an argument similar to what I have already offered:

> Paul's attempt to establish the superiority of the new presumes that what is dawning will be permanent. Nothing can resist or supplant the imminent advent of God's Kingdom on earth. Because of this imminence, Paul believes the new is displacing the old. We contemporary Christians will want to ask ourselves how we should interpret Paul's eschatological assumptions now that two thousand years have passed without the demise of Judaism.[8]

I have presented this argument concerning the eschatological context of Paul's thought not because it solves every problem in 2 Corinthians 3, but because it reveals the importance of the eschatological thrust of the Spirit's activity in Paul's writings and in the Christian Testament as a whole. This is an issue which will surface repeatedly, especially in Part III of this book. In the meantime, the question of how Christians might revise the doctrine of the eschatological Spirit after twenty centuries of ambiguous, often disastrous, and certainly unredeemed history must remain in the back of our minds.

Acts 7:51–53 is another passage in which pneumatology and anti-Judaism have been wedded in Christian exegesis. These verses provide the conclusive word of judgment against Jewish leaders in Stephen's stylized sermon: "You men who are stiff-necked and uncircumcised in heart and ears are always resisting the Holy Spirit; you are doing just as your fathers did" (v. 51). The distinction between Christian and Jewish faith becomes even more pronounced in the account which follows Stephen's oration: enraged, the Jewish leaders drive him out of the city and stone him to death, while he, "full of the Holy Spirit" (v. 55), prays for their forgiveness in words reminiscent of Jesus' on the cross (v. 60). Stephen, the first Christian martyr, represents the Spirit-filled person, while those Jewish leaders who rejected and killed him resist the Spirit with a vengeance.

My intention is not to deny the general veracity of the circumstances of Stephen's death as presented in Acts, but to suggest that Christians ought to read such accounts with a certain "hermeneutic of suspicion." For this account is actually the first of several idealized, highly stylized accounts in Acts of bitter confrontation between Jews who believed in Jesus and Jews who did not. To a great extent, in fact, in Acts "the Jews" becomes a phrase equivalent to those who resist the preaching of the gospel with treachery, lies, clamor and murder (9:23; 14:19; 17:5, 13; 18:12; 21:27; 23:12; 25:7). In short, the portrait of "the Jews" in Acts corresponds precisely with anti-Jewish caricatures of Greco-Roman antiquity.[9]

This caricature of "unbelieving" Jews, which apparently functioned to explain the gospel's failure to reach but a tiny minority of first-century Jewish people, has led to a kind of superiority complex in historical Christian identity. Christians, after all, have read in Acts of three decisive pronouncements of judgment against "the Jews" by Paul, who only because of Jewish hardheartedness then turns to the Gentiles, who listen with joy (13:46–48; 18:6; 28:25–28). Since the book of Acts is often characterized as "the acts of the Holy Spirit," the upshot is that "the Jews" are caricatured as those who are "always resisting the Spirit" (7:51). They are proud, stiff-necked and jealous of the success of the Christian mission.

One might hope that, in our post-Holocaust situation, Christianity's willingness to indulge in such projection and scapegoating might be chastened somewhat, given the undeniable fact that the long history of

Christian anti-Judaism helped prepare for the Nazis' secularized anti-Semitism. Yet an anti-Jewish bias of the Acts variety continues to infect the popular Christian consciousness. It is readily discernible in the following musings of Thomas F. Torrance, a modern Reformed theologian whose ideas about Jews and Judaism still typify the normal Christian consciousness:

> Now the coming of the Creator Spirit as at Pentecost is the point where man's own sinful creativity has to be broken. . . . At that point he is either re-created and emancipated from himself for genuine faith in God, or he lapses back in conflict with the Spirit into his own self-willed existence and becomes even more securely imprisoned within his own inventions. . . .
>
> Is that not the story of the recalcitrant Jews face to face with Jesus? Out of their own distinctive piety and attitude to existence they had forged their own conception of the Messiah. . . . Then when at last the Messiah actually came the conflict between their own image of God and that mediated by the Messiah was so intense that instead of surrendering to the creative impact of his Spirit upon them, they crucified the Messiah, and in a desperate attempt to force the hand of God they even resisted his Holy Spirit.[10]

Torrance's implications are clear: "the recalcitrant Jews" have no "genuine faith in God," for "their own image of God," apparently a Jewish invention, hinders them from yielding to the activity of the Holy Spirit. To be sure, Torrance avoids an extreme triumphalism by next asking whether the Church has not also been guilty of the sin of creating the divine according to its own self-willed designs. But the subtle suggestion remains that "the Jews," especially the image of the Jews as presented in Acts, provide the paradigm of self-willed resistance against the Holy Spirit.

The similar caricaturization of "the Jews" which occurs in the gospel of John is well known and documented.[11] Jesus is presented as being in almost constant conflict with "the Jews," who resist his teachings and seek to kill him. Jesus, for his part, calls them children of the devil, the consummate liar and murderer (8:44). While it would be ludicrous to deny that Jesus came into conflict with some Jewish officials at certain times in his ministry, the evidence suggests that John's gospel is far more reflective of the church-synagogue rift near the end of the first century than it is of Jesus' own life and ministry.

The relatively late date of final composition also undoubtedly influenced the unique pneumatology found in John's gospel. Jesus promises his disciples "another helper" (**parakletos**), "the Spirit of truth" who "will teach you all things, and bring to your remembrance all that I said to you" (14:16–17, 26). It is to their advantage that Jesus leave them, "for if I do not go away, the Helper shall not come to you; but if I go, I will send Him to you" (16:7). This **parakletos** pneumatology, then, provided an answer to the question apparently gnawing at the Johannine communities at the end of the first century: Where was Jesus? Why had he not yet returned? The Johannine reply was that, in the Spirit of truth, Jesus indeed was in their midst and would be forever (14:16). After all, the Johannine Christ who said "I am the truth" also promised that "the Spirit of truth . . . will guide you into all the truth; for He will not speak on His own initiative, but whatever He hears, He will speak. . . . He shall glorify Me; for He shall take of Mine, and shall disclose it to you" (16:13–14). This Spirit, then, is sent by Jesus and bears witness to Jesus—and so, in essence, *is Jesus* in Spirit with his disciples (7:37–39; 15:26–27). This Christocentric pneumatology finally takes narrative form in John 20:22–23 when the resurrected Jesus breathes on his disciples and says, "Receive the Holy Spirit."

When the unique pneumatology of John's gospel is considered in conjunction with its pervasive "Jesus versus the Jews" theme, the real dangers become evident. For this Spirit of truth functions practically as Christ contemporaneous with the Church, and so makes the Jesus of John's gospel *a living figure* for every generation of Christians. This sense of a "contemporary Christ" which John communicates explains at least partially the enormous popularity this gospel has enjoyed in the history of Christendom. But in so animating Jesus through the figure of the **parakletos,** there also lies the threat of animating the anti-Judaic bias of John's gospel, at least as it has been traditionally interpreted.

The most powerful illustration of this anti-Judaic pneumatology is found in John 15:18–16:3. Here the Johannine Jesus warns his disciples of the hatred they will experience at the hands of those who have hated and persecuted him (vv. 18–20). Jesus does not specifically mention "the Jews" in the passage, but there is no need to do so: when he says that they have no excuse for their sin because his coming has made their sin evident

(v. 22), and that they do not know the One who sent him (v. 21), and that the one who hates him hates his Father also (v. 23), evidently we hear a recapitulation of earlier verbal jousts with "the Jews" (5:37–42; 7:28–29; 8:23–24; 9:39–41). Then, when in 16:2 Jesus warns his disciples that "they will make you outcasts from the synagogue," the antagonists in question become obvious. Their actions, in fact, are an ironic fulfillment of "what is written in their Law" (for in John, Torah is not God's law but *theirs*): "They hated me without a cause."

In contrast to these haters of God, Jesus' disciples are promised the gift of the Helper, the Spirit of truth, "whom I will send to you from the Father . . . who proceeds from the Father" (15:26). This Spirit will bear witness to Jesus, and will inspire their witness as well. And so the followers of Jesus, in whom the Spirit will dwell (14:17), are defined essentially in terms of *absolute otherness* and *difference* from "the Jews," who are wholly bereft of the Spirit. The lines could not be drawn more sharply.

Koenig summarizes well for us the results of this first-century polemic for subsequent Christian history:

> Whatever theologians may make of them, these texts (unique to the Fourth Gospel) certainly suggest that with the coming of Jesus, Judaism and the Jewish people have lost all religious value. . . . Of course, it is absurd to hold John (and other New Testament writers who take similar positions) responsible for all Christian anti-Semitism. Nevertheless, as Christendom's most popular missionary book, the Fourth Gospel has played an unfortunate role in fitting out new converts with a ready-made prejudice against Jews . . . [and so] has fanned the embers of hatred deep in the psyches of otherwise moderate and tolerant parishioners.[12]

Perhaps we are now in a position to suggest a synthesis of the three strands of anti-Judaic pneumatology we have isolated from the Christian Testament: the Jews, having had a history of resisting the voice and activity of the Spirit (Acts), are blinded to the Spirit-inspired, Christic meaning of the Hebrew scriptures (2 Corinthians), and so continue to this day to be completely antithetical to the living Spirit of Christ, the truth (John). Christians, then, may understand themselves as being everything the Jews are *not*, and so as having replaced the Jews as God's Israel, the people of choice.

The fact that nearly all of what Christians have called the New Testament was written by Jews, or that the polemic against "unbelieving" Jews found in its pages can be characterized largely as in-house bickering, is not the point. The point is, its history of interpretation *in Gentile hands* has sown countless seeds of Jew-despising in the past two millennia, and it is not too much to say that Christianity finally reaped its harvest in the Holocaust. This point has already been ably argued and documented by Christian theologians such as Roy Eckardt, Franklin Littell, Rosemary Radford Ruether and Clark Williamson, among many others.[13] Little attention has been given specifically to the history of the development of the doctrine of the Holy Spirit in relation to this long-standing **adversus Judaeos** tradition, but that is another book and cannot occupy us here. Suffice it to say that pneumatology, as one of the doctrinal categories of traditional Christian theology, has been immersed as deeply in the spirit of anti-Judaism as any other. Indeed, our examination of three critical strands of anti-Judaic pneumatology in the Christian Testament indicates the fundamental importance of the doctrine of the Holy Spirit in the Church's tradition of triumphalistic claims to distinctiveness and superiority.

2. In Post-Holocaust Theologies

In this section we will examine the anti-Judaic bias in the pneumatologies of two post-Holocaust theologians, George Hendry and Jürgen Moltmann. The adjectival phrase "post-Holocaust" bears two possible connotations: a chronological one, in which any theology written after 1945 would be intended, and a more precisely ideological one, which refers to theology written intentionally in the shadow of the Holocaust's haunting questions. In Hendry and Moltmann we have a representative of each type: Hendry's work is "post-Holocaust" only in the general historical sense, while Moltmann writes with far greater sensitivity to the issues of Jewish-Christian relations as the Holocaust has raised them. Thus, the anti-Judaism in Moltmann's theology of the Spirit may be far more refined, but I will argue that its subtle presence continues to feed the sort of triumphalism that Moltmann, ostensibly, would eschew.

But the work of Hendry, an American Lutheran theologian, is another matter. His *The Holy Spirit in Christian Theology,* written in 1965, exemplifies what happens when the Christian supersessionist myth provides the context for pneumatology. The result is a virtually Marcionite reading of the doctrine, severing Christian pneumatology from its moorings in Hebrew experience and scripture.[14] Hendry, largely shunning the witness of the Hebrew scriptures, resists developing a doctrine of the Spirit as either animating creation, or as anointing Israel's judges, kings and prophets—let alone as indwelling the people Israel!—for fear of losing the "distinctiveness" of a Christian pneumatology. He writes,

> The witness of the New Testament to the gift of the Spirit is soteriological and eschatological in character; when the attempt is made to fit it into the framework of a conception that is cosmological and anthropological in character, it almost certainly loses something of its distinctiveness.[15]

Drawing especially upon the Johannine tradition, Hendry argues that, in the divine economy, the Spirit follows, and is a function of, Jesus Christ. The work of the Spirit, then, is "essentially of a reproductive nature; it has always to do with the work of the incarnate Christ."[16] Indeed, "there is no such thing as an experience of the presence of the Spirit distinct from the presence of Christ."[17]

To be sure, Hendry's virtual identification of the Spirit with Christ is consistent with Johannine, and perhaps Pauline, pneumatology. And it has historical precedent particularly in the Western church, where the **filioque** clause, with its assertion that the Spirit proceeds from the Father *and from the Son,* has exercised significant influence. But such an identification ignores the Hebrew notion of **ruach,** and the whole of the witness to the Spirit's activity in the history of Israel and its scriptures. Had Hendry written in a confessional tone that, *in Christian experience,* the Holy Spirit is the Spirit of Christ, or mediates Christ's presence, one might agree. But his limitation of the Spirit's activity to reproducing that of the incarnate Christ is an arbitrary reading of scripture, and invariably leads to a Christian exclusivism that confines God's Spirit to the Church.

Hendry is not unaware of the inner tensions which his exclusively Christological understanding of the Spirit creates. He asks himself,

> If the Holy Spirit is in an exclusive sense the Spirit of Christ, does this mean that the New Testament recognizes no presence or activity of the Spirit in the world prior to the historical advent of Christ? That would seem to follow from the insistence of the New Testament on the novelty of the Spirit. . . . But if we insist on the Christocentric reference of the Spirit, what, then, are we to make of those passages in the Old Testament which speak of an activity of the Spirit in creation and in the life of man? . . . The difficulty is a crucial one for Trinitarian theology.[18]

It is evident that much of Hendry's difficulty stems from his neo-Marcionite hermeneutic. The only real solution would involve a serious and sustained attentiveness to the concept of the Spirit in the Hebrew scriptures, which would in turn involve a reversal of the traditional Christian subsumption of the Spirit under Christ in the divine economy.[19] Hendry, it would seem, has virtually sundered Christ and the Spirit from the history of Israel; as a counter-move, I would suggest that God as Spirit—the same Spirit who "brooded" over creation and who called Abram out of Ur of the Chaldeans—is the one who brought forth Jesus out of Israel's history and called him to *be* the Christ (Lk 1:35; 4:17–21). Rather than thinking of the Spirit as simply reproducing the work of the incarnate Christ, as Hendry does, it would be more faithful to the whole of scripture to envision the Spirit as *producing* the Christ within the processes of Israel's history, as the gospel genealogies suggest. In short, it is more faithful to the Spirit of the God of Israel to understand the incarnate Christ in terms of the Spirit's work and empowerment (Acts 10:38), rather than the Spirit in terms of Christ.

Again, instead of Hendry's large claim that "there is no such thing as an experience of the presence of the Spirit distinct from the presence of Christ," would it not be sufficient, and equally faithful to biblical tradition, to make the smaller claim that for the Christian or the person shaped by Christian tradition, any experience of God's Spirit will inevitably be Christocentric? Surely the witness of the Hebrew scriptures to the presence of the Spirit in creation in general (Gen 1:2; Ps 33:6), in the creation of humanity (Gen 2:7; Eccl 9:7) and in the history of the people Israel (Is 63:10–11) should open the possibility of other manifestations of the Spirit within human experience that are at least not explicitly Christocentric. It may be threatening to a Christian triumphalist mentality to suggest it, but it seems likely that the Spirit or divine presence is experienced, interpreted and formulated in accordance with the narrative and symbolic traditions in which an individual or community participates.

Such a suggestion liberates pneumatological thinking to contemplate the probability of the Spirit's activity on a far wider and more diverse scope. It also appears to run counter to the famous **filioque** clause of the Western Church, which tended to narrow the Spirit's activity and influence to a specifically Christological focus. Hendry, in fact, surmises that the phrase found its way into the faith of the Western Church due to "a general sense of the inadequacy of the [Nicene] Creed to express the distinctively Christian apprehension of the Holy Spirit as the Spirit of Christ."[20] The problem with the **filioque,** though—aside from its dependence entirely on a strained reading of a single verse (Jn 15:26)—is that its ideational context is an ahistorical, speculative understanding of the

triune God, rather than the history of the God of Israel even as interpreted
in the synoptic gospels. For in that history, if there is a "procession" it is
the procession or "forth-going" of Jesus from the history and people of
Israel through the work and calling of the Spirit who is God. I would
suggest that the Spirit "proceeds" from God only in the sense that the
word "spirit" connotes the one God in God's outreach to and presence in
creation, and particularly to and in the people Israel. To take such a view
of the Spirit is, then, to alter radically the terms of the **filioque**: the Spirit
proceeds from God the Father of Israel as God's own covenantal presence, and the Son (Jesus) issues from the interactive history of that same
Spirit with the people Israel.

Such an understanding of the Spirit, to be sure, conflicts with
Hendry's operative theme of "distinctiveness": his concern is to demonstrate the specifically and distinctively Christic nature of the divine Spirit.
It might be argued that in this emphasis he is simply following the tradition of the Western Church, whose theologians have only sporadically
and hesitantly connected pneumatology with creation or anthropology.[21]
But Hendry's desire to affirm a *distinctiveness* in the Christian doctrine of
the Spirit leads him closer to *discontinuity:* the Holy Spirit, for him, is the
Spirit of Jesus Christ, operative exclusively in eschatological salvation,
and so is discontinuous with a theological vision of creation and humanity. Such discontinuity, I have suggested, is little more than a revived
Marcionism, a theological posture which in itself is anti-Judaic. This becomes most evident when Hendry stresses humanity's need for the eschatological vitality of the Spirit, a need best illustrated for him in the cross
of Jesus:

> The cross is the final crisis in the history of Israel; it marks the end of
> Israel. But, more than that, it constitutes the critical foundation in the
> life of the New Israel, for the crucifixion of the Messiah is not only the
> definitive demonstration of the incapacity of Israel, but it demonstrates
> the incapacity of man as such. . . . Thus the renewal of man is an escha-
> tological reality . . . [which] registers in history as the crisis of history,
> the crisis in which history is confronted with the limits of its own
> possibilities.[22]

For Hendry, here echoing neo-orthodox themes, the cross represents
an almost apocalyptic judgment upon Israel, after which it has no further
life, history or meaning. For the Church, however, living in the renewing
power of the eschatological Spirit, the cross provides its foundation as

"the New Israel"—a phrase which has been prominent in the history of Christian self-understanding, but which has virtually no scriptural or historical warrant. Sadly, this bald sort of displacement theology has contributed much to the history of Christian self-aggrandizement, self-defensiveness, and self-deception. It has given Christians an illusion of vitality through its solemn pronouncement of Israel's obsolescence, and contributed significantly to a history of Christian anti-Judaism which, in tandem with other historical, sociological and technological factors, came to ugly fruition in the Nazis' attempt to make that spiritual pronouncement a physical reality. In a fashion analogous to what Hendry writes about the cross, the Christian claim to vitality has been challenged deeply by the Holocaust, for there the Church's lack of love and compassion for the persecuted and destroyed Jews of Christian Europe betrayed a disturbing absence of the fruit of the Spirit. Hendry, writing two decades after that historical judgment of the Church, perhaps was too close to the Holocaust to perceive its revelatory critique of Christian triumphalism and the ideology of displacement. But for the intentionally post-Holocaust theologian, that judgment and revelation cannot be ignored.

With this in mind, it is instructive to turn to the pneumatology of Jürgen Moltmann, whose sensitivity to the issues raised by the Holocaust, as suggested earlier, is far deeper than Hendry's. This is evidenced by his attempt in *The Crucified God* to write a theodicy responsive not only to the passion of Jesus, but also in some measure to the horror of Auschwitz, and in his apparently increasing interest in Jewish theologians and their ideas. The danger, however, for Moltmann is the precise obverse of Hendry's neo-Marcionism: in his attempt to adapt Jewish concepts in his theological construction, he tends to co-opt those ideas, forcing them into a Christian baptism which robs them of their distinct Jewish identity and integrity.

For example, in *The Trinity and the Kingdom* Moltmann argues that the passion of Jesus is at the heart of the Christian tradition, a passion which involves the voluntary opening of oneself to another and the other's suffering. Christians, he states, perceive something of God's own passion in the gospel's passion narratives. Yet he transgresses this confessional stance to claim, "We *can* only talk about God's suffering in trinitarian terms. In monotheism it is impossible."[23] Moltmann proceeds to cite Aristotelian philosophy and Islamic faith as examples of a monotheism which excludes divine passion. But what of Judaism? In fact Moltmann next turns to Abraham Heschel, who developed a bipolar theology of the covenant in which "the pathos of God" arises out of the covenantal relationship God shares with the people Israel. How does Moltmann address this profound theology of divine suffering, offered not in trinitarian but in covenantal terms? He writes,

> God the Lord is a 'single' God. He is the 'only' God. But that does not mean that he is one (**monas**) in the monistic sense. On the contrary, the experience of the divine pathos inevitably leads to the perception of the *self-differentiation* of the one God.[24]

First, Moltmann has shifted rhetorically from the term "monotheism" to "monism," a word whose context is philosophical, calling to mind the often criticized "God of the philosophers" whose immutability, aseity, omnipotence and omniscience eliminate the possibility of divine suffering. In a word, Moltmann is loading the deck, apparently presenting monism and trinitarianism as the only two available options. Second, by so doing, Moltmann can argue that any human experience of the divine pathos, which in turn leads to a notion of God's self-differentiation, must finally find expression in a trinitarian theology. It would appear that he has given a nod of approval to Heschel before pre-empting his idea of divine self-differentiation in the cause of trinitarianism.

But it is highly debatable whether the self-differentiation implied in the notion of God's suffering can be expressed only in trinitarian language. For no matter how much Moltmann may assert that the trinitarian deity is "a 'single' God" or "the 'only' God," at the same time he argues passionately for a democratic, societal deity of three persons who share in common the inexhaustible divine life, "in which they are present with one another, for one another and in one another."[25] But the idea of divine self-differentiation, which Heschel suggests arises out of encounter with the God of the covenant, *does not* imply a God who can be called "they." *Self*-differentiation still suggests, indeed presupposes, one self; Moltmann's trinitarianism, particularly because of its dependence upon a societal model, suggests three. Wholly apart from the tendency toward tritheism which arises from this societal model, a subtle anti-Judaism surfaces in Moltmann's claim that it is *only* in his social-trinitarian understanding of God that divine suffering may be explicated. Yet in the very process of making his exclusivist claim, Moltmann has utilized Heschel's idea of the pathos of God.

A similar tactic may be detected in Moltmann's more recent work *God in Creation,* in which the doctrines of creation and pneumatology are intertwined through a trinitarian panentheism. Moltmann finds in the

Jewish idea of the Shekhinah a helpful category for his proposed eco-theology: "The divine secret of creation is the Shekhinah, God's indwelling; and the purpose of the Shekhinah is to make the whole creation the house of God."[26] Yet the question raised by Moltmann's abuse of "the divine pathos" in Heschel comes again to the fore in his use of the Shekhinah concept: is not his attempt to write the Shekhinah into a Christian doctrine of the trinity a theological triumphalism, particularly in light of the exclusivist claims he makes for trinitarianism? For example,

> Because God not only loves but is himself love, he has to be understood as the triune God. Love cannot be consummated by a solitary subject. An individuality cannot communicate itself: individuality is ineffable, unutterable. If God is love he is at once the lover, the beloved and the love itself.[27]

Moltmann's use of the Augustinian model of lover–loved–love for understanding God as triune is itself surprising, since it represents a step away from the God apprehended in the history of Jesus and toward philosophical speculation. Beyond this observation, though, is the same troubling insistence on a trinitarian perspective. Granted, love involves an "other" outside the solitary subject; but do not the notions of God in intimate relationship to creation, and of God in covenant with Israel, already indicate that the biblical deity is not a solitary subject? God is the *lover*. Creation, particularly as represented in our world by the people Israel in covenant with God, is the *beloved*. And God's *love* for creation need not, indeed ought not, be hypostasized into a "thing" or "force" or "person" between them. Yet Moltmann claims that God as love "has to be understood as the triune God," and later that the panentheistic vision of the mutual indwelling of God and creation "can really only be thought and described in trinitarian terms."[28] And the irony is that he imports the Shekhinah concept from Jewish thought to buttress his exclusivist argument.

Hendry and Moltmann, then, exemplify two different sorts of anti-Judaic triumphalism in Christian pneumatology. In Hendry, the Holy Spirit is presented as an eschatological discontinuity, apparently bearing no relationship to the Hebrew scriptures' witness to the Spirit of God at work in creation, in human beings as created in God's image, or in Israel as God's chosen covenant partner. The Holy Spirit, for Hendry, is the Spirit of Christ—and *that* understood narrowly as the Spirit of eschatological salvation. And while Hendry admits that such a bifurcation of God's activity presents serious difficulties for trinitarian theology, he prefers those difficulties over any qualification that might compromise what is, for him, the radical novelty of Pentecost. In Moltmann, the triumphalism is far more subtle; he finds value in the Jewish notions of God's covenantal suffering and animating presence in creation, attempts to incorporate them into his constructive effort, and then claims that these very notions make sense only from a Christian trinitarian perspective. His procedure bears some resemblance to the bland triumphalism of Karl Rahner's "anonymous Christian" approach to adherents of other religions: they and their beliefs are, on the deepest level, really Christian— they just need us to make it plain to them.

B. FIVE THESES IN RESPONSE TO THE PROBLEM

Having offered a brief survey of the problem of anti-Judaism in Christian pneumatology, and recognizing the need for a radical reversal of this trend in every aspect and doctrine of Christian teaching, I now submit five programmatic theses which underlie the present attempt at theological reconstruction of the doctrine of the Holy Spirit:

(a) An attentive reading of history reveals that Christian anti-Judaism, while hardly the sole factor, was a prominent and necessary factor in the socio-economic, ideological and historical forces which converged in the secularized anti-Semitic policies of the Nazis prior to and during World War II. The deeply rooted anti-Judaic bias in the Christian tradition also hindered the exercise of Christian compassion toward European Jews during the thirteen years of Nazi persecution and mass murder. *It is thus morally incumbent upon the Church and its theologians, out of the principle of love of neighbor, to labor tirelessly to overturn Jew-hatred in Christian teaching.* If there were no reason for doing so other than the Holocaust, it would be far more than enough, for the interpretation of one's religious tradition in a fashion responsible to the contemporary historical context is an ongoing task. While the task of continuous reinterpretation is inevitable for peoples of all religious and cultural traditions, it should be a conscious undertaking for Christians and Jews, since for both history has been, and continues to be, the arena of God's interpreted activity and so a vital component in the revelatory process.

(b) But the Holocaust is not, in fact, the sole basis for a reversal of traditional Christian attitudes toward Jews. Rather, *the very heart of Christian faith, resting as it does in the prevenient faithfulness of God, receives a self-inflicted death blow if Christians deny God's continuing covenant faithfulness to Israel.* Such a denial has functioned all too often as the basis for the Christian claim to legitimacy and priority, as in the claim in Hebrews 8:6–13 that Christianity represents a new and better covenant over "the first . . . [which] is becoming obsolete and growing old [and] is ready to disappear" (v. 13). Christians traditionally have conveniently read Jeremiah's prophecy about a renewed covenant through the lens of the book of Hebrews and its abbreviated quotation, thereby often gaining the impression that God cares not for the Jews (v. 9). But a further reading of Jeremiah 31, beyond verse 34, would instruct Christians that the sun, moon and stars, and the sea and its tides, will sooner vanish than will "the offspring of Israel . . . cease from being a nation before Me forever" (Jer 31:36). God's covenant faithfulness to Israel is, or ought to be, axiomatic for Christians and their theologies—out of regard both for the Hebrew scriptural witness and for a sure sense of God's utter reliability.

(c) A Christian affirmation of God's continuing covenant with the people Israel leads also to an affirmation of God's intimate presence with and among them. As Michael Wyschogrod has argued so forcefully in *The Body of Faith,* God's is a corporeal election of Israel; God the Spirit is committed to an "earthly" indwelling of the people of the covenant.

> If you walk in My statutes and keep My commandments so as to carry them out . . . you will thus eat your food to the full and live securely in the land. . . . So I will turn toward you and make you fruitful and multiply you, and I will confirm My covenant with you. . . . *Moreover, I will make My dwelling among you, and My soul will not reject you. I will also walk among you and be your God, and you shall be My people* (Lev 26:3, 5, 9, 11–12).

For Christians to take seriously God's covenantal commitment to indwell Israel means that *whatever the Church might claim about God's Spirit at work, either in its midst or, more broadly, in creation, must be consonant with the prior scriptural witness to God's presence in and with Israel.* An attentive reading of Israel's history up to the present moment must also contribute its insight into the meaning of divine presence—and perhaps of divine absence as well.

(d) Such an attentive reading of Israel's history means that it is time for responsible, post-Holocaust theologians to begin to learn from the halakhic, haggadic, theological, philosophical and mystical writings of Jewish scholars throughout the centuries. Too often Christian theologians have tacitly assumed that, after Jesus, Jewish religion and thought have no more validity, veracity or vitality. That assumption is sadly mistaken. But *the Christian motive for learning from Jewish theologies ought not to be in order to absorb them into an already closed and self-assured Christian theological system, but to receive from them forgotten or suppressed truths about God, creation, humanity, covenant and redemption.*

Once Christians take seriously God's ongoing covenant with the Jews, then what H. Richard Niebuhr called an "appropriation" of Jewish wisdom, religiosity and history may occur. In his classic *The Meaning of Revelation* he could write, "Through Jesus Christ Christians of all races recognize the Hebrews as their fathers,"[29] but fell short of seeing that a full appropriation of the God of the covenant means that Christians also recognize the Jews of history, up to and including the present, as their sisters and brothers (Rom 11:28–29). Such an appropriation would also help the Church to be open to the revelatory critique of Christian faith and practice which Jewish thought might offer; again, in Niebuhr's words, "To . . . have others communicate to us what they see when they regard our lives from the outside, is to have a moral experience. Every external history of ourselves, communicated to us, becomes an event in inner history."[30]

Certainly it is true that a Christian appropriation of the history of the "other" is not limited to the history and faith of the Jewish people. John Cobb has rightly stated that "our identity is richer as it is co-constituted by more strands of memory," so that "we will not want . . . to close ourselves to other traditions whether religious or secular."[31] At the same time, I am arguing that Jews have a biblical, (theo)logical and post-Holocaust historical priority on the agenda for Christian theologians who endeavor to listen to, and learn from, other communities and their narratives.

(e) While *the language of Christian theology* has many contexts—for example, the life and worship of the Church, the particular tongue and culture in which it finds expression, and the socio-economic exigencies of both those who speak it and those who hear it—Christian theologians must nonetheless recognize that it *has a primary context: God's ongoing covenantal dealings with Israel.* Just as Paul van Buren has argued in the case of Christology, so every other consideration of Christian theology, including pneumatology, must allow this context a (theo)logical priority. If traditionally the doctrine of the Holy Spirit has been understood primarily in a Christic context, that doctrine will be revisioned when a new emphasis is placed upon Christ's own context in the story, vocabulary, imagery and framework of Israel.[32]

This is not a suggestion that all sense of novelty in the Christian faith be erased, but a recognition that novelty arises only within continuity, within its context of relevant possibilities. Otherwise, it is not novelty but anomaly. Too much Christian theology has been written as though anomaly were a virtue, as far as Christianity's relationship to Jewish faith and thought is concerned. And while biblical faith points to a God who makes all things new, this God is also faithful to covenant, still the God of Abraham and Sarah, of Isaac and Rebekah, of Jacob and Leah and Rachel, of Moses and Maimonides, of the Baal Shem Tov and Buber. No other God is the One who "gives us the victory through our Lord Jesus Christ" (1 Cor 15:57). To borrow van Buren's catchy phrase, "God was not double-crossing Himself in the cross of Christ."[33]

These theses are the theological presuppositions which, taken together, provide the foundation for a reconstruction of the Christian doctrine of the Spirit in a way which affirms God's covenant faithfulness to Israel, and so also reverses Christian anti-Judaism. To extend the building metaphor, in this attempt at reconstruction I have found the pneumatological work of two theologians, van Buren and Geoffrey Lampe, to provide invaluable architectural drafts. In the following, final section of this chapter, I want to suggest why and how this is so.

C. AN ALTERNATIVE DIRECTION FOR PNEUMATOLOGY

With his three-volume work *A Theology of the Jewish-Christian Reality,* Paul van Buren is probably the one Christian theologian who has most fruitfully labored to rewrite Christian theology upon the presupposition of God's continuing covenant with Israel. While pneumatology has not been a predominant theme in his writings, he does nevertheless provide clues about the new direction which an intentionally post-Holocaust Christian pneumatology might take.

In his introductory volume *Discerning the Way,* van Buren indicates the obvious parallel between the notion of the Shekhinah's presence with Israel and that of the Spirit with the Church. Noting the "feminine" character of both, van Buren suggests that they denote God's "maternal reaching out and gathering to himself, as has happened to us Gentiles in the Way."[34] This surprising occurrence in history—that Gentiles, through the Jew Jesus, have come to worship the God of Israel—is the amazingly gracious work of God the Holy Spirit. Since this surprise is the starting point for Gentile reflection upon the God of Israel who works in history, van Buren argues that trinitarian thought should reverse the traditional order of Father, Son and Spirit and begin instead with the Spirit. Such a reversal, it should be noted, already begins to overturn the Christian tendency to think of the Spirit as derivative from the Son and so, by implication, as delimited by the Church.

For van Buren, then, as he further clarifies in *Christ in Context,* the Holy Spirit is the God of Israel in presence and activity. Therefore, "to speak of the Spirit is neither more nor less than to speak of the effects of God's outgoingness, of God's covenantal self-determination not to be without God's covenant partners nor to do his work without their cooperation."[35] Because van Buren here draws especially from David Hartman's reflections upon the Jewish covenant as an open-ended relationship capable of assuming various forms and meanings through history, he differs from the understanding of the Spirit which tends to predominate in traditions informed by the theologies of Calvin and Wesley. For van Buren, the Spirit does not present "the things concerning Jesus of Nazareth as complete in themselves, needing only a means of applying their effects in a later time."[36] This traditional pneumatology understands the covenantal work of God and humanity to have been fulfilled in the "completed work" of Jesus the Christ, so that the Spirit becomes the principle of subjective appropriation of that work. Against this rather static view, van Buren argues that the Spirit draws the Church "to Christ who leads it to the God of Israel and the Israel of God, so that it will join Israel in God's praise and in taking up responsibility for how it walks today and into the future."[37] The Holy Spirit, the Spirit of the God of Israel, thus intends to lead the Church into fellowship with Israel, and into walking in the responsible, covenantal process of historical relationship to which God called Israel through Torah.

To think of the Holy Spirit as *the Spirit of the God of Israel,* as van Buren suggests we ought, is a distinct departure from the Church's tendency to think of the Spirit as *the Spirit of Christ.* Of course, in Christian experience the latter is also true, but if the notion of "the Spirit of Christ" is placed within the ideational context of "the Spirit of the God of Israel," then "the Spirit of Christ" assumes a new meaning. No longer does the phrase suggest a Spirit who is derived from, a function of, or simply a stand-in for, Christ. Rather, it denotes the Spirit of Israel's God: the God who labors in Israel's history, and who has produced through that history the Christ, the "anointed one" who is a light to the Gentiles and in whom the Gentiles trust (Is 49:6; 11:10).

Furthermore, to think of the Spirit as denoting Israel's God in "outgoingness" or "covenantal self-determination" is to work against the traditional idea of the Spirit as a distinct hypostasis either beside God or within the Godhead. Van Buren, in fact, joins a significant chorus of contemporary theologians in warning that it is not proper for English-speaking Christians to talk about "God in three Persons," since the modern conception of "person" as a self-conscious center of willing and acting is a misleading translation of what the Fathers intended when they spoke of **hypostasis** or even of **persona.** The Holy Spirit is "the Holy Spirit of the one God," and it is best not to emphasize the Spirit as someone or something distinct from the one God. Here the influence of Geoffrey Lampe upon van Buren becomes evident—an influence van Buren freely admits.[38]

If van Buren places pneumatology securely within the context of Israel's story as a people in covenant with their God, Geoffrey Lampe's pneumatological context tends more toward the universal and the anthropological: the Spirit is God "in his personal outreach," God in personal creative interaction with the human spirit.[39] The Spirit is God at work "incarnately" in the evolutionary processes of creating authentic human beings, that is, human beings in open, personal relationship to their Creator. Lampe understands Jesus, then, not as a "second Adam" who restores to a lost humanity the possibility of open relationship with God. Rather, Jesus is a "true Adam" in whose life the human potential for communion with God finally and first comes to full fruition, and so is one who embodies for us the "continuous incarnation of God as Spirit in the spirits of men."[40]

Lampe's understanding of Spirit as God's immanence in the evolutionary processes of creation, then, leads him to a continual interest in not overestimating the novelty or radical distinctiveness of the Christian experience of the Spirit. "Rather," he writes, "we should lay great emphasis on the continuity of God's creative work in the process of cosmic evolution, in the development of man, and especially in the continuing creation and salvation of human beings . . ."[41] The event of Jesus must be placed, and so interpreted, within the perspective of an evolutionary process in which God's Spirit interacts intimately with human beings to make them more fully human, i.e., more deeply aware of, and open to, the personal presence of God.

His emphasis upon continuity of divine presence means that Lampe, while not often referring specifically to God's covenantal presence in Israel's midst, at least is not anti-Judaic when he does make such references. But on the whole his approach is *too* universalistic, *too* broad in its sweep; while he rightly stresses the uniformity of God's action in creation, he tends to forget that the divine activity assumes diverse and particular forms as it becomes mediated through different religious and cultural structures of meaning. His pneumatology would be enriched by the corrective which van Buren's particularist, Israel-centered method offers, just as van Buren's pneumatology might be aided by a more conscious reflection upon the Spirit's activity outside Israel on broader anthropological and cosmological levels. Both dimensions, after all, are loci of the Spirit according to the witness of the Hebrew scriptures and rabbinic writings.

There is, indeed, within Jewish thought a history of interpretations of God's presence—both particularly within the people Israel, as van Buren makes explicit, and more universally with creation and humanity, as Lampe indicates—which must be taken seriously as providing the pneumatological context for the alternative interpretation of the Holy Spirit to be offered in this work. The following chapter is an exercise in the task of interpreting, and thus appropriating, that history of interpretations.

NOTES

1. Paul van Buren, *A Christian Theology of the People Israel* (New York: The Seabury Press, 1983), p. 277.

2. Quoted by Philip E. Hughes, *Paul's Second Epistle to the Corinthians* (Grand Rapids: Wm. B. Eerdmans Publishing Co., 1962), p. 103. Hodge's sentiments, to be sure, are fairly representative of the "superiority complex" of traditional Christian spirituality.

3. *Ibid.,* p. 108.

4. George S. Hendry, *The Holy Spirit in Christian Theology* (London: SCM Press Ltd, 1965), p. 28.

5. In "Re-Reading Paul after van Buren," an unpublished response to van Buren's *A Christian Theology of the People Israel* (January 1987), presented to the Fellows of the Center for Contemporary Theology, Shalom Hartman Institute of Jerusalem.

6. John Koenig, *Jews and Christians in Dialogue: New Testament Foundations* (Philadelphia: The Westminster Press, 1979), p. 52.

7. *Ibid.*

8. *Ibid.*

9. See Dixon Slingerland, " 'The Jews' in the Pauline Portion of Acts," *Journal of American Academy of Religion,* LIV/2 (Summer 1986), pp. 305–321.

10. Thomas F. Torrance, *Theology in Reconstruction* (Grand Rapids: Wm B. Eerdmans Publishing Co., 1975), pp. 255, 256.

11. John T. Townsend's "The Gospel of John and the Jews: The Story of a Religious Divorce" presents a fine summary of the problem, and his footnotes provide an excellent bibliography; in Alan Davies, ed., *Anti-Semitism and the Foundations of Christianity* (New York: Paulist Press, 1979), pp. 72–97.

12. Koenig, pp. 130, 131.

13. See, for example, Eckhardt, *Elder and Younger Brothers* (New York: Charles Scribner's Sons, 1967); Littell, *The Crucifixion of the Jews* (New York: Harper & Row, 1975); Ruether, *Faith and Fratricide* (New York: The Seabury Press, 1974); and Williamson, *Has God Rejected His People?* (Nashville: Abingdon, 1982).

14. Marcion was the second-century Christian who saw such a divergence between the "God of love" revealed by Jesus and the "God of law" of the Jews that he concluded they could not be the same deity, so he rejected the Hebrew Bible and its inferior god. But that rejection necessitated a drastic pruning of the Christian authoritative texts, too, for he detected in many of those texts a distinctly Jewish element which did not fit with his notion of the gospel's radical newness. The obvious tendency of his work was to dehistoricize and de-Judaize both Jesus and the apostolic proclamation. Though the Church denounced him as a heretic, the general anti-Marcionite tactics of the Fathers actually contributed to the Church's anti-Judaic leaning: the problem, it was suggested, was not with the "old" law or with the God who gave it, but with the rebellious, inferior people to whom it was given: the Jews. See David P. Efroymson, "The Patristic Connection," in *Anti-Semitism and the Foundations of Christianity,* pp. 98–117.

15. Hendry, p. 16.

16. *Ibid.,* p. 23.

17. *Ibid.,* p. 89.

18. *Ibid.,* pp. 27, 46.

19. See Chapter 2 of this study, "Ruach, Pneuma, Shekhinah: The Divine Presence."

20. Hendry, p. 41.

21. Wolfhart Pannenberg offered a useful summary of this problem in "The Doctrine of the Spirit and the Task of a Theology of Nature," *Theology,* Vol. LXXV, No. 619, pp. 8–21.

22. Hendry, p. 127.

23. Jürgen Moltmann, *The Trinity and the Kingdom: The Doctrine of God* (San Francisco: Harper & Row, Publishers, 1981), p. 25.

24. *Ibid.,* p. 27.

25. *Ibid.,* p. 198.

26. Moltmann, *God in Creation: A New Theology of Creation and the Spirit of God* (San Francisco: Harper & Row, Publishers, 1985), p. xiii.

27. *Ibid.,* p. 57.

28. *Ibid.,* p. 98.

29. H. Richard Niebuhr, *The Meaning of Revelation* (New York: The Macmillan Company, 1941), p. 115. Niebuhr's thoughts on "appropriation" on pp. 114–120 comprise an especially potent passage of a book whose importance will endure.

30. *Ibid.,* pp. 84, 85.

31. John B. Cobb, Jr., *Process Theology as Political Theology* (Philadelphia: The Westminster Press, 1982), p. 55.

32. See van Buren's recently published third volume of *A Theology of the Jewish-Christian Reality,* entitled *Christ in Context* (San Francisco: Harper & Row, 1988). In many ways the present work is an attempt to extend van Buren's Christology to the area of pneumatology, though there are also significant differences between us in method and content.

33. van Buren, *Discerning the Way* (New York: The Seabury Press, 1980), p. 83.

34. *Ibid.,* p. 76.

35. van Buren, *Christ in Context,* p. 265.

36. *Ibid.,* p. 268.

37. *Ibid.*

38. Both in personal conversation and in *Christ in Context,* van Buren has disclosed Lampe's influence upon his own thought about the Spirit. In *Christ in Context,* van Buren summarizes Lampe's thesis: "that the experience of the post-Easter presence of Jesus and the experience of God as Spirit were one and the same thing, both referring to the experience of God as he works upon and within the human spirit" (p. 265).

39. Lampe, *God as Spirit* (London: SCM Press Ltd, 1977), pp. 11, 23. Alasdair Heron, in his book *The Holy Spirit* (Philadelphia: The Westminster Press, 1983), rightly notes Lampe's affinity with process theology, and (wrongly, I think) criticizes him for a shallow treatment of the Church Fathers' trinitarian thought.

40. *Ibid.,* p. 23.

41. *Ibid.,* p. 96.

2. Ruach, Pneuma, Shekhinah: The Divine Presence

Part I of this book represents an attempt to address the problem of Christian exclusivism and triumphalism, particularly in relation to Jews and Judaism, from the vantage point of pneumatology. The burden of the argument in Chapter 1 was to show how traditional pneumatologies have contributed to a spiteful and finally destructive anti-Judaism, and then in response to suggest a new direction for pneumatology. This direction is predicated upon the assumption that God continues in covenant faithfulness to Jews today, and so also that their history of interpretations of God's presence, both in their midst and in the world, ought to be of especial importance to a post-Holocaust reconstruction of Christian pneumatology. Consequently, it also entails a reversal of attitude: from disparagement, or even a liberal tolerance of Jewish religious reflection, to a careful and appreciative listening. In this chapter, then, I shall attempt a theological appropriation of certain key terms denoting the divine presence—**ruach, pneuma, shekhinah**—which come to the fore in the process of such listening.

What follows is not intended to be an exhaustive examination of these terms in their historical and literary contexts; rather, it is a selective theological appropriation of these terms in which two issues serve as the controlling questions in this interpretive task. Those issues can be presented well in the form of an argument: I believe that the concept of "spirit" originally and best refers not to a distinct hypostasis either beside God or within the Godhead, mediating between God and the world, but to *God's own personal presence and activity in the world.* I believe it was an unfortunate development when Christian reflection moved toward a philosophically substantive trinitarianism that understood Spirit as "the Holy Spirit," in the sense of a third hypostasis who (or "which," as the early theological confusions make unclear) derived his or its identity and

41

mission from the Son. This Christocentric view of the Spirit—particularly in the Western Church, where the **filioque** clause has predominated—has tended to limit the Spirit's activity and influence exclusively to the Church. This limitation in turn has made it difficult for Western theologians to engage effectively both the universalist and particularist aspects of God the Spirit's activity in the world, well attested to in scripture. In other words, the Church, recognizing that its apprehension by God and experience of God's presence has occurred through Jesus as the Christ, has hypostasized that presence, called that presence "the Holy Spirit," and assumed that this presence of the Holy Spirit was essentially if not exclusively Christic in its every manifestation. In this chapter I want to explore, among other things, the possibility that there is an essential connection between the hypostasizing of Spirit and the exclusivist claim.

This argument raises the two questions which control the interpretive approach of this chapter toward the terms **ruach, pneuma** and **shekhinah** within the history of Jewish interpretations of divine presence: (i) Did these terms connote a distinct, mediatorial being independent from God, or did they more often serve as circumlocutions for God's presence and activity? (ii) How did the religious communities deal with the tension between universalist and particularist visions of God's presence, i.e., how did the claim for the divine presence among the Jews color their notion of God's presence among all human beings, or in creation in general? It is likely that the answers to these questions, which will arise from the proposed theological appropriation of **ruach, pneuma** and **shekhinah,** can make important contributions to a reconstruction of Christian pneumatology. Following this relatively brief hermeneutical detour, I will in this chapter next suggest how a process understanding of God's presence may aid in a Christian retrieval of the rabbinic ideas of the presence of the Shekhinah, and then reflect upon what such a retrieval might imply for Christian trinitarianism.

A. DIVINE PRESENCE IN JEWISH EXPERIENCE: AN INTERPRETATION

1. *Ruach* in the Hebrew Scriptures

> The wind blows wherever it pleases and you hear the sound of it, but do not know where it comes from and where it is going; so it is with everyone who is born of the Spirit (Jn 3:8).

This quotation certainly could be offered as a counter-argument to the suggestion in the previous chapter that the Johannine pneumatology represents only a radical discontinuity with the Hebrew conception of spirit. For these words, attributed to Jesus, summarize well the notion of **ruach** found in the Hebrew scriptures: **ruach** is wind or breath, i.e., air in movement, as well as spirit. Or it may be more precise to say that, whatever else spirit connoted, it was experienced and expressed among the ancient Hebrew people as the rush of wind and a blowing breath. The words of this verse suggest not only the dynamism of **ruach**—blowing "wherever it pleases"—but also its unfathomable ambiguity—"you do not know where it comes from and where it is going."

Both elements of dynamism and mystery are vital to an adequate appropriation of biblical Israel's history of interpretations of God's presence. At the same time, both elements prohibit any neatly ordered, systematic presentation of a biblical theology of spirit. If it is the case that the biblical authors generally betray little interest in a systematic theology, it is all the more so when the concept in question resists ready categorization as stubbornly as does **ruach,** the wind which is invisible but whose effects, nonetheless, can be discerned.

This notion of **ruach** as the invisible, ambiguous and yet efficacious divine activity exercised an important role in Israel's formative memory of the exodus from Egypt (Hag 2:5). According to Exodus 14:21, it was a strong east wind which blew all night, turning the sea into dry land, which was interpreted as God's liberating activity on Israel's behalf. In Moses' subsequent hymn, then, it was a blast of God's nostrils which piled up the waters, and God's **ruach** that caused the sea to cover the Egyptians (Ex 15:8, 10). The very fact that, in this formative narrative, Israel's pursuers were destroyed underscores the "sense of the devastating impact of God on men and on their world" which **ruach** conveyed.[1] God's powerful breath, even when blowing in Israel's behalf, has a dark ambiguity about it. The same creative spirit which bestows life upon Israel also deals death to Pharaoh.

If the exodus memory did indeed provide the central motif for Hebraic reflection about God, Israel and the world, then one may hear its echoes in the creation narrative of Genesis 1. For just as God's **ruach** parted the chaotic seas through which the liberated Jews passed, so "the Spirit of God was hovering over the surface of the waters" of the chaotic void, preparing the waters for God's creation (v. 2).[2] "By the word of the Lord the heavens were made, and by the breath of His mouth all their host" (Ps 33:6). But again, there is something of a somber, divine unpredictability suggested in Genesis 6, when God the creator becomes God the destroyer by allowing the watery chaos to break forth and swallow the

earth. Even so, God's wind once more passes over the chaos in 8:1, causing the water to subside and preparing for a new creation through Noah.
Repeatedly in the Genesis narratives, then, the **ruach** of God, God's own
presence as spirit-breath, presides over the divine shaping of chaos into
creation. God's Spirit is God's animating personal presence, imparting
life to all of creation.[3] The observable fact that in death a creature stopped
breathing lent credence to the idea that the Creator's spirit-breath ani-
mated all living things.

If **ruach** denoted God's active and creative presence throughout creation, in a more particular sense it suggested divine intimacy, God's
"point of contact," with human beings. The classic narrative which so
graphically portrays this intimacy is Genesis 2, according to which "the
Lord God formed man of dust from the ground, and breathed into his
nostrils the breath of life; and man became a living being" (v. 7). It is often
noted that the word translated here "living being," **nefesh,** is also used of
the rest of God's creatures (2:19; 9:10), and our prior interpretation of
ruach as God's animating breath through all of creation would also serve
as a warning against any attempt to give Adam an exclusive significance
over the other creatures. Yet the assertion of Genesis 1 that humanity,
male and female, was created in God's image may find its finest exposition in the intimate imagery of God bending over and breathing **ruach**
into the clay form. What distinguishes Adam from the other creatures is
God's particular "drawing near" to the human through the in-breathing
of God's Spirit.

Henry van Dusen, in *Spirit, Son and Father,* recalled Emil Brunner's
suggestion that the image of God be understood as humanity's awareness
of, and capacity for relation with, God—and then suggested that the further necessary step was the acknowledgement that the divine Spirit bestows this awareness and gives this relationship.[4] Both Genesis 2 and van
Dusen, then, would press for an understanding of the image of God as a
dynamic, pneumatic giftedness. Thus, when the Hebrew scriptures speak
of the **ruach** of a human being, this indicates no internal essence or natural
possession, but rather the animating, intimate, human-creating activity of
God. Alasdair Heron, too, has recognized the biblical conviction that
the human **ruach** is God-bestowed, not an essence or property human
beings possess in and of themselves. In commenting upon Psalm 51:10–
11—"Create in me a clean heart, O God, and renew a steadfast spirit
within me . . . and do not take Thy Holy Spirit from me"—he writes,

It is a moot point whether the second use of **ruach** here should be translated as 'Spirit' or 'spirit,' as God's own **ruach** or the **ruach** of man which he renews. The two senses are so intimately bound up together that to insist on the one rather than the other is to drive into the text a distinction which was not . . . in the author's mind. So **ruach** even as applied to man has an implicit reference to God as man's creator and sustainer; thus it becomes a linking term which refers both to God and to human life in its dependence upon God.[5]

The animating activity of the divine **ruach,** whether in creation in general or, more specifically, in creating human beings toward relationality, provides the basis for the many other effects associated with the Spirit in the Hebrew scriptures. The divine Spirit was recognized in people especially gifted in such diverse pursuits as agriculture, architecture, jurisdiction, politics, poetry, artistry and prophecy. The divine inspiration (**in spire** = "breathe into") involved in these human contributions to Israel's societal, religious and cultural life did not entail a denigration of human ability or the natural order, but rather their enhancement by the animating Spirit. In Wolfhart Pannenberg's words, "These phenomena . . . present just outstanding examples of life. They exhibit a particularly intensified life and are therefore attributed to an exceptional share in the life-giving spirit."[6]

If, then, **ruach** at this level of interpretation suggested God's accessibility to human beings, who through God's in-breathing also partake of **ruach,** there is certainly a sense in which Moule is correct to suggest that "spirit" connotes the "immanence of the transcendent God."[7] Yet at the same time, as I have already suggested, "spirit" also connotes God's otherness, God's darkness, ambiguity and mystery. One need only recall the strange and unpredictable behavior of some of Israel's Spirit-endowed judges and ecstatic prophets to get a sense of the mystery of **ruach.** Further, **ruach** is also used in the Hebrew scriptures at times to refer to destructive and malevolent spirits. Heron writes,

> It is significant that all these 'evil spirits' come from God. . . . The Old Testament in fact offers very little by way of demonology, but it can and does use **ruach** to speak of a good or evil influence coming from God and exerting an impact on the lives of individuals or groups.[8]

It appears, then, that when Israel wanted to speak of God's dynamic and mysterious activities in the world, and especially among human be-

ings, **ruach** was a favored term. To be sure, it was not the only term
denoting divine presence; other metaphors included God's arm, hand,
finger, face, presence, name, glory, word, wisdom and angel, among
others. Each metaphor bears its own distinctive nuances, so that it would
be misleading to flatten them out and claim that they all "meant the same
thing." Yet each metaphor involved an analogy from human experience
—breathing, hearing a word, seeing a face, touching a hand—to hint at
some aspect of the one God's multitudinous and mysterious workings in
creation. These anthropomorphic metaphors are precisely that—metaphors—and in their early usage normally were not hypostasized into mediatorial beings. "Thus," in Richard Killough's words, "the Hebrew Bible's
understanding of God and God's Spirit is thoroughly monotheistic. It is
one indivisible God who creates, inspires and empowers. To speak of
God's Spirit is to speak of God."[9] And to speak of God is to speak of the
mysterious One whose activities are finally beyond human ken. No
word gets to the heart of this active, yet elusive, divine presence better
than **ruach**.

Perhaps due at least partially to the occasional ambiguity of God's
activities in Israel's tumultuous history, then, there arose the gradual
movement in Hebraic thinking to associate God's Spirit with prophecy.
The prophet depended upon the **davar** or word of God in order to discern
the ways of God's **ruach** in the world, and so to interpret those ways to
God's people. Thus **ruach** and **davar** tended increasingly to occur together: "the former stresses God's staggering, often inconceivable, alive-
ness; the latter, the fact that he wants to be recognized and known."[10]
Though the prophets certainly affirmed the mysteriousness, indeed the
ambiguity, of God's ways, their belief that as prophets they received the
word whereby to interpret God tended to empty the notion of **ruach** of
much of its inscrutability. The struggle toward a more thoroughly ethical
consciousness, too, led to the gradual moralization by the prophets of the
notion of the Spirit. The Spirit eventually was so thoroughly identified
with the prophetic calling that, among the post-exilic Jews, it commonly
was considered "the Spirit of prophecy." A certain intellectualization and
moralization of **ruach**—in itself not dangerous, and probably a positive
development except when it also means a certain exclusivist "taming" of
deity—took place.

> The Old Testament . . . in its highest and normative conception of God
> as Spirit, knows him to be that Almighty Sovereign Person, for whose
> eternal covenant-partner man is created and destined. . . . Indeed, as

Yahweh increasingly becomes a 'clear-cut personality' in the Old Testament development, the prophet more and more loses his character as God-filled, and his nature as a God-sent messenger comes to be emphasized.[11]

Though in this passage Arnold Come suggests a positive, almost evolutionary development in the Hebrew conception of **ruach,** I would suggest that something also was lost or suppressed in this development: the wild, ecstatic, uncontrollable and unpredictable aspect of **ruach** which connotes so well the divine ambiguity from the human perspective. Once this aspect of the human experience of God's presence is forgotten, exclusivist claims can surface much more readily.

Before proceeding to pre-Christian Hellenistic Judaism, two important factors in this brief theological appropriation of **ruach** should be noted: (i) it pointed to God's own active presence in creation and particularly among human beings—"God at his most empirical," in H. F. Woodhouse's fine phrase—rather than to a separate hypostasized "being" who mediated God's presence or activity; and (ii) its increasingly close connection to the concept of **davar** in the classical prophets—and so the tendency toward an increased intellectualization and moralization of "the Spirit of prophecy"—involved something of a denial or suppression of the darker, dynamic, less predictable aspects of deity. While in many ways this process was a good and necessary development of Israel's faith, and while the prophets warned against turning the Holy One into a manageable deity, it appears nonetheless that an overidentification of **ruach** with the **davar** of prophecy tended to make the Spirit quite comprehensible. A community whose God is easily interpreted is also more prone to make exclusivist claims on the deity's presence and activity. Though it would be simplistic to posit a necessary connection between the intellectualization and moralization of religious experience on one hand, and the development of an exclusivist mentality on the other, the tendency for such a union is evident.

2. Pneuma in Pre-Christian Judaism

While in classical Palestinian Judaism the messianic hope of an age of the universal outpouring of God's Spirit flourished (Jl 2:27–32), in Hellenistic Judaism the interpretation of God's Spirit as **pneuma** took a decidedly different tack. In its cosmopolitan, pluralistic setting, this notion of **pneuma,** informed to a certain extent by Stoic ideas, involved something of an expansion of the idea of God's **ruach** as animating, perhaps even permeating, all the world. The most significant examples of this idea occur in the Wisdom of Solomon: "The spirit of the Lord fills the whole earth"; "Thou sparest all things because they are thine, . . . for thy imperishable breath is in them all" (1:7; 12:1).

Though the Stoic conception of **pneuma** as the divine substance immanent in the world undoubtedly did exercise some influence upon Hellenistic Judaism,[12] a far more important factor was the close connection made between **pneuma** and **sophia,** wisdom. Here the wisdom tradition in Jewish religious thought, particularly in the personification of Wisdom in Proverbs 8 and 9, found novel expression. Since both **sophia** and **pneuma** referred to the presence and activity of God in the affairs of this world, "it is not . . . surprising that some representatives of Hellenistic Judaism should have discerned a particular link between **sophia** and **pneuma** and sought to spell it out."[13] In the Wisdom of Solomon, **sophia** is described in terms of **pneuma,** and in some passages the two are virtually identified: "Who ever learnt to know thy purposes, unless thou hadst given him wisdom and sent thy holy spirit down from heaven on high?" (9:17; cf. 1:6; 7:7).

Equally important, of course, is the close affinity the Wisdom of Solomon suggests between this Spirit of Wisdom with God, particularly in 7:22–30, which very likely was inspired by the biblical notion of the **doxa** of God:

> For in wisdom there is a spirit intelligent and holy . . . all-powerful, all-surveying, and permeating all intelligent, pure, and delicate spirits . . . she pervades and permeates all things because she is so pure. Like a fine mist she rises from the power of God, a pure effulgence from the glory of the Almighty. . . . She is the brightness that streams from everlasting light, the flawless mirror of the active power of God and the image of his goodness. She is but one, yet can do everything; herself unchanging, she makes all things new; age after age she enters into holy souls, and makes them God's friends and prophets, for nothing is acceptable to God but the man who makes his home with wisdom.

Marie Isaacs argues convincingly that this **pneuma/sophia** in Hellenistic Judaism, even when personified, is not an intermediary nor in any way independent from God. Rather, like **doxa,** it is a circumlocution for God, a way of indicating God's own presence and activity.[14] It is her thesis, then, that **sophia** is more rightly understood as a literary device than as an intermediary hypostasis. She writes,

The author of the Wisdom of Solomon does not seem concerned with the production of systematic theology. Hence there are a number of occasions in the book in which wisdom is not personified, i.e., the device of personification is not consistently employed. Far from such personification being used to overcome any difficulty which the author felt about the possibility of God making contact with the world without the services of an intermediary, God is . . . frequently spoken of as acting Himself. Were the author attempting to postulate any notion of intermediary agency, one would have thought that he would have been far more careful to make a clear distinction between God and wisdom. Therefore, it seems most unlikely that the Wisdom of Solomon presents wisdom as an intermediary.[15]

Isaac's conclusion, then, is that there exists no substantial evidence of a doctrine of intermediary beings in Hellenistic Judaism. Both **pneuma** and **sophia,** as well as their combination in the notion of the Spirit of Wisdom, instead are ways of referring to God's active presence in creation and in the affairs of human beings, much like **ruach** in the Hebrew scriptures. Similarly, Lampe writes that "this Wisdom-Spirit is a symbolical representation of God's activity, not intended to be interpreted literally as a distinct being."[16] If Isaacs and Lampe are right, then there is no more support in Hellenistic Judaism than in the Hebrew scriptures for the idea of the Spirit as a hypostasis in any way distinct or distinguishable from God.

It is significant to note, too, that this association of the divine **pneuma** with **sophia** continued also the tendency to intellectualize and to moralize —perhaps to domesticate—the notion of spirit. It is Wisdom's function to guide people according to God's will, and thus she finds her true home among the people to whom Torah was given: Israel, "God's friends and prophets." Indeed, in Ecclesiasticus she is virtually identified with "the covenant-book of God Most High, the law which Moses enacted to be the heritage of the assemblies of Jacob" (24:23). Baruch, too, envisions the heavenly Wisdom as having taken earthly form in Torah: "The whole way of knowledge he found out and gave to Jacob his servant, and to Israel, whom he loved. Thereupon wisdom appeared on earth and lived among men. She is the book of the commandments of God, the law that stands for ever" (3:36–4:1). There is in pre-Christian Jewish thought, accordingly, an important sense in which the ideas of Spirit, Wisdom and Torah were interfused in the attempt to elucidate God's "drawing near" to Israel. "God's personal outreach towards men, and his communion with them," writes Lampe of this period, "are mediated through, and as it were incarnated in, the Torah and the written words of the prophets."[17] God's presence was experienced as address and command, given in the written word, and offering fresh inspiration and instruction "through the channel of scriptural exegesis, where the exegete is moved to discern the application of God's word, addressing him through the text, to his contemporary situation."[18]

It is arguable, then, that the mode of God's presence as experienced by Israel became increasingly a *textual* presence: God as Wisdom, alluring Israel to live by her precepts; God as Word, addressing Israel in command. **Pneuma,** while not losing entirely a universal or cosmological significance, became understood primarily through the Torah-structured life. This was a particularly important development among Hellenistic Jews, since it contributed to a strong sense of religious identity amid pagan cultures and religions. For example, even the cosmopolitan Philo, who often spoke of the divine **pneuma** in the cosmos and of **pneuma** as pointing to humanity's creation in God's image, was equally apt to consider **pneuma** the unique gift of God's revelatory Spirit to the Jews, exemplified in Moses.

A potential danger arose, however, in the tendency to assume that this valid and vital experience of God's pneumatic presence as Wisdom–Word–Torah was the definitive mode of God's activity: not only did the exclusivist claim place boundaries upon God, but it also, ironically enough, paved the way for a similar claim by the Church, as Isaacs indicates:

> Jewish claims to supreme revelation mediated through their cult hero, Moses, [were] taken by Paul and applied to the Christian church and her Lord. Furthermore, the term **pneuma,** which had been honed by Diaspora Jews for the purposes of polemic, and used by them as a weapon against the pagan world, [was] adopted by Paul in his debate against Judaism to make those self same assertions for the supremacy of Christianity. Thus, the very term **pneuma,** which had been claimed by Judaism as her own, [was] taken over by Paul and used by him against his erstwhile co-religionists.[19]

It would be pointless to fault either Judaism or Christianity for having made claims to a monopoly on God's Spirit; it seems that such exclusivist assertions were vital to religious communities struggling for a sense of identity and validity in a large and threatening world. It is doubtful, however, that such claims can continue to be made in the same way today, not simply because of our increasingly pluralistic consciousness, but because they finally represent a domestication of deity which belies the mystery and dynamism of God as Spirit.

The end result of this brief interpretation of **pneuma** in pre-Christian Judaism, considered in the context of our two controlling hermeneutical questions, parallels the points made in the previous section on **ruach:** (i) among Hellenistic Jews, there was little if any hesitation about speaking of God's contact with, and activity in, the world, so it appears that **pneuma** did not function as an independent intermediary for God, but rather as a way of speaking of God's presence and activity in the world; and (ii) the intellectualization and moralization of the Spirit, which had begun with Israel's classical prophets, became even more pronounced in the identification of Spirit with Wisdom, and of Wisdom with Torah. God's presence became experienced among the Jews in an increasingly Torah-structured, textual, hermeneutic mode. Certainly this interpretation of God's presence was to become profoundly deepened in rabbinic Judaism.

3. Shekhinah in the Rabbinic Writings

In the rabbinic literature, the word which was most often utilized to refer to God's presence was the title "Shekhinah," meaning literally "dwelling," and derived from the verb **shakhan** ("to dwell"). In the Hebrew scriptures the verb often refers to God's indwelling the people Israel, and more specifically God's presence in the Temple. Apparently the noun derivative "Shekhinah" first appeared in rabbinic reflection in the Targum Onkelos sometime in the first four centuries of the common era.[20]

The early usage in Onkelos suggests that "Shekhinah" was added to the text whenever God was spoken of as dwelling, or causing the divine name to dwell, among the camp of the Hebrew people. For instance, "And let them make me a sanctuary, that I may dwell among them" became "And they shall make before me a sanctuary and I shall cause my Shekhinah to dwell among them" (Ex 25:8). Apparently its usage not only suggested "God in action . . . the emphatic declaration of the nearness of God,"[21] but also furnished both a detour around the Bible's troubling anthropomorphisms, and a way to protect from overuse the divine name and its sanctity.

The term "Shekhinah," according to Ephraim Urbach, is prevalent in halakhic midrashim, where, again, it refers to God's manifestations, descents and goings forth in Israel's midst. It suggests not simply divine presence, but divine nearness and even intimacy. Urbach writes, "We may sum up as follows: In Tannatic literature the term Shekhinah is used when the manifestation of the Lord and His nearness to man are spoken of."[22] Since in the Hebrew scriptures Israel is often affirmed to be God's special dwelling place (e.g., Ex 29:45–46; Deut 23:15; Ez 36:26–27; Zech 2:10–12), Shekhinah referred especially to God's indwelling of the people Israel, the land of Palestine, and the Temple in Jerusalem.

This interpretation of Shekhinah as denoting God's intimate nearness suggests that, in the rabbinic writings, Shekhinah did not refer to a being separate from God. This, admittedly, has not been the unanimous reading of Jewish thinkers. Max Kadushin reports that the medieval authorities Yehuda Ha-Levi and Maimonides both insisted that the Shekhinah was created by God and not to be identified with God. Nahmanides, however, disagreed with Maimonides on this question, and Kadushin argues that rabbinic usage supports Nahmanides. It was used consistently as a reverential appellative for God in a special context: "It is employed as a name for God only when the Rabbis speak of God's nearness to man."[23] Urbach, too, citing strong support from Gershom Scholem, argues that "a survey of all the passages referring to the Shekhinah leaves no doubt that the Shekhinah is no 'hypostasis' and has no separate existence alongside the Deity."[24] And Abelson indicates that the rabbis had no intention of suggesting a dualism of deities, since they were concerned stringently to avoid the very sin of "two deities." Shekhinah was a literary device, not unlike other appellatives for, or attributes of, God which could be literarily personified but were not to be ontologically hypostasized:

> Wisdom is . . . only God's wisdom, no matter how near an approach to personality there may be in the various descriptions of the term; and in the same way 'Spirit' is 'God's Spirit' and 'Holy Spirit' is 'God's Holy Spirit'; and similarly right through the Rabbinical literature. . . .[25]

At this point it is useful to note that, in regard to the two controlling questions of this chapter, the term "Shekhinah" in the rabbinic literature (i) referred not to a divine or semi-divine being alongside the God of Israel, but was a way of alluding to that God as present and active among, and even intimate with, God's people; and (ii) while not entirely devoid of reference beyond the people, land and holy sites of Israel, seemed not to carry as much cosmological significance as **ruach** and **pneuma** could. There is a sense in which Shekhinah is identified much more closely with the people Israel and their circumstances and concerns.

Two prominent themes which were important to rabbinical reflection on the Shekhinah help to illustrate the tendency toward ethnocentricity in the use of the term. The first is the phrase "the wings of the Shekhinah," which primarily denoted proselytism, in the sense that the proselyte to Judaism was entering beneath the protective aegis of the Shekhinah, God's intimate presence. The second is the idea of the exile of the Shekhinah (**Shekhinta b'Galuta**), or God's sharing of Israel's exile following the destruction of the Temple in 70 CE.

This latter notion is especially important for our purposes, since the problem of God's presence in the midst of senseless suffering and evil will be the particular problem of Part II of this study. It is important to recall that rabbinic Judaism was born in a disruptive time in which the challenges of suffering and evil to traditional faith were deeply felt. One prominent strand in the rabbinic tradition, drawing from the Deuteronomic code of rewards and punishments, asserted that the destruction of the Temple and much of Jerusalem was God's just retribution for the sins of Israel, and that, consequently, the Shekhinah had departed from Israel; "God's indwelling presence was repelled by the sins of the people."[26] This traditionalist view, however, did not square with the profound Jewish experience of God's love and compassion, nor with the covenant of perpetuity to which the Hebrew scriptures witnessed. There arose, then, an alternative strand in the tradition, associated with Rabbi Akiba, which reassuringly taught that God's presence, the Shekhinah, never departed from the people Israel and indeed was exiled with them, sharing their suffering. With that reassurance came also the assurance that, one day, both God and God's people would be redeemed together.

> "My heart shall rejoice in Thy salvation" (Psalm 13:6). R. Abbahu taught: This is one of those difficult verses which declare that the salvation of the Holy One, blessed be He, depends upon the salvation of the people of Israel. Note that it is not written "My heart shall rejoice in my salvation," but rather "in Thy salvation," by which David meant: Thy salvation depends upon our salvation. We will be redeemed together (Midrash Psalm 13:6).

The idea of the Shekhinah's accompaniment with the Jews into exile placed new emphasis upon the concept that the God of the covenant was a suffering God, a God whose heart revealed a deep involvement with, and commitment to, Israel. Thus the Shekhinah signified not only God's intimate presence, but God's exilic suffering *in relationship to, and together with, Israel.* The notion of the Shekhinah strongly communicated God's particular(ist) presence with the Jewish people in a time of exilic crisis. In the context of Christian anti-Judaic claims which surfaced in the decades and centuries following the Temple's destruction, the rabbinic reaffirmation of God's suffering presence with Israel was crucial to Jewish faith, as Norman J. Cohen indicates:

> ... this motif ... was used to counter the virulent Christian propaganda which stressed that the downfall of Jerusalem, the destruction of the Temple and the exile of Israel were a manifestation of God's having forsaken the Jewish people. The **tannaim** and the early **amoraim** responded to the taunts of the Church Fathers by denying that Israel had been abandoned by God and its place taken by the 'true' Israel, the Church. Indeed the downtrodden Jewish nation was still God's covenanted partner and He continued to dwell amongst them under all circumstances.[27]

Yet another phrase, "the confinement of the Shekhinah" (**tsimtsum ha-Shekhinah**), which denotes a unique concentration of God's presence in a particular place, contributed even further to a particularist slant in reflection upon the Shekhinah. But in a significant way, it was not a particular place but a particular activity—the process of **halakha,** or the study and application of Torah—which was to become a primary locus of God's presence among the Jews. According to Urbach, the term "Shekhinah" appears but twice in the Mishnah, and both occurrences involve the divine presence when the Jewish community gathers around the sacred text. In the words of R. Halafta of Hanania, if ten men sat down together to occupy themselves with the words of Torah, the Shekhinah would also be there in their midst; according to R. Hanania ben Teradion, it would take but two.[28] In either case it is a communal interpretive process, a religious community confronting, and being confronted by, its sacred text—and in this process God's presence is experienced.

This creative, communal encounter with the text, which involved an ongoing process of reinterpretation in ever-changing historical contexts, became for the rabbis a primary, though not exclusive, means for God to be present to God's people. Certainly it is David Hartman's argument in *The Living Covenant* that, in rabbinic experience, the locus of God's presence was discovered in engagement with Torah as a living and dynamic interpretive process, in contradistinction to Christian caricatures of "the Law" as an unyielding burden. In Hartman's words,

The enormous concern with exegesis and fine legal distinctions should not be thought to have diminished the vitality of the covenantal passion for God. Rabbinic teachers brought the religious intensity of the living God present at the revelatory moment of Sinai into their daily experience of the study of Torah. That study, they claimed, should indeed be felt as an experience akin to revelation. It should take place "in dread and fear and trembling and quaking" just like the Sinai experience (Berakhot 22a). If even only two people sit together and occupy themselves with the Torah, the divine presence rests between them (Pirkei Avot 3:6).[29]

Or, as Abelson has written, "The Law is . . . the first agent which made possible the Immanence of God. Through the Law God is near, His love is realisable, communion with Him is a possibility."[30] It should not be surprising, then, that Deuteronomy 30:11–14 was a favorite passage among the rabbis, for it stressed that God was present in the address and command experienced in engagement with Torah:

> For this commandment which I command you today is not too difficult for you, nor is it out of reach. It is not in heaven, that you should say, "Who will go up to heaven for us to get it for us and make us hear it, that we may observe it?" Nor is it beyond the sea, that you should say, "Who will cross the sea for us to get it for us and make us hear it, that we may observe it?" But the word is very near you, in your mouth and in your heart, that you may observe it.

The rabbinic emphasis upon an ever-renewed encounter with Torah complemented their belief that with the deaths of Haggai, Zechariah and Malachi, the prophets of the second Temple, "the Holy Spirit ceased out of Israel"—meaning not God's active presence, but the gift of prophecy (Sota 13:2). While, as I argued in the section on **ruach,** the association of the Spirit with prophecy can be interpreted as a narrowing of the concept, it would appear that the mode of God's presence tended to be even further narrowed in the rabbinic tradition to the textual. In Lampe's words,

> There was the general assumption that the primary locus of revelation is the written word. . . . [Therefore] in the rabbinic writings the Holy Spirit . . . is not conceived of as a force or influence, still less as a being, distinct from God, but rather as a poetical and dramatic personification of the divine inspiration embodied in, and mediated through, the written word of scripture. The Holy Spirit of the rabbinic literature is really

almost synonymous with God as he addresses men through the
scriptures.[31]

It should be stressed that God's presence as address was not simply
through the scriptures, but mediated by the communal interpretive processes of the rabbinic tradition. This communal, halakhic accent is suggested by the sometimes laboriously long and varied quotations from a
number of rabbis, offering their interpretations of a given text before
attempting either a new interpretation or a creative synthesis of all the
others—which, to be sure, would itself be a new interpretation. It was in
the midst of the rabbinic community's engagement with Torah—whether
two men or ten—that the Shekhinah dwelled.

It also must be noted that while in the above quotation Lampe refers
specifically to the Holy Spirit, the same can be said of the Shekhinah. It is
true that the term "Holy Spirit" for the rabbis generally connoted the
voice of God in the scriptures, and "Shekhinah" tended more to suggest
God's comforting and sustaining presence particularly in the context of
Jewish suffering. Nonetheless, the fact remains that the terms are frequently interchanged in the rabbinic writings. There are many passages in
the Talmud and the Midrash in which one version may use "the Holy
Spirit," and another may report precisely the same thing of the Shekhinah.[32] And in our own time, R. Joseph Soloveitchik has written elo-
quently of the descent and contraction of the divine presence into the
"empirical realm" of the halakha, so that the Shekhinah is circumscribed
and experienced in the Torah-structured life.[33] Thus it is arguable that, for
the rabbis, *both "the Holy Spirit" and "the Shekhinah" were terms which
referred to God's presence, experienced most fully in the communal encounter with the divine address and command of the sacred text, and in
faithful response to the word that is heard.*

Interestingly, however, Abelson indicates that the term "Holy Spirit"
appears far less frequently in rabbinic writings than "Shekhinah," quite
possibly due to the Christian adoption of "the Holy Spirit." The parallel
usage of the two terms is found mostly in the later rather than earlier
rabbinic literature, so that this usage "belong[s] to a period when the
breach between Judaism and Christianity was a long-accomplished fact,
and all controversy had long been silenced."[34] Thus it would seem, as has
already been suggested in the context of the idea of the exile of the Shekhinah, that Judaism's early confrontation with Christianity drove the
rabbis to an increasingly exclusivist use of "Shekhinah" to denote God's
presence among the Jewish people.

Yet for all of this, the rabbis did not allow the exclusive/inclusive tension to be collapsed completely. While "the confinement of the Shekhinah" suggested God's special indwelling of the people Israel through the covenant constituted by the gift of Torah, it did not imply God's withdrawal from the rest of creation. A favorite rabbinic analogy was drawn between the confinement of the Shekhinah and a cave on the seashore: though when the tide comes in the sea fills the cave, there is yet an unfathomable abundance of water outside the cave.[35] Similarly, while "the wings of the Shekhinah" did refer usually to proselytization, it could at times bear the more inclusive meaning of God's protective presence over all of creation, "brooding over the face of the water . . . as a dove broods over its nest" (T.B. Haggigah 12a). Urbach sums up the matter well:

> The omnipresence of God-Shekhinah is one of the primary postulates. The dicta that speak of the Shekhinah do not attempt to describe her, but to explain and reconcile her with the manifestation and presence of God at fixed places and times, whilst avoiding the solution of positing the existence of powers that are separate and emanate from the Lord.[36]

Our two controlling questions, then, may be answered in these ways: (i) the Shekhinah referred not to a being separate from God, but to God's own presence among the Jews, experienced primarily in the communal interpretive context of engaging and practicing Torah; and (ii) while this textual sense of presence—along with Jewish reaction to Christian claims that God had deserted Israel—certainly contributed to an exclusivist interpretation of the Shekhinah, the rabbinic tradition also left room for a more inclusive, universal and cosmic understanding of the term.

What might this theological appropriation of the terms **ruach, pneuma** and **shekhinah** suggest for a reconstruction of Christian pneumatology? It is important to note, first, that these terms served as *ways of referring to God's presence and activity, rather than to a being or beings hypostatically distinct from God.* This, I would suggest, is an important consideration for a doctrine of the Holy Spirit written with attention to the context of Israel's history of interpretations of divine presence. Second, the usage of these terms in their religious communal contexts indicates *the continual tension felt between God's presence among the people Israel and their intuition that God must also be present and active in the world and peoples outside Israel.* I shall address these two issues in the following two sections of this chapter but, for methodological reasons, will begin with the second before moving on to the first.

This second issue, with which I shall begin, might be approached in this way: While the rabbis indicated that the halakhic process was a primary means for God's presence, the Shekhinah, to be experienced among the Jewish people, there was little reflection among them concerning the mode of God's more universal presence in creation and humanity; it was simply affirmed. Yet in the rabbinic ideas about the Shekhinah there lie some possible hints about the manner and mode of God's active presence in creation. By drawing upon those ideas, and by bringing them into conversation with an understanding of God's cosmic presence suggested by contemporary process theology, I intend in the following section to begin reconstruction of pneumatology in such a way as to explicate in closer relation the universal and particularist aspects of God's presence as Spirit.

B. A PROCESS APPROPRIATION OF THE SHEKHINAH

The rabbinic tradition tended to understand God's presence, the Shekhinah, in terms of the halakhic process of study and ethical application of Torah, and so tended also toward a sense of exclusivity about God's presence even while allowing that the Shekhinah was omnipresent. On the other hand, the process theological tradition, understanding God's presence in the world primarily as "initial aim," speaks far more readily of the divine presence in its inclusive or universal dimension. It is conceivable that a conversation between these two traditions may yield an enriched vision of God's alluring presence in creation as well as in particular cultural and religious communities.

In process theology, to speak of the world is to speak of a continual process of becoming in which the basic realities, or what Whitehead called "actual occasions," are relational energy-events. Every occasion is relational because it becomes itself only through receiving the contributions of other occasions and deciding how to appropriate and integrate those contributions in its own becoming. Simply put, the world is a complex web of interrelational events, ever becoming and ever contributing themselves to the becoming of others. "This becoming," writes Marjorie Hewitt Suchocki in her lucid and insightful book *God–Christ–Church,* "is through-and-through relational; relativity is therefore constitutive of existence, and not simply accidental to it. . . . Relationships are the beginning and ending of each unit of existence."[37]

Process theology affirms God's universal presence in this dynamic, relational view of the world by suggesting that God is present subliminally to *every* occasion of becoming as the principle of novelty. God influences every occasion in its foundational base or beginning, and so is present as the "initial aim," as Whitehead called it. Or, in a phrase which has become popular among some process theologians, God is the "power of the future" whose call makes possible more than a simple repetition of that which completed occasions contribute to a new occasion's "concrescence" or becoming.

> God-relatedness is constitutive of every occasion of experience. This does not restrict the freedom of the occasion. On the contrary, apart from God there would be no freedom. . . . It is God who, by confronting the world with unrealized opportunities, opens up a space for freedom and self-creativity.[38]

Just as the world provides a rich context of possibilities and influences in each occasion's becoming, so God is also present, and God's presence provides novel possibilities for that occasion which are in harmony with those of other occasions. "Whether or not these possibilities for harmony are achieved depends upon the decisions of the world," Suchocki writes. "Each occasion, in the solitude of its own concrescence, decides its orientation toward God and the world."[39] According to the process model, then, at the most basic level of existence every event exercises freedom in relation to God and the world according to its capacities, so that there is a sense of radical openness—a sense which even God shares—about the direction the world will take at any given moment. It is important to understand that this activity of God, the results of which cannot be predetermined due to the contingencies of freedom, operates at the fundamental level of every single occasion or energy event. Suchocki writes,

> The aim received from God orients the occasion toward an optimum mode of harmonizing the feelings received from the world. *Every* occasion is touched by God. But this touch comes at the very base of an occasion's beginning: Whitehead calls it the *initial aim*. Since this aim is at the foundation of each momentary existence, and since consciousness is a late phase of each occasion, the touch of God is necessarily in the preconscious stage of those occasions that develop consciousness. . . . Ordinarily God is hidden in the world.[40]

God in the process view of reality, then, is *present* to each and every moment of becoming as its co-creator, offering a direction to that mo-

ment which, if followed, would contribute to the divine vision of beauty
and harmony. God's presence in the world, usually, is not experienced as
coercive or manipulative, but as persuasive and alluring, much like the
figure of Wisdom personified. Equally, God's presence is experienced
precisely in the "initial aim" or lure toward harmony (**shalom**) offered to
each occasion of becoming. That is, God's presence is not ethereal substance or static fullness of being which "fills" creation like so much blood
in a circulatory system; rather, God's presence is experienced precisely in
the presentation of the initial aim, or in the call forward "in each moment
into a yet unsettled future," the lure of "new and richer possibilities for
our being."[41] God's presence, then, is not "simple presence" in and of
itself; it is, rather, as "initial aim" a dynamic calling toward future possibilities. This is not wholly unlike the presence of the Shekhinah, experienced
in rabbinic Judaism as a presence experienced in living according to the
halakhically structured divine command. The presence of God as Shekhinah, who "draws near" to those who practice righteousness, presents a
sense of allurement to continue in self-transformation in accordance with
Torah. Process thought, then, offers a way to extend the dynamic sense of
the Shekhinah's presence in rabbinic reflection to the larger context of
creation; from this perspective God, to use John Cobb's simple but telling
phrase, is "the One Who Calls," ever beckoning creation to new and
higher possibilities of complexity and harmony. Apart from the upward
call of God present in the "initial aim" as offered to every new occasion,
all existents would tend toward entropy and dissolution. In this regard,
God's presence in the "initial aim" is ever creative, and so also corresponds to the earlier explored notion of **ruach** as God's dynamic spirit-
presence who overcomes the threat of chaos in forming creation.

God's presence as "call," or as presentation of the "initial aim" to
new occasions, according to the process model, is universal. Nothing
comes into existence apart from God's alluring presence. But, as Suchocki
has indicated, this means that God's call functions predominantly on the
level of preconsciousness, even in beings which develop consciousness—
who themselves are, after all, only "the tip of the iceberg" we call the
world. In her words,

> Consciousness, in process thought, is a late development in the concre-
> scent process of each moment. . . . God's action upon us must be at
> [the] depth level, since God's action launches us upon our way of be-
> coming—that is what the initial aim is all about. But if God works in us

at such depths, then in principle it is a rare thing for God to be part of our conscious awareness.[42]

The One Who Calls, then, calls mostly **in cognito,** "hidden in the world," quietly and subliminally alluring creation forward.

Nonetheless, it is also true that, among human beings, this call from God finds more explicit, conscious and historical expressions through the mediation of human cultural and religious traditions. I would suggest, in fact, that God's universal presence in the "initial aim," in the case of human beings, is "shaped" according to the particular social, cultural and religious patterns of particular peoples; "if God provides initial aims to every occasion whatsoever, then the very faithfulness of God requires that the divine harmony be fitted to a diversity of conditions."[43] God is, necessarily, a co-creator of every moment of every creaturely existence. Such a statement includes not only every human being individually considered as a composite series of occasions, but also by implication every human culture. Co-creatorhood means that no human culture is created solely by God, but equally that no human culture is devoid of God's alluring, animating presence in the aims which God provides. This means also that no cultural, artistic or religious expression of the divine presence is unambiguous in either its origins or its effects.

God's presence, then, "takes shape" in a variety of ways according to the particular culture, religion or ethic in which God is present as co-creating call. The particular expressions of God's presence which have occupied us in this chapter have been those of certain Jewish religious communities, not because God is not present in others, but because the history of interpretations of God's presence among the Jewish people is of axiomatic value to Christian self-understanding and theology. It is my argument that, while God's presence as Spirit is structured and so appropriated differently in Judaism and Christianity (not to mention the wide diversity among their many sub-groups), it is nonetheless the case that God's interpreted presence in and among the people Israel provides the proper ideational context for understanding God's interpreted presence in the Church. This is particularly so in a process model, for its emphasis upon the essential relatedness of all occasions should nudge Christians toward a self-understanding which incorporates on a fundamental level Christianity's historical and theological rootedness in the Jewish people's interpretations of their history with God.

I have also suggested that the rabbinic notion of the Shekhinah as

God's presence, experienced in the address and command of Torah engagement and in faithful human response, resonates well with the process conception of God's universal presence as "initial aim" or address to every occasion of becoming. In both cases God's presence is not static fullness of being, but is experienced as an address or command which functions as a lure toward new possibilities in human existence and behavior. "Remember the day you stood before the Lord your God at Horeb. . . . Then the Lord spoke to you from the midst of the fire; you heard the sound of words, but you saw no form—only a voice" (Deut 4:12). "Only a voice"—but a voice whose address opens the one who "has ears to hear" to the upward call of self-transformation.

Additionally, it should be recalled that a fundamental tenet of process theology states that God cannot properly be viewed only as the provider of the "initial aim" to every occasion of becoming. Recalling the commitment of process thinkers to a thoroughly relational view of reality, it must be added that God, too, as the most eminently "social" of all entities, receives and integrates all events into God's own becoming. This creates possibilities for speaking of real suffering in God, an idea which resonates well not only with a Christian theology of the cross, but also with the Jewish notion of the Shekhinah's suffering in and with the Jewish people.[44] In addition, it means that the nature of the initial aims which God may present to new occasions depends significantly, even if not entirely, upon what God receives and integrates from completed occasions. "In a process world," Suchocki writes, "God acts with the world as it is, leading it toward what it can be. The aims of God will transcend the given, but must also reflect the given."[45] God graciously works with creation *as it is in every moment,* and thus can only offer new possibilities which, while transcending its present situation in accordance with God's ideal vision, are relevant to that situation. This again underscores the sense of *co-creatorhood* implied in process theology, particularly (though not exclusively) as it concerns itself with God's relationships to humanity.

These reflections about the meaning and mode of God's presence to creation in process theology may be useful in providing a universal or cosmological basis to much of what the rabbis said about the Shekhinah in the Jewish community. If this is indeed the case, then the way is opened for a process pneumatology founded in Jewish-Christian conversation which can embrace both the universalist and the particularist aspects of the Spirit's activity.

First of all, it is clear that the rabbis affirmed that the Shekhinah, as

God's presence, was in some sense omnipresent. A reticence to engage in metaphysics may have prevented the rabbis from much reflection upon *how* God was present to all of creation. They were more certain of their own experience: for them, the Shekhinah was present in the communal study, interpretation and application of Torah, for it was through this hermeneutical process that God's presence was experienced as address and command. On this interpretation—which, it must be admitted, cannot be claimed to exhaust the meaning and modes of divine presence in rabbinic reflection—the Shekhinah would not be a static presence so much as a lure to live according to the Torah's precepts as interpreted by the rabbis. Hence in Hartman's words, "The living word of God can be mediated through the application of human reason (the autonomous spirit) to the revealed norms of Torah . . . dramatically capturing the experience of God's commanding presence."[46]

Is it possible that, with the help of process theology, God's *universal* presence might be understood in an analagous way? God's presence in creation is not static or immutable or ethereal quiddity; rather, God is present as the invitation to, and even the demand for, self-transcendence. This is the essential thrust of God's presence to the creature as an "initial aim" who calls forward each moment of creation's becoming. This address, throughout most of creation, functions on a subconscious or pre-conscious level, but on the level of human cultures and religions may find a more "human" mode of address: in prophets, in sacred writings, in art, in ethical reflection, in worship. At every level, though, God is experienced as the "Other" who addresses creation through the offering of initial aims, sharing the divine vision for that creation but not unilaterally forcing that vision upon it.

Precisely because God does not force the divine aim or vision for creation, the level of intensity of the felt presence of God would depend upon the measure of each occasion's appropriation of that presence in the initial aim. And to the extent to which a particular occasion responds positively to that aim, it makes possible even more "godly" initial aims on God's part, and more faithful responses by subsequent occasions. There is a thoroughly relational component both to the intensity of God's presence, or what is usually called God's "nearness," and to the specificity of God's aims, or what is more often called God's "voice." Thus, while in process thought God is present to every occasion, God can be "more present" depending upon the measure of response God's aims have received in a particular nexus of occasions. In Whitehead's words, "Every act leaves the world with a deeper or a fainter impress of God. He then passes into his next relation to the world with enlarged, or diminished, presentation of ideal values."[47]

This view of God's presence corresponds well with rabbinic reflection upon the Shekhinah. Urbach indicates that, in speaking of God's presence as the Shekhinah, the rabbis did not intend some concept of immanence **per se,** according to which the divine presence in the world was an immutable, undifferentiated quality which permeated all things equally. Rather, "the Rabbinic view is that God's presence in the world and the modes of His theophanies are linked to man's conduct and deeds,"[48] i.e., to his responses to Torah. Or again, in Abelson's words, "The Holy Spirit may be acquired by any one provided he orders his life in conformity with the highest and the best. It is not vouchsafed by Heaven miraculously, i.e., without any sufficiently evident pre-existing cause."[49] This is not in any way to qualify Christianity's sense of the free graciousness of God's presence given to human beings, except as it actually *is qualified* or *conditioned* by their own receptivity and responsiveness to divine aims.

The rabbinic tendency to link a sense of God's presence to human response to Torah was, to be sure, in tension with the broader affirmations of God's presence throughout creation. Here process theology provides a bridge: God's presence does in a sense penetrate all of creation in the provision of initial aims to every occasion, and yet the intensity of God's presence and the "godliness" of the aims depend upon the prior responses of completed occasions. Thus, while God is present to every person, the intensity of God's presence and sense of God's nearness depend upon that person's openness and faithfulness to God's previous aims (or address) to her or him. Yet it is not simply a matter of individual response. In a process-relational worldview, the individual's response occurs within, and is itself significantly conditioned by, the context of his or her historical community's overarching response to the divine call.

The presence of God, then, is experienced as a lure, resistible by human beings, the responses to which condition the intensity and godliness of God's subsequent initial aims for new occasions. Such an understanding of God's presence, in fact, can be found in Song of Songs Rabba vi:

> The original abode of the Shekhinah was among men. When Adam
> sinned it ascended away to the first heaven. With Cain's sin it ascended
> to the second ... [and so on through seven men]. Corresponding to

these, there arose seven righteous men who brought the Shekhinah down, back again to earth.[50]

While process theology's notions of intensity and specificity of divine aims may replace the spatial metaphor of rabbinic thought, the result is similar: God's presence is thoroughly dynamic and relational, depending upon the responses of creation, and especially of human beings. This means that the extent to which God can truly be present to creation depends largely upon how the creatures respond to God's overtures. While God's vision for creation—so beautifully expressed in the Hebrew word-concept **shalom**—and God's commitment to lead creation in the direction of that vision both remain constant, process theology recognizes that God's vision can become distorted and God's will frustrated by the creature. In rabbinic language, human responses of love and faithfulness can bring the Shekhinah near, while self-centered, faithless responses thrust the Shekhinah away. To be sure, God remains present in the offering of the "initial aim" to every occasion, but the nature of that aim, or how nearly it conforms to God's ideal purposes for creation, is greatly dependent upon the free responses of prior, now completed occasions.

Because "God in every moment works with and upon the world that is given to him, in that moment,"[51] the fate of both the world, and of God in relation to the world, depends largely upon human responses to God's call. Both rabbinic and process thought, then, can view the human being as "a co-worker with God in the work of creation."[52] There is also in both, correspondingly, a strong sense in which God and creation can only be redeemed *together* through cooperation. This particular rabbinic theme of mutual redemption was to gain even greater significance a millennium later in kabbalistic literature—a development which will be of particular importance in Part II.

C. A CHRISTIAN INTERPRETATION OF DIVINE PRESENCE

The argument of Chapter 2 thus far has been that the Jewish word-concepts **ruach, pneuma** and **shekhinah,** which provide the proper context for understanding what the phrase "Holy Spirit" should mean for Christians, refer not to hypostases separate from God but provide ways for referring to God's dynamic presence and activity among the people Israel and in creation generally. Then, in section B of this chapter, a process theological model provided the means for suggesting *in what sense* God might be understood to be present to creation, and then how that presence is experienced differently according to particular human cultures or religions.

The next step in the argument is that this Jewish ideational context, particularly as interpreted through the process model, provides Christian theology with a more adequate understanding of the Holy Spirit. Just as the terms **ruach, pneuma** and **shekhinah** functioned in particular Jewish communities of faith to refer to God's presence, so "Holy Spirit," as a term used by the Church, ought to refer to God as present and God as active: first of all in creation; then more intimately in human beings, created in God's image through the in-breathing of the Spirit; then in particular cultural and religious structures, co-created by God the Spirit and human communities, in which God's presence is interpreted and so "shaped" in distinctive ways.

Even as I write that Christian pneumatology properly begins with the idea of the Spirit in creation, suggested especially by the appropriation of **ruach** earlier in this chapter, it should be clear that an important concern of the argument is to avoid a vague notion of universalized, undifferentiated divine presence. A primary affirmation of the Spirit's animating presence in creation is, after all, founded upon the particular perspective of the Hebrew scriptures. Thus, the real starting point is an affirmation of God's presence among the people Israel, and a conviction that their scriptures faithfully reflect God's doings—a conviction without which Christianity is rootless. If Christians, who believe that the Holy Spirit animates the Church, can affirm also God's ongoing indwelling of the people Israel, then such an affirmation opens the distinct possibility that God's **ruach** blows through the worship, prayer and lives of the people of yet other religious communities. My utilization of process thought, which, to be sure, *assumes* God's universal presence, represents an attempt to give that possibility a metaphysical foundation.

To say that the Spirit's presence is active in both Church and Synagogue, and consequently quite probably active in other religious communities, is assuredly not to mean that God is experienced in the same way by all peoples. Because God works with what is the "given" in every moment, God must also provide aims for human beings which are relevant and realizable in their socio-historical context. "Diversity," Suchocki writes, "is the means toward actualization of the divine harmony."[53] There is a vital importance in the particularity of the structure of experience of various cultural or religious communities—not to mention the particularity of various sub-groups and even individuals within those communities—which greatly determines how the Spirit is appropriated and interpreted in a given context. Consequently, it is highly appropriate that God's universally animating presence as it impinged upon rabbinic Judaism was referred to as the Shekhinah—and indeed still is by many modern Jews—while God's universally animating presence in the Church is normally named the Holy Spirit. Indeed, just as rabbinic Jews experienced the Shekhinah through the Torah-structured life, so Christian experience of the Spirit has been rightly Christocentric, even to the extent that the Christian Testament often identifies the Spirit as the Spirit of Christ (Rom 8:9; Gal 4:6).

It is natural and perhaps inevitable that both Israel and the Church would have assumed themselves to be exclusive bearers of the divine presence, as exemplified particularly in their early fight over who would lay claim to possession of **pneuma.** But if Christians listen attentively and seriously to the writings they consider to be holy scripture, they must acknowledge that God continues to be present in and among God's people Israel (Jer 31:35–37). Similarly, when Jews listen attentively and seriously to their prophets, they must acknowledge that God's liberating activity extends graciously to other peoples (Am 9:7), and that indeed an important aspect of the prophetic hope for the eschatological age was an in-gathering of Gentiles to share in God's presence with the people Israel (Is 19:24–25; Zech 8:23). In fact, the prophetic vision of the universalist impulse of God's Spirit is exemplified **par excellence** in the promise to Joel, and ought to chasten any tendency to think of God's **ruach** in exclusivist categories:

> And it will come about after this that I will pour out My Spirit on all humanity; and your sons and daughters will prophesy, your old men will dream dreams, your young men will see visions. And even on the male and female servants I will pour out My Spirit in those days (2:28).

D. IMPLICATIONS FOR CHRISTIAN TRINITARIANISM

The interpretation offered in this chapter of the Jewish people's usage of **ruach, pneuma** and **shekhinah** suggests that the terms did not refer to hypostases separate from God which mediate between God and the world, but nearly always functioned as tropes for God's own active nearness to creation, to humanity, and particularly to Israel. It has been argued, too, that this history of Jewish interpretations of God's presence ought rightly to provide the proper context for Christian reflection upon the Spirit. This double line of argument immediately raises questions concerning the Christian doctrine of the triune God as traditionally stated.

It is clear, as Isaacs has shown, that Hellenistic Judaism's notion of **pneuma** was important to the writers of the Christian Testament in their use of the same word-concept. The fluidity and virtual interchangeability of terms such as wisdom, word, glory, spirit and Torah, all of which in Hellenistic Judaism were nuanced referents to God's active presence, is also evident in early Christian writings. But because the authors of those writings were attempting to talk about the significance of Jesus of Nazareth, these terms which referred to God's nearness tended to find a new locus and meaning in the proclamation of Christ (Jn 1:1–14; 1 Cor 1:30; Col 1:15–16). Jesus was God's wisdom, the Word become flesh, the one in whose face God's glory shone, even a life-giving spirit (1 Cor 15:45). Thus, while the **pneuma** of Hellenistic Judaism undoubtedly exercised a measure of influence upon the pneumatologies of the Christian Testament, that influence was felt far more in those early attempts to formulate a Christology. While it is also true that the foundations of a Spirit Christology can be found particularly in the synoptic gospels and in Acts, the figure of Jesus came increasingly to be seen as the mode of God's presence and activity in the world, without explicit reference to the Spirit. "The reason is not far to seek," writes Alasdair Heron:

> In this essentially universal, cosmic perspective [of Hellenistic Judaism] there is room for one comprehensively mediating principle between God and the world, God and men, but it is not at all obvious that *more* than one is either necessary or desirable.[54]

Heron has a point: the cosmic function and significance of **ruach** in the Hebrew scriptures, and of **pneuma** in Hellenistic Jewish literature, became absorbed by the figure of Christ, particularly as that figure was interpreted through the Logos idea and imagery. As the glorification process of the human figure of Jesus into the pre-existent, divine agent of creation occurred in the early Church, it "made it difficult to say in what way he differed from the Spirit," Cyril Richardson writes. "For he fulfilled precisely the function of the Logos (Jn 1:1), which was the same as that of God's vital breath or power or word."[55] For obvious reasons, the comparably amorphous notion of "Spirit" was not easily identified with, or as readily limited to, the figure of Jesus as were Wisdom and Word. Thus, while "Spirit" did not disappear by becoming completely absorbed into Christology, the functions by which **ruach** and **pneuma** were understood in Jewish interpretation were indeed absorbed. "Spirit," in Lampe's words, "was thus gradually detached from its old association with 'Wisdom' and 'Logos', and was superseded, in what became orthodox Christology, by 'Logos-Son' as the way of expressing the outreach of God to men in Jesus."[56]

There was, nonetheless, a measure of flexibility yet in the early patristic reflection upon the Spirit. Early Christian thinkers such as Theophilus, Clement and Irenaeus, for example, continued to identify the Spirit with the concepts of Wisdom or Logos, and so also at times with the pre-existent Christ. Such a move was particularly useful to Irenaeus in his battles with Marcion and gnostic influences upon the Church. By following Hellenistic Judaism in its identification of Wisdom with the Spirit, he could provide a link between the work of the Spirit prior to, and following, the advent of Jesus. But the Marcionite impulse, combatted in its overt forms by Irenaeus as well as others of the early Fathers, found covert expression in the increasing rigidity of Christological formulation under the force of Platonic thinking. With the virtual restriction of Christology to the pre-existent Logos-Son model, "to an even greater extent than in the thought of the New Testament writers, it became difficult to assign a significant role to the Holy Spirit as a third hypostasis."[57]

Consequently, Christological development in the opening centuries of the Church's life tended to reverse the witness of the synoptic gospels: those early witnesses to Jesus understood him to a significant extent as a Spirit-conceived, Spirit-filled man, and so pneumatologically; on the other hand, the developing Christology understood the Spirit as a divine power or presence applying the benefits of Christ's work to believers, and so Christologically. This inversion certainly reached a zenith in the Western Church's inclusion of the **filioque** into the creed late in the sixth century, for now the Spirit was said to proceed from the Father *and the Son,* and so was increasingly interpreted Christomorphically. God's Spirit had become "the Holy Spirit," a third hypostasis in the Godhead, and then had become, at least functionally, the Spirit of Christ.

This development not only made it difficult for Western theologians to appreciate the biblical notion of **ruach** as God's presence in nature and in history, as was noted in Chapter 1, but also made much easier the Church's triumphalist claim to an exclusive corner on the presence and activity of God. "Eventually the Western Church . . . identified the Spirit and the Church virtually as one, so that the Church became the embodiment of the recalled and indwelling Christ"[58]—precisely since the Spirit's role became reduced almost exclusively to recalling Christ and providing the mode of Christ's presence in the Church.

My proposed response to this sort of pneumatological exclusivism involves first a reaffirmation of the universalistic, cosmic aspects of **ruach, pneuma** and **shekhinah,** as already offered in Section A of this chapter. But it also involves a de-hypostasizing of the Christian notion of the Holy Spirit, in such a way that Christians would come to understand the Spirit, as Jews historically have interpreted **ruach, pneuma** and **shekhinah,** as a way of speaking about the one God in personal outreach and address to creation, and particularly to human beings. Thinking of the Holy Spirit as the third hypostasis in the Godhead, particularly when that thinking is combined with the **filioque,** has led Christians to a far narrower and generally exclusivist notion of the Spirit as the Spirit of Christ. Thus, even when they *do* speak of the cosmic function of the Spirit, it is with a Logos-Christological bent which affords them, at least implicitly, a privileged perspective on all questions involving God, creation and humanity. Perhaps this is where the Eastern Church, with its insistence upon the single procession of the Spirit from the Father, might contribute to a more adequate pneumatology. Yet its confession historically has been as oblivious as the Western Church's to the primary context for proper Christian theology and self-understanding: Israel's history and scriptures. In that context, the doctrine of single procession yields a different reading: *the Spirit "proceeds" from the Father alone because "the Spirit" is a way of referring to the One God of the Sh'ma, also called the Father, in "process-ion" from God's own self toward the "other" through dynamic address and command: first toward creation in the word of "letting be," then to humanity in the word of shared responsibility, then to Israel through Torah, and also to the Church through one of Israel's sons, Jesus of Nazareth.* Only in this last sense can the Church confess that, *in its own experience,* the Spirit proceeds from the Son. And of course this confession does not exclude the possibility—indeed the probability and, from a process view, the inevitability—that God's outreaching presence in the "initial aim" animates other religious and cultural communities as well.

Such an understanding of the Spirit, to be sure, does not square with popular Christian piety's view of the Spirit as a distinct person, indeed as "the third person of the Trinity." Yet at the same time, if it is true that "Holy Spirit" is the Church's phraseology for referring to the personal presence of God, it is inadequate to think or speak of the Spirit as an "it," a force or influence from God. Surely the Holy Spirit is *personal* and ought to be referred to in personal terms,[59] but that does not necessitate developing a trinitarian doctrine which understands God, either explicitly or implicitly, to possess more than one center of consciousness. Along this line Hendrikus Berkhof has written,

> The Spirit is Person because he is God acting as a Person. However, we cannot say that the Spirit is a Person distinct from God the Father. He is a Person in relation to us, not in relation to God; for he is the personal God himself in relation to us.[60]

Similarly, C.F.D. Moule:

> Where Spirit is most reasonably spoken of as personal is in precisely the contexts most characteristic of the New Testament. When Spirit is the mode of God's presence in the hearts and minds of his people, then there is a good case for personal language. But this still does not force upon us a third eternal 'Person' (in the technical sense) within the unity.[61]

By thinking of the Spirit as God's personal presence in relationship to human beings—and I would add to creation as a whole—we are moving nearer to Paul's explication of the Spirit in 1 Corinthians 2:10–13, which may well have been influenced by the Hellenistic intertwining of **sophia** and **pneuma**. For in this passage the Spirit is clearly God's own Spirit, the Spirit of wisdom. Here Paul draws a parallel between divine and human psychology: "For who among men knows the thoughts of a man except the spirit of the man, which is in him? Even so the thoughts of God no one knows except the Spirit of God" (v. 11). Here the Spirit is no more a separate hypostasis than is a human being's own self-consciousness an entity distinct from himself or herself. Rather, the Spirit is God's own deepest self, searching "even the depths of God" (v. 10). Yet, what is remarkable is that God can, and does, impart "the Spirit who is from God" to human beings, "that we might know the things freely given to us by God" (v. 12). Consequently, "Spirit" signifies also the *dynamic share-ability* of God, God's own self-impartation and outreaching.

It must be acknowledged that Paul's identification of divine wisdom with Christ in the larger context of this passage (1:30, 2:16) gives his notion of God's Spirit a typically exclusivist slant. But the point here is that, in this passage, the apostle seems to suggest an understanding of the Spirit that is consonant with the Jewish interpretations of **ruach, pneuma** and **shekhinah:** God's own active, outreaching presence in creation and among human beings. Spirit denotes the movement of God, reminding us that, in Berkhof's words,

> God is a living, acting God. In creation he transmits his life to a world outside of his being. In the act of creation, he therefore becomes a life-giving Spirit. As Spirit he sustains and develops his created world, he elects and protects Israel, he calls and governs her leaders and prophets.[62]

The Spirit, then, is not a separate entity or hypostasis within the Godhead, much less another god. The Spirit is the one God of Israel at work in creation, in humanity, and particularly in God's people Israel, luring and calling them forward through the address and command of Torah to new depths of love and responsibility. Christians confess that the same Spirit, "the Spirit of Yahweh," is the origin and strength of Jesus of Nazareth (Lk 4:18, 19), the death, resurrection and apostolic proclamation of whom has brought the Gentiles near to God (Eph 2:11–18), the One Jesus called "Abba." *Spirit, Son of Israel, Abba:* I am arguing for a functional, historical, Israel-centered understanding of God's triunity which begins with the Spirit, for "Spirit" denotes the graciously "other-ward" and "outward" movement of the God of Israel. As Berkhof writes, "Spirit–Son–Father. These three names in their togetherness point to a movement of the one God, not to a static community of three persons."[63]

By beginning trinitarian reflection with the Spirit as God's active, alluring presence in creation, and as the animating call to human beings to grow in the Creator's image of response-ability, there is ground for opposition to much of traditional Christianity's triumphalistic exclusivism. For the pneumatological starting point effectively reverses the Logos-Son doctrine's assimilation of those cosmological and redemptive roles which Jewish traditions had ascribed to God's **ruach, pneuma,** or **shekhinah**—God's intimate presence. As long as Christian theologians speak of the Logos as God's creative and redemptive presence, they cannot but think of Jesus. The Logos orientation, therefore, has tended to work against any truly dialogic approach to other religions, for even at its most charitable, it must finally seek a "hidden Christ" in the other's faith.[64] By affirming a universal Logos at work in creation, all the while in the background remembering John's proclamation that the Logos became flesh in Jesus (Jn 1:14), the best one can do is Rahner's "anonymous Christian" approach—the same old triumphalism in new dress.

This exclusivist triumphalism can be countermanded by pneumatological methodology which begins with Spirit as God's creative and alluring presence in creation. With this approach, Christians could confess the Spirit to be the originating source of Torah, of Jesus, and of any other means through which or whom God calls human beings to transformation of themselves and of their societies toward the divine vision which the ancient Hebrews characterized as **shalom.** Rather than being able to claim exclusive rights to God's presence, the Church would acknowledge itself to be composed of those peoples who have been gathered together, by God's animating **ruach,** to worship the God of Israel through Jesus as the Christ, the Anointed of the Spirit. We Christians would confess that the Spirit of God beckons us to transformed lives through hearing the word of the gospel, all the while acknowledging the distinct possibility that the same Spirit is calling other peoples through different mediating structures. After all, according to the writings we consider to be authoritative scripture, God *first* drew near to the Jewish people, to sanctify them through Torah (Lev 19). It is *we* who were once far from the covenants and commonwealth of Israel, without knowledge of God and without hope, who have now, in God's Spirit, drawn near to God through Jesus (Eph 2:11–18). Such wondrous, surprising grace, it seems, should restrain us from the tendency to exclusivism, and so also free us to consider with care how the Spirit of the living God of Israel might be liberating and leading yet other peoples into the glorious freedom of the children of God—a freedom for which, according to Paul, all of creation yearns, and toward which it strains (Rom 8:19–23).

NOTES

1. Heron, *The Holy Spirit,* p. 4.

2. C. F. D. Moule's disclaimer in *The Holy Spirit* (Grand Rapids: Wm. B. Eerdman's Pub. Co, 1978) concerning the Spirit's cosmic function in the Hebrew canonical scriptures includes a dismissal of Genesis 1:2. He writes that it can be interpreted "simply" as "mighty wind." But it seems to me that he is missing the possibility that the ancient Hebrews might not have been inclined to distinguish so finely between a wind and God's presence as Spirit. Indeed, the Exodus account would tend to dissolve such a distinction.

3. Cf. Eduard Schweizer, "What is the Holy Spirit? A Study in Biblical Theology" in *Conflicts About the Holy Spirit,* eds. Hans Küng and Jürgen Moltmann (New York: The Seabury Press, 1979), p. x.

4. van Dusen, *Spirit, Son, and Father* (New York: Charles Scribner's Sons, 1958), especially ch. 5, "The Holy Spirit and Man."

5. Heron, p. 7. See also Moule, where he writes of the "ambivalence of 'spirit' as man's spirit and yet also God's Spirit, on loan, as one might also say, to man from God" (p. 8).

Incidentally, if the half of Psalm 51:11 which I deleted from quotation, "Do not cast me away from Thy presence," is read with "And do not take Thy Holy Spirit from me" to form a parallelism, then the verse suggests that God's Holy Spirit and God's presence are two ways of pointing to the same reality.

6. Pannenberg, p. 10.

7. Moule, p. 13.

8. Heron, p. 5.

9. Killough, "A Reexamination of the Concept of Spirit in Christian Theology," *American Journal of Theology & Philosophy* Vol. 6, No. 2 & 3, p. 141. See also Heron: "The **ruach** of Yahweh is not detachable, as it were, from Yahweh himself: it is his living impact here and now" (p. 8).

10. Schweizer, p. x.

11. Arnold B. Come, *Human Spirit and Holy Spirit* (Philadelphia: The Westminster Press, 1959), p. 128.

12. Marie Isaacs, in her fine study *The Concept of Spirit: A Study of Pneuma in Hellenistic Judaism and its Bearing on the New Testament* (London: Heythrop College, 1976), mentions David Hill's argument that a tendency arose to understand "spirit" as independent from God when **ruach** was translated into the Greek **pneuma,** since with **pneuma** the Greek notion of substance would inevitably also be conveyed (p. 14). Isaacs is inclined to disagree, but Hill still presents an interesting possibility.

Echoing Isaacs' perspective, Ephraim Urbach, in *The Sages—Their Concepts and Beliefs* (Jerusalem: The Magnes Press, The Hebrew University, 1979), while acknowledging the influence of Stoic doctrine upon **pneuma** in the Wisdom of Solomon, nonetheless holds that **pneuma** for Hellenistic Jews was "not immanent in the world and linked to its physical conception, but is the breath of life, which the Creator breathed into Adam" (p. 40).

13. Heron, p. 36.

14. Isaacs, pp. 21–26.

15. *Ibid.,* p. 54.

16. Lampe, *God as Spirit,* p. 42.

17. *Ibid.,* p. 64.

18. *Ibid.*

19. Isaacs, p. 135.

20. See Urbach, pp. 41–44.

21. J. Abelson, *The Immanence of God in Rabbinical Literature* (New York: Hermon Press, 1969; first edition 1912), pp. 207, 206.

22. Urbach, p. 43.

23. Max Kadushin, *The Rabbinic Mind* (New York: The Jewish Theological Seminary of America, 5712:1952), p. 225.

24. Urbach, p. 63.

25. Abelson, p. 200. Similarly, Urbach mentions G. F. Moore's argument that the concept of the Shekhinah was "a verbal smoke to conceal the difficulty presented by the anthropomorphic language" (*The Sages,* p. 41). Though I agree, I might add that it would be more appropriate, given the biblical imagery, to call it a verbal cloud.

26. Norman J. Cohen, "Shekhinta Ba-Galuta: A Midrashic Response to Destruction and Persecution," *Journal for the Study of Judaism,* Vol. XIII, No. 1–2, p. 148.

27. *Ibid.*

28. Urbach, p. 42.

29. David Hartman, *A Living Covenant* (New York: The Free Press, 1985), p. 185. Similarly, he writes, "In their daily life, too, Jews met the living God in present experiences, since sacredness was brought into that daily life and normal human experiences were endowed with transcendent significance. . . . God's commanding presence is an immediate reality, since all of life is placed under the normative guidance of His **mitzvot**" (*ibid.,* pp. 223–224).

30. Abelson, p. 296, 297. It is doubtful that "immanence" is the happiest term for describing the rabbinic conception of God's nearness. Abelson admits that it is a philosophical concept, and that the rabbis were not, strictly speaking, metaphysicians. Yet he argues that the term is acceptable "if we give a wider and looser connotation to 'Immanence' " (p. 52). For an incisive critique of Abelson's attempt to understand rabbinic thought through the lens of this concept, see Kadushin, *The Rabbinic Mind,* pp. 255–256.

31. Lampe, p. 60.

32. Abelson, p. 207. See also Kadushin, *ibid.,* p. 251, n. 126.

33. Joseph B. Soloveitchik, *Halakhic Man* (Philadelphia: The Jewish Publication Society of America, 5743:1983), pp. 47–63.

34. Abelson, p. 379.

35. Urbach, p. 50.

36. *Ibid.,* p. 47.

37. Marjorie Hewitt Suchocki, *God–Christ–Church: A Practical Guide to Process Theology* (New York: Crossroad, 1984), pp. 9–10.

38. John Cobb and David Griffin, *Process Theology: An Introductory Exposition* (Philadelphia: The Westminster Press, 1976), p. 29.

39. Suchocki, p. 43.

40. *Ibid.,* pp. 43–44.

41. John B. Cobb, Jr., *God and the World* (Philadelphia: The Westminster Press, 1969), p. 55. See also Robert Neville, "The Holy Spirit as God" in Alex Steuer and James McClendon, Jr., eds., *Is God GOD?* (Nashville: Abingdon, 1981).

42. Suchocki, p. 193.

43. *Ibid.,* p. 199.

44. This will be explored further in Part II, "The Spirit of God and the Problem of Evil."

45. Suchocki, p. 94.

46. Hartman, p. 40.

47. Alfred North Whitehead, *Religion in the Making* (New York: The New American Library, 1960), p. 152.

48. Urbach, p. 51.

49. Abelson, p. 208.

50. As quoted by Abelson, p. 136.

51. Cobb, p. 91.

52. Abelson, p. 114.

53. Suchocki, p. 199.

54. Heron, *The Holy Spirit,* p. 37.

55. Cyril Richardson, *The Doctrine of the Trinity* (Nashville: Abingdon Press, 1958), pp. 47–48.

56. Lampe, p. 133.

57. *Ibid.,* p. 214. The doctrine of Christology, as well as pneumatology, suffered a significant loss with the triumph of a Logos-Son model as the Church's paradigmatic expression of Jesus' significance. For the same glorification of Jesus to the status of pre-existent Word, which emptied the notion of Spirit of any significant role in creation or redemptive history, also tended to tear the figure of Jesus out of the context of God's history with Israel and to place it in the alien context of a heavenly triad, Father–Son–Spirit. The synoptics' witness to Jesus' earthly relationship to the One he called "Abba" was projected into an ahistorical, other-worldly love between the Father and the Son. The more abstract trinitarian reflection became, the less it needed the narrative-historical context of God's dealings with God's people Israel—a practical Marcionism—though it is Israel's own sonship which provides the most adequate context for an interpretation of Jesus' filial relationship to God, the God of the exodus (Mt 2:15).

58. Killough, "A Reexamination," p. 143.

59. The instincts of some conservative denominations to guard a notion of "the personality of the Holy Spirit" against a "liberal" interpretation of the Spirit as a force, power or influence from God are, I believe, sound. It is, after all, the one personal God of scripture with whom we have to do in the Spirit. Unfortunately, the word "personality," suggesting as it does a distinct center of consciousness, generally either presupposes, or else leads to, a "tritheistic committee" image of God.

60. Hendrikus Berkhof, *The Doctrine of the Holy Spirit* (Richmond: John Knox Press, 1964), p. 116.

61. Moule, p. 50. Actually, this is not a particularly novel or unique approach to pneumatology. Several other theologians have offered similar interpretations of the Holy Spirit:

Cyril Richardson: ". . . the distinctive role of the Spirit . . . cannot be made to reflect some third mode of being in God, distinct from the basic paradox [of absoluteness and relatedness] with which we began. It can only be understood as one of the variety of ways in which God comes into relation with his world, and . . . is implicit in the second term—God in his relatedness" (*The Doctrine of the Trinity,* p. 70).

Paul Tillich: "The Spirit of God is the presence of the Divine Life within creaturely life. The Divine Spirit is 'God present'. The Spirit of God is not a separated being. Therefore one can speak of 'Spiritual Presence' in order to give the symbol its full meaning" (*Systematic Theology* Vol III [Chicago: The University of Chicago Press, 1963], p. 107).

Hans Küng: "The Holy Spirit is none other than God himself . . . in his closeness to man and the world as the one who seizes hold of man but cannot be seized, the one who gives but is not at man's disposal, the one who creates life but also judges. The Holy Spirit is therefore not a third party or a thing between God and man, but God's personal closeness to man" (*Conflicts About the Holy Spirit,* eds. Küng and Moltmann [New York: The Seabury Press, 1979], p. x).

And, of course, Geoffrey Lampe: ". . . 'the Spirit of God' is to be understood, not as referring to a divine hypostasis distinct from God the Father and God the Son or Word, but as indicating God himself as active towards and in his human creation. We are speaking of God disclosed and experienced as Spirit: that is, in his personal outreach" (*God as Spirit,* p. 11).

What *does* distinguish the interpretation of the Spirit in the present study is the employment of this particular pneumatological approach in a context of Jewish-Christian conversation, and within an intentionally post-Holocaust framework.

62. Berkhof, p. 115.

63. *Ibid.,* p. 116. Berkhof continues, "Therefore, the three names in the New Testament: God (Father)–Christ (Son)–Spirit are not meant to express a kind of tripartition in God, which would distinguish the Christian faith from Jewish monotheism (an old misunderstanding, still alive). On the contrary, in using these three names together the Apostles want to confess the unity of God, the fact that in the great movement of Spirit, Son, and Father we have not to do with three entities, but with one and the same acting and saving God" (pp. 116–117).

The notion that the doctrine of the triune God distinguishes Christian faith from an inferior Jewish monotheism can be traced back to Tertullian. It is undoubtedly one of the most pernicious uses to which trinitarianism has been put.

64. An example of this Logocentric triumphalism can be seen to work even in John Cobb, a theologian noted for his sensitivity to the issues of interreligious dialogue. Cobb, in his book *Beyond Dialogue* (Philadelphia: Fortress Press, 1982), spends all of his fourth chapter showing how Buddhist concepts of "emptiness" and "nirvana" fundamentally contradict the Christian vision of God, self and world. But in the following chapter he proceeds to fudge on the issue by choosing as his conversation partner the Amida "Pure Land" sect, which evidences some remarkable similarities to Protestant emphases upon salvation by faith through grace. In the final chapter, Cobb arrives at the assertion that what Pure Land Buddhists call "Amida" is the Logos, which became Christ (i.e., incarnate) in Jesus.

In this argument he has built on his Logos Christology presented in *Christ in a*

Pluralistic Age (Philadelphia: The Westminster Press, 1975), where "Christ" names the Logos, or principle of creative transformation, as incarnate in the world and, for Christians, especially in Jesus. Thus, he is able in an extremely attractive fashion to reappropriate the venerable Logos tradition of such early theologians as Clement of Alexandria and Justin Martyr. The real problem is that Cobb has modernized what they themselves did in a remarkably powerful way: preempt all other truth-claims, absorbing them within the Logocentric vision of John 1. Though certainly this is preferable to vilification and deliberate ignorance of religious, philosophical and cultural traditions outside Christianity, in the final analysis it is the same old Christian triumphalism in new, more attractive dress. As long as Cobb operates with such a Logocentric vision, he has already incorporated the other before dialogue, let alone mutual transformation, can begin. In the Logos doctrine of Justin, Clement, and by all appearances Cobb after them, the "other" tradition already stands within and under the cosmic Logos interpretation. Unless that Logos perspective is relinquished, it seems to me that authentic transformation is unlikely to occur.

II. THE SPIRIT OF GOD AND THE PROBLEM OF EVIL

Before we can repledge our troth
to the ancient God or present him
with our complaint—these twin stances
of our modern prayer and protest—
we must make certain that it is still
the ancient God whom we seek.

Arthur Cohen, *The Tremendum*

3. Text and Presence:
A Hermeneutic of Exile

   In Chapter 2 it was noted briefly that the rabbis responsible for shaping the Jewish religious tradition after the destruction of the second Temple in 70 C.E. carried a weighty burden. With the disappearance of the Temple—the revered symbol of God's presence with the people Israel in the land of Israel—it was on their shoulders to reconceive Israel's covenant with God in accordance with its ominous circumstances of extremity and exile. How could the God of the covenant have allowed the Temple's destruction, Jerusalem's ransacking, and the exile of the people Israel from their God-given land? How might God's presence be interpreted in this situation?

   Two answers dominated. The first was simply a retrieval of the Deuteronomic code of rewards and punishments; the destruction and exile were God's just punishment "for our sins" (**mi-penei hata'einu**), to use a rabbinic phrase. According to this view, God's indwelling presence, repulsed by Israel's sins, had already departed from the Temple even prior to its destruction. The other reply, as noted in Chapter 2, involved an affirmation of the Shekhinah's faithful presence with the people Israel; in Rabbi Shim'on's words, "Wherever they [Israel] went in exile, Shekhinah was with them" (Megillah 29a). God, bound by covenantal commitment to the people, even went into exile with them, sharing in their agonies. In this connection some rabbis loved to quote Isaiah 63:9, "In all their afflictions, he was afflicted."

   Both answers were responses to the hermeneutical challenge of reinterpreting the community's religious tradition within the context of a new historical situation, and certainly both helped, in their own ways, to sustain the exiled Jewish people in the midst of their doubt and confusion. Yet it was the second answer, that of **Shekhinta b'Galuta,** or "the

Shekhinah-in-exile" in company with the people Israel, which reflected a greater sense of interpretive freedom with the tradition and of rabbinic imagination in interpreting God's presence. Because it encouraged an awareness of divine faithfulness and companionship with the Jewish people, it was also the answer which most deeply captured their hearts and minds. Yet the fruition of what might be called a "hermeneutic of exile" was not fully to arrive till more than a millennium after the idea of the Shekhinah's exile first found its way into rabbinic reflection.

It should be remembered that, even among those rabbis who entertained the notion of the exile of the Shekhinah with the Jews, the underlying, traditional ideas about God's power and providence were maintained. There remained a strong commitment to the idea that God rules God's world, and that in good time all injustices against Israel would be righted (Avodah Zarah 1:1–3). Though God might share in Israel's exile out of a deep covenantal love, that same love insured that God's might would eventually right all wrongs. To be sure, there were differing opinions regarding the measure of responsibility God had entrusted to the Jewish people for ushering in the messianic age. While David Hartman in his book *The Living Covenant* draws heavily on those rabbinic teachings which emphasized human responsibility through interpretation of, and obedience to, Torah, there was also a significant and influential rabbinic tradition which stressed God's own liberating activity in the future redemption of Israel.[1] Thus, while God might share temporarily in Israel's exile, it was an exile which God underwent voluntarily and from which God might liberate both Israel and God's own self at any time.

This is not to deny what was suggested in Chapter 2 concerning the human, and particularly Jewish, capacity either to "draw the Shekhinah near" through obedient response to the command of Torah, or to "press against the feet of the Shekhinah" through disobedience.[2] It is, though, to point to a tension in rabbinic thought between a traditional idea of God's omnipotent providence in the world and the idea of the Shekhinah's exile, whether due to Israel's sins or to the unjust oppression of Israel by the nations. There is no question, however, that the latter idea was incorporated into, and understood within the context of, the former. Thus, while the sense of God's presence might be dulled or even lost through individual or corporate disobedience, or through the vicissitudes of historical crisis and calamity, there remained an underlying confidence in God's ultimate ability to manifest an overwhelming presence, to end all exiles and to right all wrongs. Exile was a temporary condition. There was no question that, in the final analysis, God exercised omnipotent control.

It was precisely this traditional assumption of God's omnipotent providence in history which underwent erosion in the Jewish religious tradition which will be under consideration in this chapter—the tradition loosely called the Kabbalah. Since "kabbalah" means simply "tradition," and can essentially be used to refer to any Jewish mystical or theosophical text, attention will necessarily be focused upon the ideas of two prominent figures in medieval Jewish mysticism: Moses de Leon (d. 1305), who is generally recognized today as the author of most of the Zohar, or "Book of Splendor"; and Isaac Luria (1534–72), whose ideas especially continue to exercise influence not only in Jewish theology, but occasionally in contemporary Christian thought as well.[3]

It was in this body of literature that Jewish suspicions about divine omnipotence and providence—suspicions which were veiled, largely hidden, yet lurking occasionally at the dark edges of some rabbinic thinking —broke surface and asserted themselves in all their radicality. One might suggest that, in the Kabbalah, a hermeneutic of exile displaced the dominant rabbinic hermeneutic of certainty and divine power. In this hermeneutic, in fact, many suppressed notions about God, creation and human beings found new and powerful expression in a mythically tragic vision of the world. Unlike the medieval Jewish philosophers with whom they were contemporaries, the kabbalists did not ignore the darker forces of the primitive and terrifying, even demonic, underbelly of existence. One might argue that, in a sense, their writings represented something of a revival of the darkness and ambiguity in deity which were suggested in the early Hebrew notion of **ruach.** As Gershom Scholem has written,

> The fact of the existence of evil in the world is the main touchstone of this difference between the philosophic and the Kabbalistic outlook. . . . [Most Kabbalists] have a strong sense of the reality of evil and the dark horror that is about everything living. They do not, like the philosophers, seek to evade its existence with the aid of a convenient formula; rather do they try to penetrate to its depth.[4]

It is a worthwhile task to appropriate some of the ideas of these two imaginative religious geniuses primarily for this very reason: as Scholem suggests, they allowed the reality of evil to have full sway in their thinking. There is a deeply tragic temper in their theosophies which is appropriate to the post-Holocaust, post-Hiroshima age in which we find ourselves. We may not follow their mythologies literally, but their tragically exilic vision of God, self and world may inform us nonetheless.

Furthermore, a theological appropriation of these medieval kabbalists is pertinent to this present study of God as Spirit, or of God as actively
present to creation, among human beings, and particularly in Israel. For it
is precisely in those times of deepest human anguish and senseless suffering that God's presence, indeed God's reality, may be most deeply challenged; the experience of evil "interrupts" ordered and orderly discourse
about life's meaning and beauty, slapping our privileged assumptions.
And it was, again, such experiences of evil which de Leon and Luria took
quite seriously in their deliberations about God in God's relationship to
creation. It should be remembered that Part I of this study ended with a
reference to Romans 8, in which Paul writes of the groaning of all creation
for redemption, "the freedom of the glory of the children of God" (v. 21).
Two millennia later, creation groans all the more under humanity's technical "triumph" called the Holocaust, and the additional technical threat
of nuclear annihilation foreshadowed by Hiroshima and Nagasaki. The
fundamental affirmation of Part I—that God is universally present in and
to creation—is now interrupted by the harsh reality of evil, and must
be tempered with the Kabbalah's deeply tragic sense. Since process-
relational theology is often criticized for not having taken seriously
enough the problem of evil, or of having been naively optimistic about the
possibilities of "creative advance" in the world,[5] it is likely that such a
confrontation of process theology with the kabbalistic myth of exile will
be instructive.

Finally, a theological appropriation of kabbalistic themes is particularly pertinent to this study since the primary rabbinic referent to God's
presence in the world, the Shekhinah, was also an important symbol in
kabbalistic literature. To be sure, the figure of the Shekhinah, like so
many of the rest of the terms and concepts of rabbinic thought, underwent
profound transformation in the Zoharic-Lurianic myth. Yet this very
transformation may suggest something about how God's presence might
be interpreted by those who take seriously the prevailing sense of God's
absence in our suffering, destitute, violent world. It may, in short, provide
a model for an intentionally post-Holocaust pneumatology.

The following two sections of this chapter represent an attempt at
pneumatological appropriation of de Leon and Luria. In the final section
of this chapter, by bringing the Zoharic-Lurianic myth into conversation
with deconstructionist readings of theology, I will suggest a contemporary
hermeneutic of exile—of absent presence—which will provide a frame-

work for interpreting God's presence as Spirit in the midst of senseless human suffering and radical evil.

A. THE ZOHAR: ENCOUNTERING EVIL

When one enters the interpretive world of the Zohar, de Leon's mystical midrash mostly on the five books of Moses, one encounters an imaginative way of reading the biblical text in which symbolism is infinitely rich, meanings are multi-layered, and imagery is fluidly overflowing and intermingled. Nothing is simply what it appears to be on the surface; God, humanity, Israel, creation, and in particular the biblical texts are all profusely complex in their symbolic and dynamic interrelatedness. The power of the Zohar, writes Daniel Matt, "lies in its capacity to stimulate the imagination; its inner meaning is an evocation of yearning for the divine flow."[6]

The "divine flow" to which Matt alludes already gives some indication of the different way of envisioning God in the Zohar. It involves a thoroughgoing rejection of the impassible transcendent deity of Aristotelian thought, which, to be sure, had made significant inroads into Jewish as well as Christian thinking. Contrary to this philosophical theism, in de Leon's mythic commentary one finds a dynamic, complex, interactive, passible deity. This dynamism—truly a divine "flow" which also courses through creation—is expressed through the concept of the **sefirot,** which are the active forces or attributes which emanate from God, pulsing back and forth and throughout the immensity of the divine life. Indeed, the **sefirot** represent the kabbalistic attempt to write what David Blumenthal has called a "psychology of God,"[7] to plumb the depths of God's own infinitely rich, and often troubled, psyche.

The word **sefirot** originally means simply "numbers," and functioned in an earlier Jewish mystical work, the "Book of Creation" (**Sefer Yetsira**), to refer to the ten numerals of the decimal system which, in combination with the twenty-two letters of the Hebrew alphabet, composed the archetypal elements of creation. In the Zohar, there are still but ten **sefirot,** but their function is to refer theosophically to God's own pulsating being. They denote a dynamic process of the complexly interrelated attributes (including both male and female sexuality) within God's own self and, because they are divine attributes, function at the same time as the means by which human beings can perceive and contact God. They are not, however, intermediary beings between God and creation; rather, they are "various phases in the manifestation of the Divinity which proceeded from and succeeded each other."[8]

The **sefirot,** according to the Zohar, are the attributive emanations of **En Sof,** the hidden, infinite, unfathomable aspect of God. Nothing can be said or even imagined about **En Sof** by finite minds, except that **En Sof** is Nothingness **(Ayin).** Thus, God's own endless movement from **En Sof** to the **sefirot** is understood to be God's own transition from silence to speech, from incommunicability to communication. It is the divine movement into linguisticality, God issuing into words, for the world of the **sefirot** is the hidden world of language, of divine names. But it is worth emphasizing that this linguistic process occurs within God, and does not denote a multiplication of deities; in the words of the Zohar, "He is they, and they are He" (III:70a)—"He" meaning God in aweful unutterability **(En Sof),** and "they" meaning God in interactive communicability **(sefirot).** Scholem writes, "The God who manifests Himself in His **sefirot** is the very same God of traditional religious belief, and consequently, despite all the complexities such an idea involves, the emanation of the sefirot is a process within God Himself."[9]

Because of the rich, interrelated and overflowing symbolism of the sefirotic system, it is difficult to offer a simple schema of what each **sefirah** denotes in its relation to all the others. There is a dynamic circumincession among the sefirot, "an infinite reflection of the **sefirot** within themselves,"[10] which belies a simple, one-to-one correspondence between a particular **sefirah** and a particular attribute or characteristic of God. Indeed, three centuries later another kabbalist, Moses Cordovero, was to complexify further this map of the divine psyche by developing the concept of **behinot**—"the infinite number of aspects which can be differentiated within each **sefirah**"[11]—in order primarily to explain the already complex relations among the **sefirot.** For the kabbalists, then, God's consciousness was an ever-expanding, ever-deepening interconnection of what Harold Bloom has called "relational events."[12] The Zohar, near its beginning, describes the sefirotic interconnectedness in this way:

> ... three issue from one and one is established on three; one enters between two, two give suck to one, and one feeds many sides, and so all are one (I:32b).

"And so all are one": the rich, multivalent consciousness of God finally finds uniform expression in creation in the last **sefirah,** known variously as **Malkhut** ("kingdom"), **Keneset Yisra'el** ("Community of Israel") or, most familiar to us, **Shekhinah** ("indwelling presence of God"). In the Zohar, the Shekhinah is God's face turned toward creation; indeed, it is God's interface with the universe, the *sefirah* through which the flow of divine complexity touches the world. According to Scholem, in kabbalistic thought the Shekhinah is

> . . . the last attribute through which the Creator acts in the lower world. It is "the end of thought," whose progressive unfolding demonstrates God's hidden life. . . . Appearing from above as "the end of thought," the last **sefirah** is for man the door or gate through which he can begin the ascent up the ladder of perception of the Divine mystery.[13]

There is, accordingly, some continuity between the rabbinic conception of the Shekhinah as God's presence, and the kabbalistic notion of the Shekhinah as the **sefirah** through which God interacts with creation. Though set in different perspectives, both still refer to God's active presence in creation. And because the last **sefirah** is also called **Keneset Yisra'el,** the intimate connection made between the Shekhinah and the people Israel in rabbinic reflection continues also in kabbalistic literature. Indeed, through the identification of the Shekhinah and the Community of Israel, the people Israel were understood virtually as the mystical embodiment of divine presence and activity in the world—a female embodiment, at that, which receives its "soul" from the divine flow of the masculine or kingly aspect of God, the **sefirah** called **Tif'eret.**

The dynamic interconnection of God with the world, through the particular sefirotic identification of the Shekhinah with Israel, provides the key for understanding the kabbalistic vision of divine and cosmic instability. The divine, emanative flow of energy circulates among and through the **sefirot,** and down through the Shekhinah among the Jewish people. Their response to the divine flow determines whether or not God's psychic energy is "recycled" back up to and through God in a healthy fashion. Just as "spiritual and psychological wholeness [in human beings] is achieved by meditating on the qualities of each **sefirah,** by imitating and integrating the attributes of God,"[14] so the degree to which such integration is accomplished by the people Israel determines the extent of integration and stability within God's own psyche. God's "personality," one might suggest, is in the Zohar forged through God's own interaction with the Jewish people, particularly those Jews who take up responsibility for mystic relationship to the God of Israel. In contradis-

tinction to the classic philosophical idea of God's aseity, in the Zohar God
is a profoundly relational self.

Scholem mentions another set of symbolic terms in the Zohar which
even more clearly illustrate God's own arrival at self-conscious identity
through interaction with creation, Israel in particular. It is the symbolism
of I, You and He, and Scholem's account of it is especially lucid:

> God in the most deeply hidden of His manifestations, when he has as it
> were just decided to launch upon His work of creation, is called He.
> God in the complete unfolding of His Being, Grace and Love, in which
> He becomes capable of being perceived by the 'reason of the heart' and
> therefore of being expressed, is called 'You'. But God, in His supreme
> manifestation, where the fullness of His Being finds its final expression
> in the last and all-embracing of His attributes, is called 'I'. This is the
> stage of true individuation in which God as a person says 'I' to Himself.
> This divine Self, this 'I', according to theosophical Kabbalists—and this
> is one of their most profound and important doctrines—is the Shekhi-
> nah, the presence and immanence of God in the whole of creation. It is
> the point where man, in attaining the deepest understanding of his own
> self, becomes aware of the presence of God. And only from there, stand-
> ing as it were at the gate of the Divine Realm, does he progress into the
> deeper regions of the Divine, into His 'You' and 'He' and into the
> depths of Nothing. . . . [So] the Zohar identifies the highest develop-
> ment of God's personality with precisely that stage of His unfolding
> which is nearest to human experience, indeed which is immanent and
> mysteriously present in every one of us.[15]

There is, then, a real movement in God from undifferentiated simplicity, or "Nothingness" (**Ayin**) to an experience of self-conscious identity, or "I" (**Ani**). God's "I" is the Shekhinah, God in dynamic interaction
with human beings at the point where they, too, say "I." This is reminiscent of the explication of the Spirit of God in 1 Corinthians 2:6–16, where
Paul the apostle draws an analogy between human self-consciousness on
the one hand, and the deepest self-awareness and self-manifestation of
God on the other, calling both dimensions "spirit." Furthermore, it is in
the confluence of these dimensions that God and humanity are able to
communicate (to say "I") to one another; "for the Spirit searches all
things, even the depths of God" (2:10), and then shares those depths with
those who have "the mind of Christ" (2:16). Though he does not refer
specifically to this passage, Roman Catholic process theologian Bernard
Lee reflects this Pauline understanding of the Spirit when he writes that

"God's Spirit is where God's deep story is. Our spirit is where our deep story is. Through the immanence of God's Spirit in the human spirit, the deep story that is intended for history is transmitted."[16] There is possible, then, a Christian interpretation of the Spirit as God's deepest and fullest "I," communing with human beings on an analogous level of self-consciousness, which corresponds rather well with the Zoharic notion of the Shekhinah as "the highest development of God's personality" which is also "nearest to human experience" (Scholem).

The essential point of difference—and it is a crucial one—is that, in the Zoharic tradition, God's self-consciousness in the Shekhinah is radically vulnerable to the responses, actions and even thoughts of the human partners. While in Paul the communication of "depths" is essentially one way—from God to human beings—and while Lee writes that the Spirit's communion with spirit is the way in which "the deep story that is intended for history is transmitted," in the Zohar there is an intermingling of the depths of the divine and human stories. God and humanity, in fact, share the same tragic story—a story of alienation and suffering, a story of yearning for a lost cosmic unity. This means that human sin not only affects human beings, but also affects and even "infects" the divine life, causing destabilization and self-alienation in God.[17] This effect of human rebellion upon God is best portrayed in the myth of the exile of the Shekhinah.

According to the Zohar, evil has its origin in the sin of Adam, but this sin acquires a new interpretation. In de Leon's commentary on Genesis 3, the "tree of the knowledge of good and evil" becomes a symbol of the Shekhinah. Adam's transgression lay in his meditation upon, and worship of, the Shekhinah alone, thereby isolating the Shekhinah from the other **sefirot** in general and from her husband, **Tif'eret,** the "tree of life," in particular. This divorce caused a disruption of the unity of the cosmos, a "cutting of the shoots" (**qizzez ba-neti'ot**), a phrase which in rabbinic literature had referred to heresy. Here, Adam's sin is a heresy of cosmic proportions; it is heteropraxis which *inter-rupts* the relational flow within God, and between God and creation. The Shekhinah, God's (feminine) presence, by Adam's sin is sundered from the sefirotic union and banished from the Garden, abandoned and vulnerable. Adam, also banished from the Garden, stumbles upon the Shekhinah and together they go into exile. "Adam brought death upon himself and all the world, and caused that tree in regard to which he sinned to be driven out along with him and his descendants forever . . ." (Zohar I:237a). Through Adam's interrupture of deity, all the higher **sefirot,** the conduits of divine consciousness, have been closed off. The Shekhinah is alienated and vulnerable to the attack of demonic powers, and so relates to the world under the aspect of the "tree of death" rather than the "tree of life."

Similarly, the Zohar speaks symbolically of human sin as having caused a separation of the **sefirot** of "strict justice, rigor and divine judgment" (i.e., God's "left hand") from God's own self. In sefirotic symbolism, as long as **Din,** God's rigorous judgment, is balanced with **Hesed,** God's loving kindness, then there is harmony in God's psyche, represented by **Tif'eret,** God's beauty, the "tree of life." When, however, human sin creates an imbalance in God's psyche, there are violent repercussions in the world below. Scholem writes,

> The quality of stern judgment represents the great fire of wrath which burns in God but is always tempered by His mercy. When it ceases to be tempered, when in its measureless hyper-trophical outbreak it tears itself loose from the quality of mercy, then it breaks away from God altogether and is transformed into the radically evil, into Gehenna and the dark world of Satan.[18]

All this means that the **sitra ahra,** the "dark side," is actually an aspect of God, sundered from God's loving mercy and wreaking havoc on the world—due largely to human sin. With these symbolic expressions, **Shekhinta b'galuta** and **sitra ahra,** the Zohar attempts to speak of the divine struggle with evil, and with evil's consequences for and in God's own being. There is no question that the Zohar drifts occasionally toward an ultimate dualism, but finally avoids this conclusion by understanding this struggle to occur within God's own self. Even the tearing away of the **sitra ahra** from God's **hesed** can be mended, though the process of reunification of divine being was to become a central issue only with Luria's reflections. What is crucial here, in the midst of this highly symbolic and often mystifying language, is to recognize the Zohar's serious struggle with the problem of evil.

It is precisely at this point that kabbalistic thought presents a challenge to process theologians, who can claim that God "affects all and is affected by all"[19] and yet apparently suppress the possible consequences of their claim. In Chapter 2 it was noted that, in process thinking, human recalcitrance does affect the specificity and clarity of subsequent initial aims which God may offer to new occasions, but God's own nature considered under its "primordial" aspect apparently is considered impervious to sin, suffering and evil in the world. Process theologians, on the whole, maintain a basic confidence in God's capacity to weave a world of harmony and beauty even out of the worst of our sufferings. A theological appropriation of the kabbalistic myth poses the question of whether the process vision either of human sin or of divine vulnerability is radical enough. What effects might human sin, senseless suffering, and radical evil be exercising upon God? How, for example, can God integrate the Holocaust's horrors into the divine psyche?

It is apparent that, in this connection, the notion of divine wrath in Christian tradition needs to be retrieved and reinterpreted. Perhaps it points to God's passionate response to sin, suffering and evil, a response which at times may burn "out of control," as it were. Many of the biblical narratives whose anthropopathisms have posed problems to theologians —such as the Flood, the destruction of Sodom and Gomorrah, the **Akedah,** or God's mysterious attempt to put Moses to death (Ex 4:24–26)— could then be taken more seriously as indicators of this unfathomable divine rage and fury.

But the possibilities of the notion of the Shekhinah's exile as a way of explicating the radical effects of evil upon God the Spirit are of more central concern here. In this connection, we recall first that the Shekhinah is, for the Zohar, God's own self-consciousness, God's "I" in relation to creation and human beings in particular. Consequently, the exile of the Shekhinah, due to human sin, suggests that God's own ability to grasp the divine self-consciousness is debilitated. God becomes, as it were, "unsure of himself"—self-alienated, unable to say "I" clearly and distinctly—due to a deeply tragic spurning of God's love by human beings. One might say that God's sefirotic speech has been interrupted by human sin.[20] This deeply relational God, more truly a God who "affects all and is affected by all," is in need of the proper human therapy—right meditative prayer and halakhic observance—in order to be restabilized. To be sure, the Shekhinah or divine presence provides sustenance and help to those who would pray and live with the proper devotion, so that there occurs a relational and mutual "therapy" between God and Israel. Nonetheless, the kabbalistic vision is of a God who needs human beings in order to speak clearly, and thus to relate rightly, to creation. "The impulse below calls forth an impulse above."

The highly mythical character of such language ought not to prevent us from a recognition of the significant contribution which the Zohar can make to a contemporary theology of the tragic—one which knows itself to be interrupted by evil, one which is written intentionally "after Auschwitz." It must be remembered, after all, that the **Shekhinta b'galuta** myth itself was an historical commentary; the Shekhinah's exile corresponded with, and was the cosmic, prototypical expression of, the centuries-long **galut** of the Jewish people from the land of Israel. The myth had, therefore, a deeply historical character, for it provided an interpretation of the historical circumstances of the people Israel, as well as a reinterpretation of the Jews' authoritative texts in the *con-text*—a text read alongside—of those circumstances of suffering, persecution, and exile.

This reinterpretation of scripture, and so also of the God witnessed to therein, challenges the prevalent religious assumption that it is within God's power unilaterally to overcome all suffering and evil in the world. It asks us to consider the possibility that God is internally related to creation, is deeply responsive to its sufferings as well as its joys, and indeed is constituted as a "personality" to a significant extent by that relationship. It suggests that God awaits, indeed needs, human cooperation in the task of completing the work of creation and divine fulfillment. It even hints that God's presence is a fragmented, fleeting, exiled presence—banished by human insensitivity and sin.

And so, in this reinterpretation of God, the Spirit tragically awaits the response of human beings to the divine flow of energy—or, in process terms, to the divine aims offered to us. That tragic sense is absent, unfortunately, from a statement by Alfred North Whitehead which otherwise contains kabbalistic overtones: "What is done in the world is transformed into a reality in heaven, and the reality in heaven passes back into the world."[21] This mutually transformative relationship described by Whitehead as occurring between "heaven" and "world," read through the kabbalistic myth of the Shekhinah's tragic exile, can be interpreted in terms of the Spirit—God's active, yet also "passive" or "exiled," presence in creation.

Yet, even with its tragic sense, there still remained in the Zohar the sustaining hope that, in the coming of the Messiah, human sin and improper meditation would be righted. In those days God, humanity and all of creation would be brought back from exile, so to speak, and so brought back into proper relation.[22] Thus in the Zohar the hermeneutic of exile was not thoroughgoing; although it was used to interpret deity far more tragically than the rabbinic notion of the Shekhinah's exile had been, it yet coexisted with a messianic hope that tempered the threatfulness of exilic thinking. Even so, the Zoharic myth represented a radicalization of the rabbinic idea of the Shekhinah's exile. The Zoharic myth was, in turn, radicalized later by Isaac Luria, who wrote after the expulsion of the Jews from Spain in 1492. We turn now to Luria's reworking of the myth of exile in his own historical context.

B. ISAAC LURIA: POSTPONING PRESENCE

The crises in Jewish experience engendered by the catastrophe of 1492 were considered by many Jews to represent the "travail of the Messiah," the birth-pangs of history which promised the dawning of redemption. This anticipated redemption, however, did not arrive—and as usually happens with the disappointment of messianic expectations, the tradition underwent further, historically informed interpretation. The tradition to be reinterpreted, in this case, was the Zohar's "hermeneutic of exile."

With the exile from Spain, the center of Jewish mysticism migrated to Safed, a village in Palestine. Here Isaac Luria (1534–1572) rethought the Zoharic themes of exile and messianic hope, and formulated a myth in which **galut** was portrayed as the very heart of existence. Here, ironically enough, was a Jew living as an alien in the land of his ancestors, and the inner tension which such an image evokes is taken up into Luria's hermeneutic of exile. Here God, humanity and creation are envisioned as ever participating within the tensions of presence and absence, indwelling and exile. These tensions find expression in the three cosmic moments of **tsimtsum, shevirah** and **tikkun,** which correspond to the traditional theological categories of creation, fall and redemption.

For Luria, the first moment in the divine drama involves the process undergone by the all-encompassing deity in order to "make room" for creation. It is a divine self-*di*vestment in which the **En Sof,** the unspeakable Allness and Nothingness with no beginning or end, withdraws or retreats from a point so that something other than the divine self can be. Since God is ultimately Nothingness (**Ayin**), the doctrine of **creatio ex nihilo** is now interpreted to mean that God creates out of God's own self through this process of **tsimtsum,** meaning, in Scholem's synopsis, "that the existence of the universe is made possible by a process of shrinkage in God."[23]

In Chapter 2 the idea of **tsimtsum ha-Shekhinah,** which for the rabbis meant the "confinement of the Shekhinah," or the concentration of God's presence at a particular holy site, was mentioned briefly. Luria's notion of **tsimtsum,** though, is an inversion of the imagery from concentration to withdrawal, from presence to absence.[24] It is God's own self-exile, "not the galut of one of the creatures but of God Himself,"[25] through which God "lets there be" an other—the realm of creation— which is not God. God's own **galut,** then, becomes the primary cosmological fact which underlies all historical or existential experiences of **galut.**

In light of the interpretation of **ruach** in the Hebrew scriptures offered in Chapter 2, it is interesting that the word **tsimtsum** may be rooted in **mezamzem,** the metaphor of holding one's breath.[26] While **ruach** usually has been considered to be God's animating presence in creation, the imagery of God holding in God's breath presents a different picture: God's presence is withdrawn, held back, inhaled, so that the other might be in its integrity. God's presence to creation, in fact, is a certain absence, a divine breathlessness. Bloom playfully suggests that **tsimtsum** denotes a divine anxiety: "God had breathing trouble, and this trouble created the world."[27] We might, in turn, play out Bloom's suggestion enough to suggest that the **tsimtsum** which is God's "breathing trouble" betrays God's anxiety about creating an other. For the profound truth which Luria's doctrine of **tsimtsum** may teach us is that the act of creation involves a profound limitation on God's part. God truly must withdraw in order to allow the other to exist (= to "stand forth") in freedom and integrity. Already in the first moment of creation, there is a postponement of divine presence, an exile of God which is simultaneously both from and into God's own self in order to "make space" for creation, to give birth to a creative space. This is the divine self-*di*vestment, a divestment of both full presence and absolute power.

The hermeneutic of exile continues to wend its way in Luria's second cosmological moment, **shevirah** or the "shattering of the vessels." God's self-exile in **tsimtsum** has made space for a world, a realm of finitude over against God's infinitude. God's next movement is one of self-*in*vestment, for the Creator emanates a light which is intended to fill and animate the finite forms or "vessels" of potentiality. But apparently God underestimates the potency of this creative light, for the vessels shatter under its impact. "This is the decisive crisis of all divine and created being," Scholem writes, for "after the crisis nothing remains as it was."[28] There is already in this second cosmological moment a brokenness in the created order, due, as it were, to a divine miscalculation. Creation becomes composed of the fragments of the shattered vessels of finitude (**kelippot**), and some of the "sparks" of divine light—the fallout of **shevirah**—become attached to, and eventually trapped by, the shattered vessels.

There is no place left untouched by this cosmic catastrophe, nothing left unbroken. Alongside this trope of brokenness stands the familiar trope of exile. As Scholem describes Luria's scenario, "Nothing is in the place appointed for it; everything is either below or above, but not where it should be. In other words, all being is in **galut**."[29] The shattering of the vessels, indeed, is a second moment of exile for God; the sparks entrapped in the **kelippot** are, in fact, the "sparks of the Shekhinah," so that this cosmic portrait of **galut** includes even "the **galut** of the Shekhinah at the very inception of its being."[30] The exile of the Shekhinah in this world is yet another metaphor for postponed presence. God as the exiled presence wanders on the edge between presence and absence, for "exile" signifies a presence which is not fully "here" or "there," but ever "outside" and "beyond" and even "untouchable"—and yet which is nonetheless also "present." In this creation myth's second moment, God is "captivated," as it were, by God's own shattered, exilic world.

The keenly tragic nature of kabbalistic thought is once again evident, for in Luria's interpretation, creation has not proceeded (from God) as God intended. We find this, of course, in the Bible as well as in de Leon's commentary, but in those cases the fall from idyllic existence is attributable to human sin. With Luria, existence is envisioned to have been exilic from the moment of its original impulse out of God. To exist is to exist in exile, and even God is not immune; indeed, exile begins in God's own **tsimtsum** and then is transposed into finite existence in **shevirah,** which itself is God's "fault." Scholem even suggests that, in Luria's guarded opinion, this "cleavage in God" is a self-catharsis, a purification of the elements of evil in the divine being.[31] In softer language, **shevirah** represents God's attempt to cope with an overabundance of **Din,** the plethora of rigorous judgment within God's own self. In either case, creation has about it a sense of God's own deep struggle to contain, let alone embody or express, the complexities of a divinely turbulent creativity.[32]

All this is not to suggest that Luria interpreted God as wholly helpless. There remains a transcendent aspect of deity which is not entrapped in the shattered creation. At the same time, this very picture entails a rift, a true alienation, within God.[33] This, again, had also been the Zohar's picture, but there it was the fault of humanity, and final redemption would arrive with the Messiah. But Luria's radicalization of the hermeneutic of exile placed the fault in the very genesis of God's creative activity, perhaps even in God's own self. If the fault is in God, this raises the question of whether God alone can overcome self-rupture in order to effect redemption. God longs to overcome self-alienation—and so also the state of exile which characterizes all existence—but cannot do so apart from the aid of humanity. This necessary human role in redemption brings us to the third moment in the divine drama, **tikkun.**

Tikkun, meaning "restoration" or "mending," refers to human responsibility to help mend the rift in God which makes for exilic existence. According to Luria, it was given to Adam, the first human being and the primal soul, to effect redemption of the fallen sparks through proper meditation and spiritual action. But Adam failed and so human history, too, has its genesis in exile, a truth symbolized in Adam's expulsion from Eden. In his failure to unite the exiled Shekhinah with the divine masculine principle, even Adam is splintered; his " 'great soul,' in which the entire soul substance of mankind was concentrated, has also shattered. . . . The sparks of Adam's soul and the sparks of the Shekhinah disperse, fall, and go into exile . . . [to be] dominated by the **kelippot.**"[34] Luria's hermeneutic of exile continues to work like an infinite puzzle, one level of **galut** providing the maze-like context for yet another. Even the ever-renewed possibility of **tikkun,** given to each person and particularly to each Jew, also entails the possibility of failure, and every failure throws existence (and God's Shekhinah) into yet deeper and more confused exilic quandaries.

Nevertheless, for Luria, the mending of creation through proper meditation and Torah observance is the achievable responsibility of human beings. The ancient hope of the coming of the Messiah as one who effects redemption of God and creation is a presence infinitely postponed, for now the messianic hope is focused on the individual Jew's own response to the call for **tikkun.** According to Scholem, "To Luria the coming of the Messiah means no more than a signature under a document that we ourselves write,"[35] a symbolic testimony to a universally completed process of **tikkun.**

Though it appears that Luria fully expected that the day of **tikkun** would finally arrive "as the logical consequence of a process in which we are all participants,"[36] his vision nonetheless had a tragically realistic edge to it, for in fact at every crucial juncture in history humanity had (and has) failed "to mend the world" (Fackenheim). Perhaps the full presence of deity, manifesting a primordial unity and fullness, is forever exiled from human experience, a postponed presence. Certainly as long as the real presence of senseless human suffering and radical evil interrupts our messianic dreams, "exile" remains an appropriate image for God, self and world.

C. A CONTEMPORARY HERMENEUTIC OF EXILE: MEANDERING MEANINGS

After having wandered, via a hermeneutic of exile, through de Leon's encounter with evil, followed by Luria's postponement of divine presence, it seems appropriate to ask how such a radically alien religious vision could arise and thrive among Jews who had been shaped by traditional rabbinic Judaism. Judaism was centered upon an authoritative text, the Hebrew Bible, and a rich and imaginative—yet also authoritative—interpretation of that Bible, the Talmud. How was there room for this mystical-mythical midrash with its darkly tragic, wildly symbolic, almost nightmarish vision of reality?

Of course, for many Jewish teachers there *was* no room in the tradition for Kabbalah. It was regarded by many with suspicion and fear. Yet, on the other hand, there was virtually a continuous line—a "kabbalah," or tradition—of esoteric mystical teaching and practice, admittedly of various expressions, among certain of the rabbis dating back to a century before the common era. Finally, though, it is apparent that the Kabbalah's true staying power, simply enough, was that it was *commentary* on the Hebrew scriptures.

I have already written in Chapter 2 about the centrality of the text in the rabbinic tradition—and the ongoing process of commentary on the text, and commentary on the commentary, **ad infinitum.** As far-reaching and imaginative as the Zohar might have been in its interpretation of the biblical text, it was just as attentive to textual minutiae as any more "orthodox" commentary could be—and sometimes more so, since it relished the opportunity to find hidden sefirotic meanings in the most unlikely phrases, words and even letters of the text. Thus, it could claim a place in the rich and dynamic Jewish tradition of creative readings and intertextuality. As Scholem has indicated, the Jewish mystics could thrive because they rooted and expressed their experience in a new, deeper, mystical reading of the authoritative text, thereby claiming to find the "coincidence of true intuition and true tradition."[37]

The written text, of course, is but one factor in the hermeneutical situation; another vital, interfacing "text" is the historical context of the interpreter or interpreting community. As the Jewish people struggled with centuries of suffering and persecution—usually at the hands of Christians—in a situation of **galut** or exile, an interpretation of the authoritative texts which could profoundly address the historical situation of oppression was a necessity. Centuries had passed, and God had not yet delivered Israel, nor consequently God's own presence with Israel, from exile. For those who were drawn to Kabbalah, a novel, radical interpretation of the scriptures was felt to be crucial for maintaining faith in the God of the scriptures.

The "text" of history in which the Jewish people found themselves during the times in which de Leon and Luria wrote, then, had a pervasive sense of **galut** on every line, and between the lines as well. An historical context such as this encourages the interpreter to a "heretic hermeneutic," as Susan Handelman has characterized it. In an era of extremity, the interpreter's need "to find meanings within Scripture to accord with contradictory contemporary experience" may readily "edge over into heresy."[38] Handelman does not intend by the use of the word "heresy" a negative judgment, for she argues that the ongoing process of reinterpretation of texts in light of new and ever-changing socio-historical *con-texts* is necessary and inevitable in any literary tradition, religious or otherwise. So it may be that the "heretical" reading is the best reading in a particular circumstance, though of course the very notion of heresy is thereby called into question. For the kabbalists' rereading of the Hebrew scriptures—based on a hermeneutic of exile responsive to their historical situation—already had precedent in the restructuring of the covenant by the **tannaim** in the decades and centuries following the destruction of the second Temple. But one need not stop the backward tracking of reinterpretation with the early rabbis, for historical-critical and sociological studies of the Hebrew scriptures reveal in biblical faith the ongoing processes of the Jewish religious community reinterpreting its tradition in ever-changing historical circumstances.[39] To what supposedly primal point might one retrace the interpretive, intertextual paths of any tradition in order to find the pristine moment of pure presence, the "orthodox" revelation by which to measure "heresy"?

The deconstructive ruminations of Jacques Derrida, particularly as they are expressed in his notion of **ecriture,** or "writing," come into play here. **Ecriture** is his name for an explicitly interpretive approach to existence, in which the interpreter lives in the awareness that all experience and thought possess a mediated character. As Robert Magliola describes it in its relevance for theology,

> Writing is God "at a remove." . . . It is precisely the "remove," the
> "silence" of God's voice, this *interval,* this *difference* . . . which *consti-*
> *tutes* the writing whereby we "know" Him, but this writing *is not* God.
> This writing is "trace," a "directional." . . . Because one follows the
> "directional" which is trace, there is "movement," "pathway," *pas-*
> *sage, procession, parcours.*[40]

"Speaking," on the other hand, designates what Derrida calls the
logocentric claim that Being is directly accessible to human thought and
discourse, "known directly through the human spirit and vented immediately through the human voice."[41] The Derridean notion of "writing"
assumes that there is no such knowable logos, no site of pure presence or
unambiguous revelation, which might negate the need for interpretation.
"The necessity of commentary, like poetic necessity, is the very form of
exiled speech," Derrida writes. Turning the onto-theological dream in-
side-out, he continues, "In the beginning is hermeneutics."[42] No unadul-
terated, crystal-clear Logos to be discovered or revealed—just the never-
ending task of interpreting what Bernard Meland called the "fallible
forms and symbols" of our cultural traditions.[43]

Luria's radical hermeneutic of exile serves to underscore the irretrie-
vability of the moment of pure presence. Literary critic Harold Bloom,
while acknowledging that the Kabbalah, like Derrida, thinks in ways alien
and unpermitted by the Western onto-theological tradition, proceeds to
claim that "Kabbalah stops the movement of Derrida's 'trace,' since it has
a *point* of the primordial, where presence and absence co-exist by continuous interplay."[44] Yet, in the Lurianic myth, that point is itself lost and
inaccessible to human reflection, for the moment of **tsimtsum,** where
presence and absence co-exist, has been eclipsed by the shattering moment of **shevirah,** by which even God is exiled. In a contemporary appropriation of the hermeneutic of exile, the "trace" is the continual attempt
to track the presence of the absent, exiled deity through **ecriture,** writing
upon writing, interpretation of interpretation.

Kabbalistic literature offers several other images which can be readily
interpreted as expressions of this sense of intertextuality. One thinks of
the kabbalistic notion of Torah as an infinitely interpretable text composed of the names of God, and so as containing in seed form all of
"reality"—which is, in truth, layer upon layer of interpretation, "hermeneutical account upon hermeneutical account, all the way down."[45] The
Torah does not yield just one specific meaning, for at its hidden heart,

waiting to be exegeted, is the great mystical name of God, whence all language, both divine and human, flows. Thus all of reality is infused with, and at bottom composed of, Torah. The divine name is, in Scholem's words, "far-reaching, all-embracing, and, unlike a human word, cannot be applied to a specific context of meaning. In other words . . . it is *the* object of interpretation par excellence."[46] This concept of Torah, demythologized, may suggest that our religious traditions can be infinitely rich resources for creative thought and interpretation, if treated neither as static deposits of facts and ideas nor as eternal expressions of an immutable deity, but as the pliable structures through which the divine presence encounters and addresses us in history. It may remind us that God can become mediately "present" to us in the interpreted languages of our religious or cultural traditions.

This point is made further in the kabbalistic theory of the **sefirot,** which attempts to describe the divine psyche through the use of divine names. Divine emanation, accordingly, is associated with a theory of language, for "the **sefirot** are the creative names which God called into the world, the names which He gave to Himself. . . . The world of divine emanation is one in which the faculty of speech is anticipated in God."[47] To begin to speak the divine sefirotic language, then, was for the kabbalist to embark on an infinite and mysterious journey of countless meanings. God's hidden language, which provided the basis for human linguisticality, yielded interminable significance. Bloom, in his *Kabbalah and Criticism,* has explored this reading of the **sefirot** with some fascinating results. He suggests that the **sefirot** are "complex figurations for God, tropes or turns of language that substitute for God. Indeed . . . they are names implying complex commentaries that make them into texts."[48] If the Zoharic pronouncement that "He is they, and they are He" comes dangerously close, in Bloom's interpretation, to the notion that God and language are identical, certainly it can, at the least, be said that language provides the mediating structures through which God's presence is experienced (i.e., interpreted) by human beings. The imagery of the **sefirot,** particularly when it is complexified by the almost infinite number of interrelationships traced by Cordovero's concept of **behinot,** invites us to consider the boundless plurality of readings of God offered by our traditions.

The tragic side of the hermeneutic of exile, however, would also remind us that, as rich as our religio-literary traditions may be, they cannot encompass deity. Existence is exile; we are never in the "full presence" of the other, including and especially God. For our relationships are mediated by linguisticality, and our language, which includes interpretation as well, partakes of the brokenness of all creation. God's holy name is itself broken in half by the cosmic exile of **shevirah,** and the letters of the Tetragrammaton remain disjointed for the duration of the exile. In the exile which is existence nothing is where it was intended to be, particularly the final **vav** and **he,** the letters in the divine name which are the **sefirot Tif'eret** and **Shekhinah.** The brokenness and corruption of our own linguistic traditions is, for the Kabbalah, a repetition of the divine inter-rupture. Language, with Adam and Eve, is exiled from Eden, "ever not quite" capable of circumscribing God, self or world.[49] As Bloom has written, "The great lesson that Kabbalah can teach contemporary interpretation is that meaning . . . wanders, like human tribulation, or like error, from text to text, and within a text, from figure to figure."[50] A contemporary hermeneutic of exile recognizes that it yields meandering meanings in the never-ending task of interpretation.

The kabbalists may therefore remind us that, if God is to be "found" anywhere, it will be precisely in the historically-conditioned process of reinterpretation of the religious community's texts and tradition. God will not be located at the end of the long task of retracing our tradition's interpretive steps to some ahistorical, pristine moment of full presence and unambiguous revelation; rather, with the rabbis who believed the Shekhinah to be present in the communal hermeneutic encounter with Torah, I believe that God is "present" to us precisely in the midst of our struggle to understand, interpret and appropriate our religious traditions in our own socio-historical situation.[51] And with the kabbalists who believed the Shekhinah to be in exile, wandering in the dark and dusty alleyways of the world, I believe that God's presence is an exiled presence, a presence/absence inscribed in our texts, yet never circumscribed by our traditions or retraced to an ahistorical ("pre-**shevirah**") point of total presence. A contemporary appropriation of the hermeneutic of exile, then, operates on the assumption that God as Spirit is never a full, immediate, unambiguous presence. Rather, the Spirit is mediated presence, textual presence, interpreted through the con-texts of the interpreter's scripture, tradition, history and self-in-community.[52]

It is rather significant to note, in this context, that Jewish mysticism has rarely talked about absorption of the self into an all-encompassing divine presence. It is much more prone to speak of **devekut,** which is usually understood to be attachment to, or devotion to, God. Furthermore, a good argument can be made that what the kabbalists wrote was not a textbook for mystics, for they wrote little about direct manifestations or experiences of God. Their writings are more mythical than mystical, more an attempt to interpret God *in* history than to evoke ecstatic experiences of the divine which would deliver them *from* history. It is important to remember that their full confrontation with the historical realities of human suffering and evil, and the deeply tragic theosophies which resulted from their vision of those realities as they impinged upon the Jewish people, were two distinguishing marks in the reflections of de Leon and Luria.

Because of their rootedness in the vicissitudes of historical exile, the kabbalists found themselves reading their traditions with a daring "heretic hermeneutic" which challenged the prevalent interpretations, a hermeneutic of exile which at the same time attempted to uncover suppressed suspicions about God, creation, humanity and evil. Though we cannot take their mythological constructions literally, the thrust of this chapter has been to show how we can appropriate seriously in our contemporary situation their "hermeneutic of exile." But in this chapter the argument has remained largely on the level of methodological considerations of the linguistic-hermeneutic basis of all human constructions of "reality," including theological constructions. In the following chapter, the retrieval of a hermeneutic of exile must be shifted onto the level of theological content in an intentionally post-Holocaust setting. For a Christian pneumatology which is founded in Jewish-Christian conversation, and is attentive to the present historical context, the **tremendum** of the Holocaust poses the greatest challenge to the task of interpreting God's presence in history and in creation. This is, nonetheless, the task before us, and if the kabbalists have taught us anything, it is that we should assume the task of interpreting our texts and traditions with full attentiveness to the pains and evils of our socio-historical situation.

NOTES

1. Hartman, of course, would agree. Indeed, he recognizes that there is an "Exodus" tradition which emphasizes God's unilateral power of liberation. For his own understanding of covenant—an understanding to which I am deeply attracted—he chooses a "Sinai" tradition which emphasizes human responsibility, before God, for how Israel's covenantal history will be shaped. See especially Chapter 10 of *A Living Covenant,* "Two Competing Covenantal Paradigms," and Chapter 6 of this study.

2. Chapter 2 of this study, pp. 53ff. Cf. Abelson, *The Immanence of God,* p. 291.

3. Like anyone else in our century who studies Jewish mysticism, I am highly indebted to the labors of Gershom Scholem. (Consult bibliography for relevant works.) I have also been greatly helped by David Blumenthal's two-volume source reader, *Understanding Jewish Mysticism* (New York: Ktav Publishing House, Inc., 1978 and 1982).

Among Christian theologians who have attempted to utilize Luria's ideas, I have already in Chapter 1 mentioned Jürgen Moltmann (esp. *The Trinity and the Kingdom* and *God in Creation*). To a lesser extent, Paul van Buren has also cast a glance in Luria's direction; see *A Christian Theology of the People Israel.* Chapter Two, "Israel's Testimony to Creation."

4. Scholem, *Major Trends in Jewish Mysticism* (New York: Schocken Books, 1941), pp. 35, 36.

5. See, for example, David Basinger, "Divine Persuasion: Could the Process God Do More?" *Journal of Religion* Vol. 64 (July 1984), pp. 332–347; Nancy Frankenberry, "Some Problems in Process Theodicy," *Religious Studies* 17 (June 1981), pp. 179–197. Certainly this criticism is wide of the mark when its target indiscriminately includes the more "empirical" process-relational thinkers like Bernard Loomer, Bernard Meland, Bernard Lee, William Dean and Larry Axel. See Dean and Axel, eds., *The Size of God: The Theology of Bernard Loomer in Context* (Macon: Mercer University Press, 1987).

6. Daniel Matt, trans. and intro., *Zohar: The Book of Enlightenment* (New York: Paulist Press, 1983), p. 293.

7. David Blumenthal, ed., *Understanding Jewish Mysticism: The Merkabah Tradition and the Zoharic Tradition* (New York: Ktav Publishing House, Inc., 1978), p. 114. The book will hereafter be referred to as Vol. I.

8. Scholem, *Major Trends,* p. 209.

9. Scholem, *Kabbalah* (Jerusalem: Keter Publishing House, 1974), p. 98.

10. *Ibid.,* p. 113.

11. *Ibid.,* p. 114.

12. Harold Bloom, *Kabbalah and Criticism* (New York: The Continuum Publishing Company, 1983), p. 28.

13. Scholem, *Kabbalah,* p. 112.

14. Matt, p. 37.

15. Scholem, *Major Trends,* pp. 208, 209.

16. Bernard Lee, S. M., "An 'Other' Trinity," manuscript form of a paper presented at the Conference on Jewish Theology and Process Thought at Hebrew Union College, New York (April 13, 1986), p. 4.

17. For a clear, concise explication of the divine dependence upon humanity in the Zohar, see Blumenthal, Vol. I, pp. 154–157.

18. Scholem, *Major Trends,* p. 237.

19. This somewhat programmatic description of God is offered by David Tracy in *The Analogical Imagination* (New York: The Crossroad Publishing Company, 1983), p. 431. He argues, or at least assumes, that it functions well as a synopsis of process theology's vision of God; cf. p. 444, n. 35.

20. According to the Zohar, interestingly enough, once the Shekhinah was driven out of the Garden, language became corrupted and remained so until the Sinaitic revelation. Yet, even as Sinai returned Israel and its language to a state of Edenic purity (Talmud, Shabbat 146a), with the idolatrous sin of the golden calf, Israel immediately cast itself and the Shekhinah back into exile (Zohar 2:193b)—presumably again with a recorrupted language. See Matt, p. 263.

21. Quoted by David Ray Griffin, *God, Power, and Evil: A Process Theodicy* (Philadelphia: The Westminster Press, 1976), p. 305.

22. See Blumenthal, Vol. I, p. 145.

23. Scholem, *Major Trends,* 260.

24. See Chapter 2 of this study, p. 54. It is noteworthy at this point that Urbach is adamant in his denial that "the term **sim-sum ha-Shekhina** (confinement of the Shekhina) as used by the Sages has nothing in common with the doctrine of **simsum** expounded by R. Isaac b. Solomon Ashkenazi Luria . . ." (*The Sages,* p. 704, n. 48). This is a rather odd way of putting it. Surely it is not incorrect to interpret Luria as having retrieved and reinterpreted the rabbinic idea of the Shekhinah's confinement. If the Shekhinah confines herself, so to speak, in the people of Israel, then in their exile the Shekhinah also is exiled. Luria's doctrine of **tsimtsum** simply gives "exile" a larger cosmological meaning and context.

25. Scholem, *Major Trends,* p. 44.

26. Bloom, p. 74.

27. *Ibid.,* p. 83.

28. Scholem, *On the Kabbalah and its Symbolism* (New York: Schocken Books, 1969), p. 112.

29. Scholem, *The Messianic Idea in Judaism* (New York: Schocken Books, 1971), p. 45.

30. *Ibid.* Later in the same book he writes, "In an age in which the historical exile of the people was a terrible and fundamental reality of life, the old idea of an exile of the Shekhinah gained a far greater importance than ever before. For all their persistent claims that this idea represents a mere metaphor, it is clear from their own writings that the Kabbalists at bottom saw something else in it. The exile of the Shekhinah is not a metaphor, it is a genuine symbol of the 'broken' state of things in the realm of divine potentialities" (*ibid.,* p. 275).

31. Scholem, *On the Kabbalah and its Symbolism,* pp. 110–113.

32. Again, Blumenthal offers a concise and clear exposition of Luria's fragmented God and world; see Vol. I, pp. 177–180.

33. In addition to the myth of the Shekhinah's exile, another powerful symbol of God's ruptured self occurs in Luria's imagery of the rending in half of God's holy name. He speaks of the first two letters of the tetragrammaton as having been ripped from the last two through the catastrophic **shevirah.** See Scholem, *The Messianic Idea in Judaism,* p. 275. It is fascinating to compare this imagery to Christian kabbalist Johannes Reuchlin's insertion of the letter **shin** into the Tetragrammaton to make of it the name of "Jesus," i.e., Joshua, or "the Lord saves." Thus in Christian kabbalism it was indeed in the coming of the messianic figure of

Jesus that the divine name/nature is not only reunited but also concomitantly reinterpreted and transformed. See Joseph Leon Blau, *The Christian Interpretation of the Cabala in the Renaissance* (New York: Columbia University Press, 1944), pp. 48, 60. See also the brief but fascinating reference to Reuchlin in Robert Magliola's deconstructive trinitarian theology, *Derrida on the Mend* (West Lafayette: Purdue University Press, 1984), p. 149.

34. Scholem, *On the Kabbalah and its Symbolism,* p. 115.

35. *Ibid.,* p. 117.

36. *Ibid.*

37. Scholem, *Major Trends,* p. 21. See also *On the Kabbalah and its Symbolism,* Chapter I, "Religious Authority and Mysticism."

38. Susan Handelman, "Jacques Derrida and the Heretic Hermeneutic," in Mark Krupnick, ed., *Displacement: Derrida and After* (Bloomington: Indiana University Press, 1983), p. 101.

39. See William Dean's discussion in *American Religious Empiricism* (Albany: State University of New York Press, 1986), pp. 2–5. Christianity too, of course, can be interpreted as another example of a process of reinterpretations of the Hebrew scriptures—initiated, indeed, by Jewish followers of Jesus—and then of the growing Christian traditions of interpretation.

40. Magliola, *op. cit.,* p. 30. He does not mention the **sefirot** in this connection, but as tropes of movement, passage and procession, they certainly fit well into the discussion of **ecriture.** For another possible theological development of **ecriture** other than Magliola's, see Charles E. Winquist, *Epiphanies of Darkness* (Philadelphia: Fortress Press, 1986), esp. Chapter 4, "Metaphor and the Accession to Theological Language." On whether or not God is **ecriture,** cf. Derrida, "Violence and Metaphysics," in *Writing and Difference* (The University of Chicago Press, 1978), pp. 79–153, esp. p. 108.

41. Dean, p. 43.

42. Derrida, p. 67.

43. See Meland, *Fallible Forms and Symbols* (Philadelphia: Fortress Press, 1976), which Dean accurately characterizes as "virtually one long radically empirical critique of recent American theological presumptions" (*American Religious Empiricism,* p. 127, n. 65).

44. Bloom, p. 53.

45. Dean, p. 16, on contemporary American pragmatist Richard Rorty.

46. Scholem, *Major Trends,* p. 295.

47. *Ibid.,* p. 216.

48. Bloom, p. 25.

49. "Ever not quite" was a phrase of William James' which process-relational theologian Bernard Loomer, who possessed a deep sense of the tragic, made his own. See Dean and Axel, eds., *The Size of God,* esp. pp. 14–17, 84.

50. Bloom, p. 82. See also Mark C. Taylor, *Erring* (The University of Chicago Press, 1984), esp. Chapter 7, "Mazing Grace."

51. On this point, see Joseph O'Leary's exemplary work in deconstructive

theology, *Questioning Back* (Minneapolis: Winston Press, Inc., 1985). For example, "Theological tradition lives only as stirred from within or from without by the essential concerns and questions of faith. If the Spirit moves in tradition . . . it is plausible to believe that his movement is mediated through these concerns and questions. An indiscriminate hallowing of all the elements of tradition blinds us to the pneumatic stirrings in its texture" (p. 135).

52. See Dean, pp. 55–58; and Louis Mackey, "Slouching Toward Bethlehem: Deconstructive Strategies in Theology," *Anglican Theological Review* LXV:3 (July 1983), pp. 255–272.

4. Holocaust and Holy Spirit

Admittedly, the two terms united in this chapter's title make a strange pair. What, after all, has the Holocaust to do with the Holy Spirit, or vice versa? What is intended by placing the terms side by side, indeed uniting them by the coordinating conjunction "and"? Is the title only valuable as an alliteration with shock value?

No. This is not theological sensationalism. It is, rather, an attempt to make as uncompromising as possible the disparity between the Nazis' attempted genocide of the Jewish people—a seemingly endless procession of mass shootings, selections, fire pits, gas chambers, ovens, hangings, ghastly tortures, inhuman medical experiments, starvings and beatings and filth—and any sense of God's presence and power interpreted as Holy Spirit. A Christian pneumatology founded in Jewish-Christian conversation must, at some point, first face and then attempt to address this disparity. And in the present work, an intentionally post-Holocaust pneumatology, this disparity resides at the very heart of the matter. For if the problem of evil—especially as posed by the dark reality of meaningless human suffering—is an interruption of normal, privileged human discourse about the goodness or significance of human existence, then that nexus of events called the Holocaust, or **Shoah,** or the **tremendum,** is an interruption *within* the interruption. It ruptures traditional theodicies, or theological justifications of God's ways in the world, with a vengeance. In our time, no other event raises seemingly unanswerable questions about God's presence, power, goodness and even existence as the Holocaust does. And a Christian pneumatology that does not attempt to allow those questions to have their way in its text cannot claim for itself the privilege of speaking of God's Spirit in the world, or in humanity's religious and cultural traditions—let alone in the Church—in this post-Holocaust hour.

Certainly there are many among both Jewish and Christian theolo-

gians who disagree with such an estimation of the Holocaust's interruptive power. Although as a Christian theologian deeply committed to
Jewish-Christian conversation I try to listen closely to the debate among
Jewish theologians, it is not mine to determine what significance the Holocaust should finally have in their deliberations about God. I tend to
agree with those who believe that the traditional Jewish theodical formulations are severely strained by, if not altogether inadequate to, the task of
interpreting what happened to European Jews in the years 1933–1945,
but that is finally not my responsibility to determine.[1]

In the matter of Christian theological responses to the Holocaust,
however, I agree with those theologians who perceive in the Holocaust a
deeply Christian problem: how is it that, in the heart of Christianized
Europe and the home of the Protestant Reformation, the massive genocide of the Jewish people could be imagined, attempted and, to a shocking
extent, actually carried out? It is a deeply Christian problem because it is
evident that the centuries-old Christian tradition of anti-Judaism contributed significantly to a Western socio-cultural tradition in which it was
quite proper to despise Jews. Those same traditions which made it easier
for baptized Nazis to hunt down, humiliate, dehumanize and murder
Jewish men, women and children also made it difficult for even serious
Christians to act with compassion in behalf of the Jews.[2] The Church's
complicity in this all-too-recent attempt to erase the biblical "people of
God" from the face of the earth raises a question not only about the moral
integrity of the Christian faith, but also about how, and whether, God's
Spirit can any longer effectively address human beings in and through
traditional interpretations of that faith.

It should be evident that the burden of this work is to offer an intentionally post-Holocaust interpretation of Christian faith, from a pneumatological perspective, which labors against triumphalism and supersession-
sionism by beginning with a foundational confidence in God's covenantal
faithfulness to, and presence among, the Jewish people. It is, in that respect, already a theological response to Christianity's tradition of anti-
Judaism as that problem has been evidenced in the Holocaust. How such
an interpretation plays itself out in the vital areas of Christology and
eschatology will be the concerns of Chapters 5 and 6. Before those matters, though, the doctrine of the Spirit must itself be cast into the crucible
of the Holocaust. In this chapter we must listen once more to the haunting
question of Wiesel's *Night,* the probing query addressed to no one in
particular beneath an apparently uncaring sky as a Jewish boy struggled

at the end of a gallows rope for more than half an hour: "*Where is God now?*"

That simple question is appropriate because, in most traditional Christian pneumatologies, including the present one, the Holy Spirit is none other than God *present* and *active* in creation and in human existence. Henry van Dusen summed up well this approach to the doctrine of the Spirit when he wrote that the two distinctive and virtually universal characteristics attributed to the Spirit are intimacy and potency, that the Spirit is "God at hand" and "God at work."[3] The second chapter of this study included the proposal of a process pneumatology which is consonant with this view of the Spirit as God near and active. But it is precisely such an understanding of God which is challenged by that question, "Where is God now?" If God as Spirit was near to the starving, suffering, murdered Jews (and others) of the death camps, how, if at all, was that presence experienced? And if God as Spirit was active in the midst of those victims, what was it that God was doing? How might the pneumatology being offered in this work address the interruptive problem of evil and suffering paradigmatically expressed in this century by the nightmare of the death camps? How might it be affected, or even transformed, by a serious encounter with these questions?

It was suggested in Chapter 3 that a contemporary appropriation of the "hermeneutic of exile" found in the Zoharic and Lurianic mythologies might prove fruitful in attempting to address, even fragmentarily, the questions raised by the Holocaust. True to the theme of intertextuality, in my case such a hermeneutic retrieval of the Kabbalah is not an individualistic undertaking; it is mediated to me through several modern Jewish thinkers who in their writings have drawn, to varying degrees and in varying fashions, from kabbalistic imagery in attempting to grapple with the question of God's efficacious presence in the present historical situation—a situation in which, in David Tracy's words, "the overwhelming absence of all meaning [is] exposed by those events in our century which are satanic explosions of anti-Spirit."[4] The Jewish theologians I have in mind are Martin Buber, Emil Fackenheim and Arthur Cohen, and it is in conversation with them that the context is provided for the theological, or, more precisely, *pneumatological,* response to the Holocaust to be offered in this chapter.

There are actually three factors which enter into the choice of Buber, Fackenheim and Cohen as conversation partners in forging an intentionally post-Holocaust pneumatology. First, all three have written about

God within a context framed by the Holocaust's questions, though this is less true of Buber than of Fackenheim and Cohen. Second, all three have drawn inspiration or imagery from the kabbalistic tradition, though this is less true of Fackenheim than of Buber and Cohen. Third, all three have been concerned about the precise issue which is the particular province of pneumatology, that of God's presence in human affairs, though it is arguable that this is less true of Cohen than of Buber and Fackenheim. It is, nonetheless, the convergence of these three factors in the writings of these three theologians which frames the conversation of the present chapter.

I intend, then, in the following section to work via conversation and critique through the notions of God's presence in the face of the Holocaust as offered, whether implicitly or explicitly, in the writings of Buber, Fackenheim and Cohen. I will then attempt a reconsideration of the process pneumatological model of Chapter 2 through the application of the hermeneutic of exile outlined in Chapter 3—particularly as that hermeneutic is strained through, and shaped by, the ruminations on divine presence discovered in these three conversation partners.

A. DIVINE PRESENCE IN JEWISH EXPERIENCE: POST-HOLOCAUST INTERPRETATIONS

1. Pansacramental Presence in Buber

One of the earliest, and perhaps the most influential, of Jewish thinkers to contribute to this century's Jewish-Christian conversation was Martin Buber. The influence of his "I-Thou" philosophy upon Christian theologians such as Emil Brunner and Ronald Gregor Smith, his classic written confrontations with Kierkegaard, and his sympathetic rendering of his "brother Jew" Jesus are all examples of his leadership in this area. At the same time, while his life did encompass the horrors of the Third Reich, Buber's explicit references to the Holocaust are scant indeed. In his defense, it should be pointed out that no one, Jew or Christian, undertook sustained theological reflection upon the Holocaust until well after the time of Buber's death. Even today, such reflection remains relatively sparse, so perhaps it is the case that Buber lived and died in a time in which the pain was yet too fresh to do anything but keep silence.

Yet to one so deeply committed to the venture and possibilities of dialogue, silence could not have the final word. It was the apparent silence of God in the face of the Holocaust, in fact, which gave rise to one of the few explicit allusions to **Shoah** in his published writings. In the haunting conclusion to his essay, "Dialogue Between Heaven and Earth," Buber acknowledged that the Holocaust put his view of human history as dialogue between God and humanity to its most formidable test:

> How is a life with God still possible in a time in which there is an Auschwitz? The estrangement has become too cruel, the hiddenness too deep. . . . Can one still, as an individual and as a people, enter at all into a dialogical relationship with Him? Can one still call to Him? Dare we recommend to the survivors of Auschwitz, the Job of the gas chambers: "Give thanks unto the Lord, for He is good; for His mercy endureth forever"?[5]

Generally, the reply Buber gave to this most central question was, "One can endure the pain, but not the God Who sent it: one rejects either Him or the image one has made of Him."[6]

To be sure, the problem of senseless suffering typically has driven modern religious thinkers precisely to this alternative: either to reject the notion of God's existence altogether, or to revise—and so, in essence, to reject—traditional formulations about God and God's relationship to creation. Thus, for most sensitive Jewish and Christian theologians who allow the **tremendum** to interrupt their thinking, any traditional notion of providence which necessitates viewing God as the causal agent of such radical evil—that God was, in Buber's words, "the God Who sent it"—is unequivocally rejected as blasphemy. Further, to suggest that God "allowed" the Holocaust, along the lines of an understanding of God's relationship to history derived from the prologue of Job, is also problematical, as Buber himself indicated.[7] How, then, **did** Buber answer the questions of God's relationship to creation, of God's role in history, or of the extent of God's responsibility for, and participation in, radical evil and suffering? The evidence suggests that Buber rejected the traditional image of the providential God.

It is important to note that Buber's responses to these issues, like so much of the rest of his thought and writing, were significantly informed by his existentialist interpretation of the myths and religiosity of the Hasidic revitalist movement which began in eighteenth-century Eastern Europe. Buber considered it one of the great tasks of his life—indeed, almost his vocation—to retrieve what he considered to be the essential spirit of Hasidism for his generation. His hermeneutic of retrieval in this regard has been legitimately criticized on several counts: for having made Hasidism appear to anticipate many of the themes of twentieth-century religious existentialism; for having downplayed or even denied the prominent gnostic elements of Hasidism; for having selected only that dimension of Hasidic literature (the legendary) which was most amenable to his existential-dialogical hermeneutic; and for having exploited even the literature which he did choose to retrieve.[8]

On the other hand, Buber indicated often that what he offered was an *interpretation* of Hasidism *for his times.* And in no act of interpretation can the interpreter's presuppositions simply be "bracketed." Perhaps Buber was not sufficiently explicit about this, or perhaps he did not even recognize the extent to which he transformed the Hasidic legends into existentialist tracts which celebrated his sense of the importance of the "here and now." In any case, every new interpretation of a tradition entails also its transformation, to one degree or another. If Buber is criticized for having misread and misused Hasidic sources, it is legitimate to counter that he, too, stood in the ongoing process of reinterpretation of tradition in new socio-historical contexts, and that every such reinterpretation involves the risk of what Harold Bloom has termed *misprision,* or creative misreading.

Buber, though, regarded himself less a misreader, and more a midwife, of Hasidism. In characteristically suggestive imagery, Buber wrote in the foreword to *The Origin and Meaning of Hasidism,* "Because of its truth and because of the great need of the hour, I carry [Hasidism] into the world against its will."[9] In this act of midwifery, many of the key ideas in Buber's neo-Hasidic philosophy were forged; among them were the dialogical nature of all authentic living, the stern refusal to bifurcate reality into sacred and profane dimensions, and a sense of the immediate, personal presence of God.

Though admittedly not a theme equally prominent, it is yet evident from his writings that the myth of the Shekhinah's exile was for him a powerful symbol of God's presence in solidarity with those who suffer; he defined the Shekhinah as "the divine participation in the destiny of His sinful and suffering creation," the earthbound presence of God "which dwells in things, wandering, straying, scattered."[10] Though Buber stressed that the Shekhinah represented God's own voluntary "descent," as it were, into fallen creation in order to redeem "the suffering creatures in the midst of their uncleanness,"[11] there was also a sense in which God's identification with the brokenness of creation led Buber to suggest that the Shekhinah too, like the sparks of a creation gone awry, was trapped—"wandering, straying, scattered"—and in need of redemption. Thus Buber, in retrieving the kabbalistic understanding of the suffering of

God and humanity, and of their mutual, even interdependent redemption, displaced the traditional image of a providential God who rules unilaterally over history.

It was argued in Chapter 3 that it is not necessary to take literally the myth of **shevirah**—the shattering of the vessels and ensuing captivity of the divine sparks, or "sparks of the Shekhinah"—in order to derive insight for a contemporary understanding of divine presence as exile. Yet this disclaimer should not diminish the poignancy of the kabbalistic vision, or its importance for Buber. For this myth narrated God's real investment in creation, God's real risk in creating a free "other," God's real suffering in the midst of creation's brokenness. As Buber wrote, "It is not merely in appearance that God has entered into exile in His indwelling in the world; it is not merely in appearance that in His indwelling He suffers with the fate of the world."[12] Here was a way of voicing the fundamental alienation, and tragic quality, of such a world as ours as somehow being shared by God's own self. God, in fact, "has fallen into duality" in the process of this skewed creation's becoming and now stands in need of redemption along with created order.

Certainly the idea of a fissure in the very being of God—a disjunction, in Buber's words, "of God's being [from] God's indwelling"—challenges every thought of God as self-composed, self-enclosed, immutable and impassible Being Itself. Instead, God's personified presence in creation is here portrayed as a tragic, alien figure who shares in the suffering and homelessness of all exiles, "wandering, erring about, dispersed."[13] The longing of all creation for harmony and unity is a longing shared even by the Creator, who has so divested himself in the world that she nearly loses herself in the world's brokenness. God has so identified with a suffering world that the divine movement from duality toward unity is inseparably bound with "every soul's becoming one within itself"[14]—Buber's existential interpretation of **tikkun**.

Hence, the Shekhinah evokes images of God as exile: the tragic lover wandering through a broken world, trying to find her way back to reunion and fulfillment. Buber's neo-Hasidic portrayal of God is of one who shares in the absurdities and horrors of our world. Buber was careful to distinguish this description of God's participation in the world from the Hindu concept of God's sport or play (**lila**), one aspect of which was the playful immersion of the divine self in the world as **in cognito** presence for a certain aeon. No, insisted Buber, the world was not God's game, but God's *fate,* a fate for which humanity held inestimable responsibility. In *I and Thou,* Buber wrote,

That you need God more than anything, you know at all times in your heart. But don't you know also that God needs you—in the fullness of his eternity, you? How would man exist if God did not need him, and how would you exist? . . . The world is not divine play, it is divine fate. . . . Creation—we participate in it, we encounter the creator, offer ourselves to him, helpers and companions.[15]

This entails an inversion of the common understanding of the God-human relationship, in which a patronizing deity is responsible for everything, including the destiny of the world and every person. Here, rather, it is God who needs redemption from exile just as surely as does every human being—an image of God which unmasks the inadequacy of the traditional understanding of God and redemption by presenting a model of divine-human participation.

If redemption is the mutual responsibility of God and humanity, what is humanity's role? Buber found his answer in his appropriation of the notion of **kavvana,** or inner direction and devotion of one's heart toward God, which for the Hasidim helped to liberate Godward the divine sparks entrapped throughout existence. No aspect of life was excluded from the need for **kavvana;** everything was to be said, done, imagined, thought and dreamed in God's presence and offered to God. For Buber, **kavvana** meant recognizing the divine presence in even the most mundane moments and places, and consciously living in that presence. In his words,

A God who so truly takes part in the destiny of His creation that He separates Himself from His Shekhinah for its sake and makes the reunification with it dependent upon the unification of creation, cannot tolerate—so teaches Hasidism—that in his life and actions man should make a fundamental distinction between above and below.[16]

If in Buber's neo-Hasidism the distinction between above and below was banished, so too was that between human and non-human, and even non-living creatures. All are members of "the community of existence" with which we are continually to "hold holy converse"; we are to perceive the divine depth in all things and so live at all times with a profound consciousness of God's presence. Buber, quoting a Hasidic rebbe, wrote, "There is no thing in the world in which there is not life. . . . And lo, this life is the life of God."[17] To understand and consciously to realize this panentheistic vision, then, provides the root experience of **kavvana.**

Furthermore, in Buber's interpretation of Hasidism **kavvana** finds concrete expression in love, for love is the very life of God within, or more precisely between and among, all creatures. To recognize God's presence in the "between," or in the profound interrelationality of all creation, and to act upon that recognition, is to love. Thus Buber, like Paul in Romans 8, moves us to recognize that the suffering of God arises out of the pains of all creation in which God shares. The panentheistic vision relativizes usual distinctions between human and animal, between living and non-living creatures. It is now a truism that much of our own suffering is due to our ecological egocentricity, our willful ignorance of the technological violence and manipulation which Western civilization in particular has inflicted upon fellow members of the community of creation. Buber found a vital corrective in his reading of Hasidism, whose message, he wrote, "might most easily be rendered through a verbal paraphrase: to love the world in God,"[18] and whose vision of human salvation he described in terms of "preserving the great love of God for all creatures, yes, for all things."[19]

It is **kavvana,** then, existentially interpreted by Buber as love in the community of creation, which accomplishes the movement toward divine unity. It is a love which suffers with a fragmented deity and with a shattered creation, a love which strives for unity and healing. Not that love overcomes the pains and contradictions of existence; it is not a privileged position from which the mysteries of evil and suffering are solved. Rather, wrote Buber, "The absurd is given to me that I may endure and sustain it with my life; this, the enduring and sustaining of the absurd, is the meaning which I can experience."[20] In Hasidism, Buber insisted, this enduring and sustaining can be accomplished only by carrying out the Hasidic watchword, "to love more."

This neo-Hasidic interpretation of the God-world relation, out of which issued the challenge "to love more" and so to bring God and creation nearer to wholeness, Buber called pansacramentalism. Every thing, every person, every experience, every time and place was a potential vehicle for the Holy, a potential sacrament awaiting recognition. Such a vision provides the basis for his conception of the I-Thou encounter, and occasionally his pansacramentalism nearly breaks through the text of his *I and Thou.* For example,

> Man can do justice to the relation to God that has been given to him only by actualizing God in the world in accordance with his ability and the measure of each day, daily. . . . The genuine guarantee of duration is

that the pure relation can be fulfilled as the beings become You, as they are elevated to the You, so that the holy basic word sounds through all of them. Thus the time of human life is formed into an abundance of actuality; and although human life cannot and ought not to overcome the It-relation, it then becomes so permeated by relation that this gains a radiant and penetrating constancy in it.[21]

It is, then, up to human beings, by exercising **kavvana** in their concrete existence, to discern and to elicit the divine dimension (the "You") in every sphere of life.

The awesome responsibility of human beings to "actualize God in the world" was, in effect, Buber's way of translating the Hasidic emphasis upon the *deed.* For the Hasidim, every human thought and action contained a holy spark, no matter how deeply buried. When it is recalled that, in kabbalistic myth, the sparks were the "sparks of the Shekhinah," it becomes clear that the centrality of the deed meant that every human act directly affected the Shekhinah, so intimately bound was she to creation and human history. Nothing is said or done on earth that does not have ramifications and reverberations in heaven—precisely because earth and heaven are united in the divine immanence, the Shekhinah. Buber, in another quotation from a Hasidic rebbe, wrote, "Even when a man does a sin, then too the Glory is clothed in it, for without it he would not have the strength to move a limb. And this is the exile of God's glory."[22]

Thus, in the myth of the Shekhinah's exile, Buber perceived something of the mystery of divine and human freedom. God in God's own freedom has "made room" for an "other," the human, who is created with the capacity for decision and action. This capacity, further, is actuated in every moment by the power of God ("the Glory") immanently active in creation. Human actions, in turn, have a certain limiting and conditioning effect upon God's freedom and power. So, for example, human sin—which is always committed in the actuating power of God—contributes to "the exile of God's glory," just as the loving devotion of **kavvana** contributes to God's own wholeness and redemption. Moreover, so intimately bound are divine and human activity that God, tragically, is "clothed" in human actions which destroy the creation just as surely as in those actions which are redemptive.

The critical question is whether Buber's neo-Hasidic retrieval of a kabbalistic view of the God-world relationship provides an adequate response to the Holocaust. It is more appropriate to the liberalism of the nineteenth century, when the dream that humanity could "realize God" flourished. The Holocaust, however, looms as a stiff challenge, if not a grim denial, of the pansacramental possibility. One may use the kabbalistic language of Hasidism to make the point: if human action determines the measure of proximity of the Shekhinah, does not the Holocaust suggest the eternal exile of God's presence? *Were* there "holy sparks" in the gas chambers? What significance has the Hasidic catch-phrase, "to love more," in the face of the Nazis' genocidal policy against the Jews? What happens to the intimate and immanent God of the Hasidim in the nightmarish slaughter of millions of men, women and children? Wiesel's whispered reply to the question, "Where is God now?"—that God was there on the gallows—might be the most suitable portrait of the Shekhinah in our century.

Apparently, Buber never consciously reflected on his neo-Hasidic pansacramentalism within the context of the Holocaust. He should have, for that event seriously challenges any optimistic hope in humanity's capacity to effect redemption and so to justify its own existence. Indeed, the Holocaust makes a nightmarish mockery of pansacramentalism; if humanity, and especially the Jewish people, is one of the Shekhinah's limbs,[23] then **Shoah** means she has been maimed, raped and left for dead, and the sacrament of creation is a mass of broken bodies and shed blood. The fact that we seem not to have learned very well any lessons from the Holocaust, and now stand ready to destroy the entire creation in nuclear war, raises the question of whether we have not already and altogether exiled God's presence from creation. To adapt Nietzsche, the Shekhinah is in exile, and we have banished her.

Buber was not wholly unaware of the challenge the Holocaust presented to an assured sense of divine presence. In the book which is generally considered his most explicit response to the Holocaust, *Eclipse of God,* he characterized our age as one in which the I-It relation had "usurped, practically uncontested, the mastery and the rule" and so "steps in between and shuts off from us the light of heaven."[24] The divine dimension of I-Thou had been eclipsed by humanity's own unresponsiveness to the divine address in history and creation. It was not a matter of God having mysteriously hidden God's face, for God was for Buber the "Present Being" who continually addresses humanity as an "I" to a "Thou." It was, rather, a matter of modern, technological humanity having stopped listening; the "I" of the "I-It" relation had become lord of humanity. It was probably the most realistic assessment of the twentieth century which Buber ever offered in writing.

Yet, remarkably, Buber ended the book on a note of hope. While the

"I-It" relation reigned supreme now, and had eclipsed God's presence in the "I-Thou" relation, this did not necessarily dictate what must also be the case in the future. Perhaps in some unforeseen moment, humanity would allow the "I-Thou" relation again to emerge, the light of God again to be seen. Undoubtedly, what lay behind Buber's hopefulness was his belief, deeply engrained in Jewish faith, in the ever-present possibility of **teshuva,** of "turning." The road toward redemption began always with the first step of "turning" back toward relationality, toward creation, toward the God who was present in every I-Thou moment.[25] This "turning" was a new beginning which was always open to human beings—and for Buber provided a note of hope after Auschwitz.

It should be evident that Buber's neo-Hasidism still provided the basis for his post-Holocaust notion of humanity's eclipse of God. For Buber had insisted for years that the deed, or human action, determined how deeply God's sacramental presence would be realized in the world. What he wrote in *Eclipse of God* was not essentially different from what he had written in the essay "Jewish Religiosity" forty years earlier:

> In the unconditionality of his deed man experiences his communion with God. God is an unknown Being beyond this world only for the indolent, the decisionless, the lethargic, the man enmeshed in his own designs; for the one who chooses, who decides, who is aflame with his goal, who is unconditioned, God is the closest, the most familiar Being, whom man, through his own action, realizes ever anew, experiencing thereby the mystery of mysteries. Whether God is "transcendent" or "immanent" does not depend on Him; it depends on man.[26]

2. Commanding Presence in Fackenheim

Emil Fackenheim's writings, particularly *God's Presence in History* (1970) and *To Mend the World* (1982), represent possibly the most searching of Jewish theological responses to the Holocaust. Fackenheim has recognized its radically interruptive power far more deeply than Buber ever did. While Buber held out for the possibility of a "turning" which could lead to redemption for God and creation—or, in his words, a powerful returning to the "I-Thou" relation—Fackenheim questions whether, after the Holocaust, such a mending of the world is possible. But he does so in his own, typically logic-jarring way: "*No Tikkun* is possible of *that* rupture, ever after. But the impossible Tikkun is also necessary."[27] For Fackenheim, logic cannot contain the mysteries of God's presence in a history which includes, and which has been ruptured by, the Holocaust.

This inadequacy of logic—particularly as theologic—is a central theme in his earlier work, *God's Presence in History*. Fackenheim opens this book by stressing that, within the structure of Jewish existence, God's presence in history is a fundamental affirmation. This affirmation is grounded in what Fackenheim calls the "root experiences" of Jewish existence, Exodus and Sinai. These root experiences are the historical events with which Jewish faith originated, by which it is nourished, and by which it continues to interpret itself within new historical contexts. Additionally, these experiences reveal for Jews a double aspect in God's presence in history; Exodus reveals God's saving presence, Sinai God's commanding presence. Fackenheim here locates a paradoxical note in the Jewish experience of divine presence: in the deliverance at the Red Sea, God is perceived by the astonished witnesses to be the "sole Power," present in and through this natural-historical event;[28] yet in the commanding voice of Sinai, that same "sole Power" which, by definition, should annul human freedom, actually addresses and so protects human freedom. "For, being *commanding*, it *addresses human freedom*. And being *sole Power*, it *destroys* that freedom because it is only human. Yet the freedom destroyed is also required."[29] The commanding voice of the sole power needs to be heard and responded to by human beings in order to bring salvation to fruition. This tension within the Jewish experience of God's presence is one that Fackenheim exploits as his argument unfolds.

The Jewish affirmation of God's presence in history, rooted in the experiences of Exodus and Sinai, has provided the framework by which Jews have interpreted themselves when faced with what Fackenheim calls "epoch-making events" such as the destruction of the first and second Temples and the expulsion from Spain. These events, while challenging Jewish faith in God's historical presence, did not destroy that faith; they could not reach as deeply into the Jewish psyche as did Exodus-Sinai. Nevertheless, epoch-making events confront the received tradition with such a magnitude that reinterpretation of the tradition becomes a necessity.

Fackenheim, to be sure, distinguishes the necessity of reinterpretation from any thought of denying or qualifying the root experiences of Exodus and Sinai. He argues that Jewish theological thought has a character of "stubbornness" which resists the temptation to lessen the paradoxical tension of faith in a sole power, whether that faith be challenged by philosophical reflection or by the vicissitudes of history. For Fackenheim, Jewish thought resists the notions of (i) God as sole power but without involvement in history, i.e., deism; (ii) God as sole power who overwhelms history, i.e., theological determinism or fatalism; and (iii) God as other than sole power, which Fackenheim argues would be theological finitism. The adoption of any one of these positions would lessen the paradoxical tension in which Jewish faith exists, but that tension is precisely the locus of faith in a God who is present in the ambiguities in history. Yet if this God is not merely present but is present as sole power, the tension must finally be resolved; "a dialectical tension develops, and this points to a future in which evil is vanquished by divine Power and human freedom, and in which divine Power and human freedom are reconciled."[30] A messianic or eschatological hope for the future, then, is a necessary component in faith in God as sole power.

The messianic hope, though, does not dissolve the contradictions experienced in the present between God as sole power and human freedom, or between divine transcendence and divine involvement in history. Fackenheim argues, rather, that the paradoxical tensions involved in faith in God as sole power are neither dissolved nor suppressed, but expressed fragmentarily in the stories, parables and metaphors of midrashim. Midrashic thinking does not aim to be logical, for logic cannot encompass the inner tensions of Jewish faith. Instead, midrashic thinking exposes and almost celebrates those tensions in what might be called a theology of **k'b'yakhol,** or an "as it were" theology, in which the limitations of human thought and language are explicitly recognized, and yet in which thought and language are daringly employed in imaginative commentary on the scriptures.

Though relatively unbound by the strictures of logic, even midrashic thought met its stiffest challenge, writes Fackenheim, in the paganization of Jerusalem in 135 CE. Perhaps the Temple's destruction in 70 could be interpreted as divine punishment "for our sins," but not the transformation of Jerusalem by Hadrian into a pagan city. For this calamity a new answer had to be found, and was found, in the notion of the Shekhinah's exile with the Jewish people.[31] But in the rabbinic idea of the exile of God's presence, the inner tension of Jewish faith in God as sole power is even further heightened:

> A God in exile still commands, for He continues to be present. His presence still comforts, for it holds out hope for a future salvation as His past saving acts are remembered. But where, we must ask, is the "sole Power" or the "Creator of the world"? . . . the exile of a God who is sole Power is inexplicable.[32]

To be sure, the inexplicability of the Almighty's exile is certainly no reason to reject the notion, either for the rabbis or for Fackenheim. But one must ask how long the paradox inherent in such a notion can be sustained—particularly after the Holocaust. If this sole power is manifested as both saving and commanding presence, where is the saving? Granted, at every Passover the Jewish people reenact and so relive the deliverance from the Egyptians, and many faithful Jews celebrated Seder in the death camps and found its litany of liberation to be particularly appropriate to their situation.[33] Yet, where was that saving presence in the camps? *"Where is God now?"* Though the God witnessed in the exodus is a saving presence in history, Fackenheim admits very early in his book—even before explicitly mentioning the Holocaust—that "except for a commanding Presence, any divine Presence in history remains, for Jewish experience, at best fragmentary."[34] And when he does turn explicitly to the Holocaust in Chapter III, it is hardly accidental that its title is "The Commanding Voice of Auschwitz," referring solely to a commanding presence.

Subtly, perhaps not even wholly consciously, Fackenheim redefines the notion of God as sole power. If the power of God is expressed in the command, then it is a power which shares itself. It awaits the obedient response of the hearers, and so accords them a power of their own in the matter of effecting redemption. And even though it is *divine* command, there is a certain powerlessness implied in that God either cannot or does not coerce obedience. Rather, the command assumes, necessitates, perhaps even makes possible, free human response. And if God's presence in history is experienced only as a commanding voice, in some fashion dependent upon human response, then this is a far cry from the image of God normally associated with a phrase like "sole Power."

Admittedly, Fackenheim nowhere claims that God is only a commanding and never a saving presence, though he comes close when he writes that, for the religious Jew, "the Voice of Auschwitz manifests a divine Presence which, as it were, is shorn of all except commanding Power."[35] Fackenheim's usage of the rabbinic "as it were" makes it possible for him to maintain faith in God's saving presence while at the same time finding no evidence of such a power at work in the Holocaust; thus, while the Holocaust is an epoch-making event, it does not negate Fackenheim's faith in God's saving power. Yet if anything raises the paradoxical tension involved in faith in God as sole power, it must be the Holocaust. This tension is, in fact, raised to the level of madness, says Fackenheim—and yet the "Voice of Auschwitz" commands Jews *not to go mad,* but rather to endure specifically as Jews.[36]

But the nagging question concerning the absence of saving presence during the Holocaust cannot, and should not, be dismissed or hidden in the paradoxical constructions of which Fackenheim is so fond. The tensions which are created between God's presence as commanding and as saving must be allowed to surface completely. To wit, if God's power is expressed in a commanding voice which awaits human response, is it possible for it also to be expressed in a salvific **coup** which bypasses human action? Granting it is possible, is it likely? Is it not possible, even likely, that God's mode of activity in history may reside somewhere in the dialectic of divine command and human response, rather than in some notion of unilateral determination of events? If it is, then the notions of God's suffering and even exile, due to human recalcitrance, make some kind of sense. Yet on the other hand, Fackenheim is not overly concerned about making sense if it means a sacrifice of the paradox of faith in God as sole power. Moreover, he finds the midrashim of divine powerlessness and suffering, or of the Shekhinah's exile, inadequate to deal with the Holocaust. In an extremely significant passage he writes,

> In the Midrash, God goes into exile with His people and returns with them; from Auschwitz there was no return. Hence, whereas in the Midrash God is only "as it were" powerless, in *Night*, Wiesel sees Him in the face of a child hanging on the gallows. [Wiesel's account follows.] . . . To stake all on divine powerlessness today, therefore, would be to take it both radically and literally. God suffers literal and radical powerlessness, i.e., actual death; and any resurrected divine power will be manifest, not so much within history as beyond it. A Jew, in short, would have to become a Christian.[37]

It is undoubtedly the case that the notion of divine exile possesses a natural attraction for at least some Christians because it accords well with a theology of the cross; it sounds a great deal like Bonhoeffer's prison musings about a weak and powerless God who is edged out of the world and onto a cross. But Fackenheim ignores the sense of divine powerlessness also found in Jewish tradition, in that a God who commands is also a God who can be rejected. A God who commands is a God who takes human action seriously, and who therefore also takes human history seriously. A God who makes the divine presence known in a commanding voice is a God whose presence *can* be exiled, even "killed," as it were, by human disobedience. But if human disobedience can deaden the Voice, alternately the proper human response can "resurrect" the Voice—in the sense of actualizing the command, not beyond history, but within it—and this was Buber's hope, though differently stated, at the conclusion of *Eclipse of God*.[38]

While the title of Fackenheim's more recent work in post-Holocaust theology, *To Mend the World,* appears to offer a more Buberian, or optimistic, evaluation of the project and possibilities of human history after the Holocaust, the text itself suggests that the title carries more than a touch of irony. For here Fackenheim claims that any mending of the world, any **tikkun** after the Holocaust, will be fragmentary at best. The Holocaust represents an aweful rupture in human history, thought, optimism and faith in God. He writes,

> For centuries the kabbalists practiced their Tikkun, their 'impulse below'—'Torah, prayer and mitzvot'—calling forth an 'impulse from above': in the Holocaust their bodies, their souls and their Tikkun were all indiscriminately murdered.... Hence in our search for a post-Holocaust Tikkun we must accept from the start that at most only a fragmentary Tikkun is possible. This is because we are situated in the post-Holocaust world. We must accept our situatedness. We must live with it.[39]

Fackenheim here utilizes the Lurianic notion of **tikkun,** or the human possibility and responsibility for mending the rift in God and creation, to deny that very possibility. There is no healing of an abyss so deep, only fragmentary attempts at understanding. All the resources of historical, socio-economic, political and religious study are helpful in such attempts, but they cannot span the chasm. "Where the Holocaust is there is no overcoming; and where there is an overcoming the Holocaust is not."[40] Fackenheim points specifically to two phenomena of the camps which resist **tikkun:** the screams of burning children, and the deadly silence of those the Nazis called **Muselmanner,** the walking dead of the camps, the living skeletons who lost all sense of self- and other-identity. These victims of the camps, especially, cannot be reconciled with any theory of redemption, or of any theodicy which speaks of the educational or character-building value of suffering. Their testimony denies a saving presence in the Holocaust.

This, then, raises again the question of God's presence in history: in what sense is it possible to say that God was present to those in the death camps? If there was no *saving* presence, was God a *commanding* presence, as Fackenheim spoke of in *God's Presence in History?*

Although he does not utilize the categories of saving and commanding presence as readily or as thoroughly in *To Mend the World,* an argument can be made that Fackenheim still "locates" God's presence at Auschwitz in the commanding voice. In the context of his ruminations upon what he calls the Holocaust's "new phenomenon," the **Muselman** or walking dead, Fackenheim mentions the testimony of one Pelagia Lewinska, a Polish noblewoman whom he calls "an honorary Jewess," who resisted the dehumanizing tactics of the Nazis by clinging to the one "command" which addressed her: "I felt under orders to live." Fackenheim comments,

> She felt under orders to live. We ask: *Whose* orders? Why did she wish to obey? And—this above all—where did she get the strength? We answer the last question by discovering that it is unanswerable. Once again 'will-power' and 'natural desire' are both inadequate. Once again we have touched an Ultimate.[41]

Fackenheim finds in Pelagia Lewinska's simple testimony an "Ultimate," a hint of God's presence in the Holocaust. It is not coincidental, either, that the experienced command "to live" is virtually identical to the now-famous "614th Commandment" which Fackenheim hears issuing forth from Auschwitz: that Jews must survive as *Jews.* His argument is that God's presence is a commanding voice which prompts, even enables, the Jew to survive, to endure, not to lose hope or to go mad. For Pelagia Lewinska, that command issued in a sense of being "under orders to live," to resist the Nazi dehumanization tactics designed to reduce human beings to living dead, **Muselmanner,** before killing them. Such resistance is reminiscent of the "sanctification of life" theme, which was an inversion of the traditional Jewish notion of martyrdom, and in the following form was attributed to Rabbi Isaac Nissenbaum of the Warsaw ghetto:

> Now is the time for the sanctification of life [**kiddush ha-hayim**] and not for the Sanctification of the Name [**kiddush ha-shem**] through death. Once when our enemies demanded our soul, the Jew martyred his body for kiddush ha-shem. Today when the enemy demands the body, it is the Jew's obligation to defend himself, to preserve his life.[42]

To be sure, there were many ways in which European Jews attempted to fulfill the divine command to live. Some resisted dehumanization through Torah study and observance, inasmuch as it was possible; others resisted through artistic expression, visual, musical, or dramatic; others through journals and diaries by which the story could later be told; yet others through armed resistance, meager though it usually was. But each avenue of resistance affirmed the "sanctification of life," the command which, for Fackenheim, issued out of the Holocaust. Yet this affirmation of those who successfully resisted Nazi dehumanization tactics cannot serve as a judgment upon those who finally could not resist. Nor can it be used to deny the fact that, had Hitler sufficient time and manpower, no "command to live" could have saved the Jews from the Nazi plan to rid the world of them. Nothing so idealistic is intended. Fackenheim's purpose is simply to find a hint of divine presence in the massive evil called the Holocaust—in the simple, enabling command to live, to resist becoming a **Muselman**—rather than to assume a traditional doctrine of providential divine presence which is subsequently challenged deeply by the Holocaust, and must be defended with theodical ingenuity.

The divine presence to which Fackenheim alludes, then, continues to be understood best as a commanding voice which can be ignored or disobeyed, rather than as a sole power. The phrase "sole Power," in fact, can possibly refer only to an ahistorical moment either prior to creation or at some eschatological end. But Fackenheim acknowledges there is no evidence available to us outside of history—a history in which the Holocaust was spawned—and that we are left with a commanding voice. While such an interpretation of God's presence in history may be insufficient to the minds of many people, Jews and Christians alike, it is the most that Fackenheim can find. It is interesting, too, that Fackenheim characterizes the Holy Spirit's presence in the Church in quite similar terms. He writes of the great **kairos** which presented itself to the Church in the years prior to, and during, the Holocaust: a critical opportunity for challenging the Nazis' anti-Jewish, and in reality anti-Christian, ideology. But the opportunity was lost, and Fackenheim writes movingly of the violence done to the Spirit in that lost opportunity:

> Never were the gates of Christian prayer more open, the Holy Spirit at once more clearly present and more vulnerable. And never was a kairos more betrayed, the Holy Spirit more wounded, than when the Word was not spoken, and instead there was a dead, murderous silence.[43]

Here, truly, are prophetic words addressed to the Church by a Jew. He is correct to speak of the Spirit as being vulnerable, as capable of being wounded. This is language highly reminiscent of the Shekhinah's vulnerability and exile—and since both Holy Spirit and Shekhinah are ways of referring to God's presence, the language is appropriate. The term "Holy

Spirit" is the Church's predominant way of referring to divine presence, while "Shekhinah" is an important way, among many others, for Jews to do the same. What is more important than this consideration, however, is that God's presence as Holy Spirit in the Church is vulnerable, woundable, perhaps even "killable," as it were. The "murderous silence" in the Church, to which Fackenheim refers, truly "quenched the Spirit" (1 Thess 5:19), if indeed the Spirit is the active presence of the God of Israel. For in the Holocaust, the Church, on the whole, deserted Israel the people of God. If God's presence among the Jews was experienced in the command to live, the Spirit in the Church should have been heard in the command to save and protect the Jews and other threatened peoples. The general failure to do so raises a serious question about the Spirit's presence to the Church after the Holocaust: Did Christian silence concerning the Nazis so deaden the voice of the Spirit that the Spirit is now a virtual exile?

One shudders at the possibility, and can only trust that the Spirit of God, in covenantal faithfulness and fortitude, continues today to draw near in address and command to the Church. Much of that trust must be founded upon those instances of Christian compassion which occurred all too rarely during the Holocaust—a prayer publicly prayed for the Jews here, a self-endangering rescue there, the occasional help offered in Jesus' name to the persecuted. Such acts also provide the models for a sorely needed reconstruction of Christian faith and practice today. But it is not enough to find and celebrate the rare Christian heroes who heard the Spirit's address, and who responded positively in the Jews' behalf; indeed, such a strategy may become an effective means of whitewashing the Church's complicity in the Holocaust and so relieving ourselves of responsibility for transformation. True repentance would mandate that the Church must labor to cleanse its tradition of those elements which have hindered the body of Christ from hearing clearly the commanding voice of the Spirit of the God of Israel.

Such issues will be addressed more directly in Part III. For the present, it is enough to note that, even after his emphasis in *God's Presence in History* upon God as sole power and saving presence, in the final analysis Fackenheim's post-Holocaust interpretation of divine presence is founded essentially upon the notion of the commanding voice—a voice which can, and apparently often does, go unheeded.

3. Dialectical Presentness in Cohen

By his own admission, Arthur Cohen's one authentically post-Holocaust work in theology was *The Tremendum,* published in 1981.

Unfortunately, Cohen's recent death means that this little book will stand alone in this regard, and that Cohen's rudimentary remarks concerning a post-Holocaust concept of God will go undeveloped by him. Nonetheless, Cohen's suggestions concerning the meaning and mode of God's presence in human affairs are sufficiently challenging, if not entirely novel, to merit consideration in this context.

A central strand of Cohen's argument lies in his denial of Martin Buber's claim that Jewish history has no midpoint, no caesura.[44] Cohen admits, to be sure, that Buber was reacting against Christianity's claim of redemption in the midst of history through the incarnation, and Buber's emphasis upon the present experience of revelation in the existential moment of encounter between God and the individual precluded the recognition of any decisive inbreaking of history. But in a fashion not unlike Fackenheim, Cohen responds that such a caesura, such a decisive intervention in Jewish history and self-understanding, has indeed occurred in the Holocaust. For Cohen to speak of the Holocaust as an intervention in Jewish history does not entail an understanding of the event as being of divine origin. Rather, it is a human deed, but one of such immense proportion that it deserves the name **tremendum** as the deadly human inverse of Rudolph Otto's conception of God as the **mysterium tremendum,** the unfathomable and terrifying, yet fascinating and strangely inviting, presence occasionally manifested to human beings.

Cohen makes it clear that, for him, the Holocaust is a **tremendum** not in the sense of manifesting divine presence, nor even as a mysterious event, but simply because of its sheer *immensity* as a pathological celebration of violence and death. It is an immense abyss in human, and particularly Jewish, history, an event which resists interpretation and assimilation by human rationality because it "denies meaning and makes mockery of meaning."[45] It resists the interpretations of history provided by traditional Jewish theology, and so challenges radically their adequacy and negates their explanatory power. For example, Cohen challenges interpreters who, in one way or another, align Sinai and Auschwitz as symmetrical, signal events in the history of the Jewish people, as when Fackenheim speaks of the "commanding Voice of Auschwitz" with its "614th commandment." "We speak about them in the same breath because their relation is negative," he writes, ". . . sundering connection rather than effecting it. The only contact that Sinai and the **tremendum** make is the Jewish people."[46]

If the **tremendum** has analogue in Jewish history, for Cohen it is found in what he calls the abysses of the Temple's destruction in 70 and the expulsion of the Jews from Spain in 1492. The first abyss of destruction and exile was bridged by the Jews' admission of guilt, by the confession that hardship had befallen them "because of our sins." Thus the received tradition was kept relatively intact. The second abyss was bridged by the mystic-gnostic reading of history offered in kabbalistic literature, in which "the agony of history [was] lifted up into a reading that allowed to God vastly more complexity and interior movement than had been envisaged by the negative theologies that preceded it."[47] This was, to be sure, a radical reinterpretation of the received tradition. The third abyss is the **tremendum,** and "this time the abyss opened and one-third of the Jewish people fell in."[48] And the question for Cohen is whether the tradition is at all adequate to bridge this abyss.

> . . . like our ancestors we are obliged to decide whether such catastrophes are compatible with our traditional notions of a beneficient and providential God. The past generations of Israel decided that they were. The question today is whether the same conclusion may be wrung from the data of the **tremendum.**[49]

Cohen believes that the question must be answered in the negative. He repeatedly raises suspicions about what he variously calls "the God of ancient meaning," "the ancient God," "the God of classical theism," and "the Jewish and Christian monopolar divinity of absolutes and superiorities."[50] A new, or at least different, understanding of God is needed in order to bridge, even precariously, the abyss of the **tremendum.** The point of this different understanding is not to explain or to rationalize evil within a theological system, in which case the system provides an interpretive context for the Holocaust. Rather, Cohen is calling for an inversion of this traditional approach to the problem of evil. His intention is, "accepting [evil's] reality, to estimate what consequence it has for our thinking about the nature, existence, and action of God."[51] This entails a serious attempt to regard the Holocaust truly as a **tremendum,** as a caesura which "inter-rupts" human history and language. It is an attempt to recognize the poverty, even uselessness, of the prevailing theodical tradition which has in the past tended to insulate itself from extreme human suffering through rationalizations about a deity of absolute power and undefeatable providence. It is the difficult attempt to make evil one's starting point in rethinking about God, rather than to assume traditional notions of God before moving to explanations of the existence of evil.

How, then, might one begin to speak about God in this post-

tremendum situation? Quite significant for the purposes of this study is Cohen's penchant to speak of a divine *presence;* he writes of God as being "in some sense, most immediately, presentness," of "the real presence of God before, even if not within, history," and of "the justification that God's presence renders to the worthwhileness of life and struggle."[52] But what is God's mode of presence for Cohen, and how is that presence manifested in the affairs of human history?

Cohen's revisioning of God's presence to creation involves an appropriation of Franz Rosenzweig's construct of God, world and humanity in dialectically interdependent relationship, with renewed emphases upon the passive receptiveness of the world, the active freedom of humanity, and the bipolar nature of deity. God, then, is both active and passive, both receptive and free, both "the absolutely existent (that abstract ground of all), remote and distant, parsed in the classical tradition by negative arguments that winnowed divinity of all admixture," and yet also "commingled with the divine concrete and caring, the presentness and immediacy that validates our own human individuality."[53] For Cohen such a vision of God is arrived at by uniting Scholem's reading of the kabbalistic God with a theological tradition of "divine speech" running through the radical Christian mystics Joachim of Fiore and Jakob Boehme, the German idealist philosopher Friedrich von Schelling, and Rosenzweig—a tradition which itself has common roots with kabbalistic thought. In this theosophical tradition, divine speech is "a movement within God that occurs in his eternal instant and in our time for everlasting," a speech-movement which calls forth the "other" of creation as God's "event of speech and love."[54] The world as we experience it, then, is an eternally ongoing event within God which overflows out of the divine plenitude. This is God's relationship to the world, understood as *creation.*

God's presence and activity is consequently defined as an overflowing speech which describes the limits and engenders the possibility for the free actions and speech of human beings, so that "his plenitude is always in the beginning of our ends and our true end."[55] God is present as the ontological context of human speech and action, "the immensity whose reality is our prefiguration,"[56] which helps to explain why Cohen could allude to "the real presence of God before, even if not within, history." The dialectic of divine speech—which sets the context for human speech and act—and human response to that speech, provides Cohen, as it did Rosenzweig, with a notion of God's relationship to humanity understood as *revelation.* In this connection Cohen writes, "When life is lived in community with God, God's name is spoken as continuous presentness, the ongoing **koh 'amar** ('Thus says the Lord') of creation answered by the response of revelation, **hinneni** ('Here I am')."[57] The divine speech creates, as it were, a receptive world, but only the active response of humanity to divine speech effects revelation.

Significantly, while Rosenzweig wrote of humanity's relationship to the world understood as *redemption,* Cohen writes in this last quotation of creation and revelation but makes no mention of redemption. Cohen, writing after the **tremendum,** is by his silence evidently suggesting that redemption neither has occurred, nor is occurring, in any recognizable way. Redemption is a responsibility which human beings have yet to assume. The common outcry over God's "silence" in the Holocaust, according to Cohen, implies the repudiation of this human responsibility and the concomitant expectation of an "interruptive miracle" on the order of Exodus. Thus the common charge that God was silent at Auschwitz is but a thin cover, often unrecognized, for a "fundamentalist theism" which results in a denial of human freedom and a return to a fatalistic ethical quietism.[58]

Rather than the "interruptive God" who is assumed in such plaints, Cohen offers a far more dialectical and subtle notion of God's speech and activity. The efficacy of divine speech depends upon the receptivity of the human will, upon the **hinneni** of human beings—and if that is so, then God's will is not unilaterally or uniformly expressed in the events of history. Against the providential God whose speech-acts are finally irresistible, Cohen writes,

> Can it not be argued no less persuasively that what is taken as God's speech is really always man's hearing, that God is not the strategist of our particularities or of our historical condition, but rather the mystery of our futurity, always our *posse,* never our acts? If [so, then] we can begin to see God less as the interferer whose insertion is welcome (when it accords with our needs) and more as the immensity whose reality is our prefiguration...[59]

In this connection Cohen mentions the rabbis' repeated rejection of a divine interruptive sign (the **bat kol** or "heavenly voice") as a valid argument in talmudic disputation, on the grounds that Torah is "not in the heavens" but has been committed to human beings, to be conserved and interpreted by them. God's speech creates the conditions for, but does not dictate the particulars of, human existence and activity. As in the Kabbalah, the created world flows out of God, but is not controlled by God. "In short," Cohen writes,

> . . . freedom within history is the continuation of creation made articulate by revelation. Halakhah, in such a view, is the ongoing elaboration of the implications of revelation . . . requiring no further miracle, for every day is the miracle of renewed freedom.[60]

Cohen's bridge over this third abyss he calls the **tremendum** is, therefore, in his own words, "one that sinks its pylons into the deep soil of human freedom and rationality."[61] As such, it entails a greater estimation of human responsibility than the prevailing theological traditions have tended to allow. Hence the value of his retrieval of kabbalistic thought, with its notions of creation as a continuous gestational outflow of God, of evil as a real and potent threat to both God and creation, and of **tikkun** as a human responsibility achievable through faithful and obedient response to Torah. There is in both the Kabbalah and in Cohen a precariousness about creation, an open-endedness that does not guarantee the happy ending of final redemption. For both, the efficacy of divine speech-action depends squarely upon human hearing-response. Thus, though he does not say so explicitly, Cohen's revisionist argument suggests that the real need is not theodicy, but anthropodicy. For it is finally and irrevocably up to human beings whether or not creation is experienced as God's ongoing speech, and so whether or not God's dialectical presentness is truly present.

B. DIVINE PRESENCE AS SPIRIT
AND A POST-HOLOCAUST HERMENEUTIC OF EXILE

1. The Point of Confluence: Divine Vulnerability

It is worth noting that, in the end, Cohen's vision of the God-humanity relationship does not differ significantly from Buber's. Relatively early in *The Tremendum,* Cohen criticizes Buber for having sidestepped hard theological thought on the Holocaust, essentially calling Buber's notion of humanity's "eclipse of God" insufficient and shallow.[62] While it is indisputable that Cohen's is far more an intentionally post-Holocaust theological work—and, for that matter, much more deeply theological in a classical sense than anything Buber, the religious anthropologist, ever wrote—his post-Holocaust revisioning of the tradition is finally not un-like Buber's. This is particularly so if the kabbalistic roots of Buber's neo-Hasidism, which may nourish a richer and more dynamic under-standing of the idea of divine eclipse, are kept in mind. It is ironic that, while Cohen summarizes—perhaps trivializes?—Buber's idea of eclipse as, "Six million died and God's speech was not heard," he later concludes his own ruminations with the suggestions that "the nature and efficacy of divine speech . . . needs to be examined," and that "God's speech is really always man's hearing."[63] And while Cohen could write that "it has to be more than the eclipse of God," in the end he utilizes that same metaphor when he writes that "there is, in the dialectic of man and God amid history, the indispensable recognition that man can obscure, eclipse, burn out the divine filament . . ."[64]

The point is not so much to counteract Cohen's criticisms of Buber, as to show his affiliation with Buber in constructing a post-Holocaust understanding of God's relationship to creation, and particularly to hu-manity. Both draw from kabbalistic literature to postulate a dynamic interdependence between God and humanity, in which the fulfillment of God's intentions for creation depend upon human cooperation. This leads to the rather tragic vision of a God who suffers (in both senses) the disobedience of human beings, a God who can be "eclipsed" or "ob-scured" by human unresponsiveness, a God who, in Cohen's words, is in some sense "constituted by his creatures [and] affected by the trials and alarums of creation."[65]

It is no coincidence that Fackenheim's theological formulations gen-erally avoid the tendency toward a tragic, suffering deity. For of the three, Fackenheim is apparently the one least interested in, or the least depen-dent upon, kabbalistic modes of thought. He tends, on the surface, to prefer a more traditional approach to the question of God's relationship to creation and history, calling God the "sole Power" and asserting the Jewish tradition's notion of God as saving presence. Yet, as I have argued already, Fackenheim allows those traditional ideas to undergo so much qualification through his emphasis upon God as a commanding voice that, finally, he is not far from the tragic vision which Buber and Cohen share. Indeed, in *To Mend the World* he has begun quite intentionally to incorporate several important kabbalistic themes into his reflections. In the end, all three envision God as one who speaks to humanity—whether that speech takes the form of address or command or even of silence is inconsequential at this point—and who awaits human response. And while Buber is most explicit about this, any idea of God which includes a measure of divine reciprocity with humanity also includes a notion of divine vulnerability and, at least implicitly, the possibility of divine suffering.

2. *Divine Vulnerability in Process Theodicy*

The relevance which this confluence in Buber, Fackenheim and Cohen has for the process pneumatology offered in Chapter 2 of this study should be evident. For the essence of the argument there was that God's presence as Spirit in creation, and among human beings particularly, is not some static, ethereal "substance" underlying the phenomenal world, but is better interpreted as the dynamic address of God's presentation of the "initial aim" to every occasion of becoming. And because each occasion exercises a measure of freedom in regard to that aim, according to its own capacities, God's vision for the world is likely never to be wholly fulfilled. God's will may, in fact, be horribly frustrated, for God's mode of presence and activity as Spirit in creation is not coercive but persuasive, in the presentation of new aims to God's creatures. And when those creatures reject or distort God's aims, God as well as they (or others) suffers the consequences.[66] The apostle Paul's dual imagery of a suffering and groaning creation longing for redemption, and of the Spirit's own intercession for the saints—and for all of creation, I would argue—"with groanings too deep for words" (Rom 8:19–26), certainly fits in this context. The difference is that, while Paul apparently expected the fulfillment of creation's longing in an imminent, apocalyptic end of history, redemption according to this model can be envisioned only as an ongoing, cooperative effort.

The biblical theme of covenant is particularly instructive at this point. God gives the Torah as an act of grace, with the underlying assumption that God truly expects the chosen people to hear and obey. It is within their power to do so. They are, then, to some degree responsible for their actions and thus for the course their history takes. Those actions, accordingly, can either further or frustrate God's intentions for creation; stated in the graphic language of midrash, the Shekhinah is ousted by sin and drawn near by righteous living. In such an understanding of covenant, redemption is historical and processive, and depends upon the faithful responses of human beings.

If this strand of Jewish tradition recognizes and affirms human responsibility and a capacity for well-doing, there is another, far more pessimistic strand which has also exercised influence in the history of Jewish

thought. Especially in the apocalyptic literature of the centuries surrounding the beginning of the common era, the accent falls upon the futility of
human action and a dependence upon God's inbreaking of wayward history to establish a reign of justice. Here, redemption is characterized as
static perfection achieved solely by God's power and irreversibly final. It is
important to note that Christianity was born and nurtured in the soil of
Jewish apocalyptic, so it should be no surprise that the Torah of the Sinaitic covenant underwent radical reinterpretation in Christian tradition.
No longer was Torah a lure to justice on earth, and so "do-able" by
human beings, but became rather a divine instrument for frustrating people into recognizing their helpless inability to please God, so that they
would rely for salvation solely upon the grace of God and not upon works.
Hence, positive human action tended to become devalued, for the only
work that truly counted for anything was God's gracious work in Christ,
whose soon-expected return would even further negate the significance of
human action in history.

In contrast, process theodicy can be legitimately interpreted as a
metaphysical foundation for a renewed appropriation of the Sinaitic view
of the God-humanity relationship, for in the fundamental recognition of
human freedom and effectiveness in history, the Torah and process
thought coincide. They both also recognize, though in differing ways, the
logical conclusion: if human beings really do exercise power in history,
then it cannot be true, let alone logical, to assert divine omnipotence. God
cannot exercise *all* power if human beings have *some* power.

What, then, is the nature of divine power and action? If human
power is expressed in free responses of compliance with or of rebellion
against God's aims, how is God's power expressed? How does God act in
the world? Most process theologians, following Whitehead's basic intentions, speak of God's action as a persuasive influencing of events, consonant with God's role as "the poet of the world, with tender patience leading it by his vision of truth, beauty, and goodness."[67] This divine
leadership of the world occurs in two modes, in accordance with Whitehead's notion of the di-polar nature of deity. First, in God's primordial
nature, God acts as Creator "*with* all creation" (Whitehead); God provides both a context of order *and* the possibilities of novelty through the
offering of initial aims to new occasions.[68] Second, in God's consequent
nature, many process theologians see the potential to speak of God as
Redeemer. This aspect of deity is called "consequent" because it is shaped
by every event which occurs in the world, for God in God's consequent
nature is the supremely relative being. God's experience of these events, in

turn, is a crucial factor in their "place" or role in the so-called "creative advancement" of the world—though, to be sure, the Holocaust radically challenges such an apparently optimistic notion.

We are, then, brought to an impasse: there are few convincing indications that human beings can bring about redemption, but history seems to belie the idea that God will unilaterally usher in a messianic age. Perhaps, in the spirit of de Leon and Luria—and, in their own ways, Buber, Fackenheim, and Cohen—the time is ripe for a post-Holocaust hermeneutic of exile.

3. *Process Pneumatology Through a Hermeneutic of Exile*

An underlying assumption of Part II has been that the "hermeneutic of exile" derived from kabbalistic modes of thought may provide an ideational context for addressing more adequately the theological questions which arise in the consideration of the Holocaust. No interpretive pattern can possibly put such questions to rest; even to assume that one could would be blasphemous. Nonetheless, I want to suggest five levels at which the hermeneutic can be said to be at work in this intentionally post-Holocaust pneumatology:

(a) The most fundamental recognition of this hermeneutic has been clearly explicated by Cohen: after the Holocaust the traditional theodicies, borne out of "orthodox" notions of the God-world relationship, are distant, ineffectual and even alienating. There is a sense, then, in which the theologian who labors on the edge of this abyss called **Shoah** experiences his or her own exile from "the ancient God" of providence, omnipotence, omniscience and every other metaphysical compliment. According to Luria, the assertion that all of life is exile, that nothing is "where it should be," includes even God—and if God, then certainly those theologians who talk about God from an intentionally post-Holocaust perspective. There is no sure and certain "place to begin"; one begins *in exile.* One cannot begin in the security of traditional notions of God and then try to incorporate the Holocaust into the picture; one must begin with lived experience—which of course includes the experience of dehumanization and mass killings in the death camps—and then ask what sort of God might be accountable for, or at work in, such a world. *On the first level, then, the hermeneutic of exile points to the problem of the disjunction between received theological tradition and lived human experience.* To live with just such a sense of exile from the received tradition, wandering through the contemporary human experience of death camps and atomic

bombs and yet straining for a sense of divine presence, is certainly consonant with the impulses of the kabbalists, whose historical extremities necessitated such an imaginative reinterpretation of the history and authoritative texts of Judaism.

But it is important to remember, too, that the kabbalists offered their
imaginative interpretation of *precisely* those texts which provided the
foundation of Jewish religious tradition. This underscores a primary affirmation of Chapter 3: that our theological traditions may potentially provide infinitely rich resources for interpreting God, self and creation when
they are not hardened into inflexible systems safeguarding orthodoxy.
They should, instead, be seen as pliable streams of interpretation which,
when appropriated imaginatively, may indeed become "living words"
through which the Spirit of God may yet address us even in this era of
death and doubt.

In other words, just as "exile" denotes a site *between* presence and
absence, even so the theologian of exile who follows the kabbalistic example will labor "on the boundary" (Tillich) between his religious tradition
and our post-Holocaust, post-Hiroshima world. While the theologian
may not begin squarely and securely from the safe site of authoritative
orthodoxy, neither can he or she think theologically from some void of
absolute absence. No one begins completely "from scratch," but always
and already in relationship to particular religious, cultural and literary
traditions which have nurtured and shaped one's thinking. Those traditions may need often to be challenged, revised or even spurned, but it is
impossible for them to be ignored. It is my argument that, in the case of
the Christian tradition, there is a deep need for imaginative reinterpretation of the tradition in response to the harsh and shocking realities of
human existence in the twentieth century, of which the Holocaust is
paradigmatic.

(b) For de Leon, such reinterpretation of his tradition included theosophical speculation on the effects which the world's evils might be having
upon God. Those effects have been discussed already in Chapter 3; what is
important at this point is to stress that the organic interrelationship envisioned in the Zohar between God and creation meant that God suffers
deeply creation's ills, and conversely that the sufferings of God are experienced in creation. God's own sense of wholeness and identity, in fact, is
put to risk, for the Zoharic myth of the Shekhinah's exile denotes a fundamental sense of alienation and lostness in the divine self as a result of
human sin. This myth narrates the *second level of the hermeneutic of exile,*

which *suggests the possibility of God's "exile" or "eclipse" by human beings.*

Despite the tendency of many modern theologians to move away from the revered notion of the impassible God and toward an emphasis upon God's suffering, no one has ventured to ask the Zoharic question: How does all the suffering and evil of the world—the lion's share of which is directly caused by, or could be relieved by, human beings—truly affect God? Process theologians, who love to quote Whitehead's aphorism about God as "the fellow-sufferer who understands," have yet to delve imaginatively into the depths of God's suffering and ask how deeply stab creation's pains. Even Grace Jantzen, who in her 1984 book *God's World, God's Body* offered a vision of the God-creation relation reminiscent of the Zohar's, retreats at this point. Though she insists that "only a God who can suffer could command respect after Auschwitz," she follows with the assurance that "we would hardly want to say that God is incapacitated by earthquakes or that his character is changed by volcanic eruptions" primarily because, "to put it crudely, God can cope with more than we can."[69] Though that is undoubtedly true, the question which the Zohar so graphically raises is: just how much can God take before reaching the "breaking point"? And if one speaks not of volcanoes but of the smoke-stacks of Auschwitz?

(c) The primary myth through which such questions were addressed in the Zohar—the exile of God's active presence in the world as Shekhi-nah from God's own self—suggests that a post-Holocaust pneumatology must recognize the vulnerability, and even woundability, as Fackenheim suggested, of the Spirit. This myth warns that human beings have the God-given capacity to "edge God out of the world" (Bonhoeffer) and so to create a godless hell on earth through their own decisions and indecisions. Though both the authoritative scriptures and the rabbinic writings witness to the abiding faithfulness of God's presence as Spirit, God's faithfulness is not, and cannot be, a substitute for human faithfulness to the task of redemption. *The hermeneutic of exile, then, on the third level, points to the problem of an adequate post-Holocaust anthropodicy, of humanity's exile from humaneness,* or of "how," in Clark Williamson's words, "in the name of God or of humanity or of all that is holy, human beings could tolerate their own involvement and complicity on such a sweeping scale in such monstrous evil."[70]

It is appropriate to mention Williamson at this third hermeneutical level because he has been one of those instrumental Christian theologians

—and among process theologians, a relatively lonely voice—who has addressed the ugly question of Christianity's historical role in making Auschwitz a human possibility.[71] Human beings could, and did, participate in the atrocities of the Holocaust partially because they were born and nurtured in Western religious, cultural and literary traditions of thought and interpretation which taught their participants to understand themselves as light and goodness and to see the "other" as darkness and evil—and no one personified the "other" like the Jew. Modern hermeneutical theory forces upon us a recognition of the formative power of the traditions which sustain our social constructs of thought and meaning—but which also have distorted and denied the value and legitimacy of people and ideas outside of those constructs. Traditional Christianity's supersessionist ideology, of course, is a most pertinent example. Williamson, accordingly, is among those who experience self-exile not simply from the all-sufficient God of ancient tradition but also from the Christian tradition of anti-Judaism, and who labor to find a new, Sinai-affirming site for constructing Christian theology. At this third hermeneutical level of anthropodicy, Williamson's work in process theology is a reminder that the challenge of renewing Christian faithfulness to God and creation cannot be met without Christians rendering a new, post-Holocaust interpretation of their faith which affirms and celebrates God's unique relationship to the Jewish people.

(d) But as Chapter 3 suggested, the hermeneutic of exile in Luria runs deeper than anthropodicy; it descends even into God's own self. The "fault" that runs through creation is hinted actually to have its origin in deity. While God is of vast complexity already in the Zohar, that sense of deep inner struggle and self-wrestling is even more pronounced in Luria's cosmic moments of **tsimtsum** and **shevirah.** In addition, the further development of the doctrine of the **sefirot** as dynamic inner forces or attributes in God, sometimes operating in tension or even in conflict one with another, only accentuates this portrait of divine ambiguity. Luria's radical hermeneutic, then, raises the possibility that God's own inner struggles, not to mention God's struggles with a wayward creation, may at times "explode" out of control, so that **shevirah** becomes an ever threatening possibility. Hence, *the fourth level of the hermeneutic of exile points to the real possibility of exile in God's own self, of divine self-alienation and struggle, indeed of divine ambiguity.*

Certainly this possibility is one which most process theologians, as well as more traditional thinkers, would prefer not to entertain. While process theologians readily dismiss the notion that omnipotence is necessary to a God worthy of worship, they do not so easily dismiss pure benevolence! The metaphysical move of Whitehead and some of his followers to separate God neatly from the ultimate metaphysical principle, which for them is "creativity," is motivated precisely by the desire to protect God from any association with, or responsibility for, evil in the world. But perhaps this is why God as conceived in process thought often seems so aseptic, bland and unmysterious: this moral God of genteel, persuasive power apparently has no "dark side" with which to struggle, no uncontrollable passions or powers with which ever to deal.[72] Certainly a contemporary appropriation of the myth of **shevirah** could help to correct process theology's tendency toward such a one-sided portrait of deity.

The biblical writings, too, tend to confirm suspicions about an ambiguity, even darkness, in God. For example, in Genesis 6 God is not only disappointed with wayward humanity—which disappointment suggests that God's knowledge is contingent upon human freedom—but God also responds to the depths of divine dissatisfaction[73] with a watery holocaust of the vast majority of living creatures. Later in Genesis, Abraham tries to talk God out of wholesale destruction of Sodom and Gomorrah. In the Exodus account, God not only invades Egypt as a destroyer of the firstborn and then drowns the Egyptian army in the sea, but also commands extensive slaughters of peoples in the Promised Land. But the classic example, to be sure, is that of Job, whose protests against his own innocent suffering, and challenges to a God who would allow such gross injustices, are never directly answered. Speaking out of the uncontrollable power of a whirlwind—recall **ruach,** and recall that some of Job's children had been killed by a "great wind" which "came from across the wilderness" (1:18, 19)—God simply proclaims God's own self as Lord of tooth and claw, as Creator of a savage nature which feeds upon itself to survive, as a Stranger whose ways are darkly and mysteriously ambiguous to human beings.

Job's God is not unlike the one who speaks in Isaiah 45:6–7, "I am the Lord, and there is no other, the One forming light and creating darkness, causing well-being and creating calamity; I am the Lord who does all these." "The logic of monotheistic faith," writes Catholic process thinker Bernard Lee in response to this Isaian passage, "is that this one Lord must take responsibility for all that is, no matter what, for God is the One Lord of all."[74] If God is in any fashion, or to any extent, responsible for the sort of world in which the Holocaust happened, then God *truly and finally is responsible.* Perhaps Christian theologians tend too quickly to let God off the hook when, actually, as Lee has suggested, Jesus on the cross is for Christians an apt symbol of God *on* the hook.

Does the suggestion of divine responsibility bring us full circle, back to the claim that God "caused" or "allowed" the Holocaust? No, for that is too simplistic a notion in a hermeneutic of exile, for which the nature of God's interaction with creation is, in the end, past finding out. But even process theologians must admit that God allowed the Holocaust in the sense that God "lets there be" a world which is an "other" with real freedom. This means that risk and contingency are part of the very fabric of things, and that the future is always radically open. God allowed the Holocaust to occur in that God allows, and probably encourages, freedom and unpredictability in this creation, and particularly, though not exclusively, in human beings. For God to create beings with the capacity to reject God's aims, however, means that God accepts the risk of "exile." It also means God is willing to accept the risk of the Holocaust, or even the destruction of the entire planet through technological rape or nuclear war.

(e) But again one might ask: does God's creation of the "other" and God's valuation of freedom mean that God cannot, in situations of extremity, intervene? As Cohen indicated, this question can only arise out of a particular understanding of divine activity in the world. It is, to be sure, an understanding derived from the scriptures; perhaps Exodus provides the best model. But Exodus should not be read as a straight historical account, as if God were one actor among many, sending plagues, hardening Pharaoh's heart, splitting the sea, and so on. Rather, Exodus should be read as Israel's theological interpretation of its ancient escape from Egypt. No doubt the events composing the Exodus could have been interpreted otherwise, for every historical event *becomes* an "event" for human beings through interpretation, and every interpretation is offered in the midst of, and as an attempt to lessen, the ambiguities of human existence. As was noted in Chapter 2, the Exodus text itself allows some of that ambiguity to remain in the narrative when it reports that God's splitting of the sea was, more immediately, the result of a strong east wind which blew all night (14:21). All of this bespeaks the *fifth level of the hermeneutic of exile, the exile from immediacy,* which *denies the possibility of an unambiguous apprehension of pure presence, of a divine site which circumvents the necessity of human interpretation.* There is little reason to suppose that God's activity was immediately evident to the Israelites, or that God's presence was readily visible; God's presence and activity was, and is, an interpreted presence and mediated activity. Indeed, much of

God's activity occurred through Moses' obedient actions, but the text also offers interpretations of a strong east wind and even Pharaoh's stubbornness as being somehow God's own mysterious activities. Thus, though the Exodus drama is told in such a way as to suggest that God's activity was visible and evident, the underlying adumbration of the text is a mysteriousness, an inscrutability, about God's presence and activity.

In any case, the ensuing account of the giving of the Torah would suggest that the deepest aim of divine liberation is to enable responsible human action. If that is a legitimate reading, then a premium is placed, not so much upon the activity of God, but upon that of human beings. And the rabbis, with their dictum "it is not in the heavens," rightly recognized that even the Torah is in human hands, to be interpreted and fulfilled in accordance with historical exigencies. Perhaps Paul van Buren has said it best in his description of "the covenant of freedom": "God is free to do a new thing out of his love for his people, and they are free to interpret God's will in new ways."[75] But it is impossible to delineate neatly between God's doings and human interpretations, and if Hartman's reading of rabbinic covenantal relationship is valid, then the two are inseparably interrelated. Human interpretation actually contributes significantly to the nature of divine activity in the world.

By way of summary, then, and in anticipation of Part III, the preceding five levels of the hermeneutic of exile give rise to these corresponding five directions for an intentionally post-Holocaust pneumatology:

(a) The disjunction between theological tradition and lived human experience points to the need for imaginative reinterpretation of our texts and traditions in order, perhaps, to hear anew the address of the Spirit of God. The kabbalists de Leon and Luria offered such interpretations for their own time, and have inspired much of the powerful imagery for the post-Holocaust theologies of Buber, Fackenheim and Cohen. The foundation for my own reinterpretation has been outlined in Part I of this study, has then been reshaped and chastened through encounter with these imaginative Jewish thinkers in Part II, and finally will be explored further for its implications for Christian eschatology in Part III.

(b) The myth of the Shekhinah's exile by human beings points to the need for further reflection upon God's own vulnerability and even pain. One might respond that it seems superfluous to speculate upon God's sufferings when it is quite evident that there is more than enough human suffering to be addressed and alleviated. Yet it is undeniable that, for Jews and Christians who long to live faithfully out of their traditions, a deeper intuition of God's own pain—for the former best exemplified in the myth of **Shekhinta b'galuta,** for the latter in the cross of Jesus, and for both as they then respond to the calling of the **imitatio dei**—may provide a potent impetus toward compassion for, and solidarity with, all those who suffer unjustly. Here Buber's interpretation of the Shekhinah myth is important, for it inspires a vision of God as remaining faithful to creation, suffering in and with God's creatures, struggling against evil, hoping patiently to lead creation to its completion in redemption, but unwilling—and perhaps unable—to effect **tikkun** without the creatures' aid.

(c) The problem of an adequate post-Holocaust anthropodicy points, for Christians, to the need for a cleansing of the Christian tradition of any elements of superiority, prejudice, or hatred toward "other" peoples, cultures or faiths. This is particularly the case in regard to the Jewish people, since the thorny problem of the Church's relationship to the Synagogue lies so very close to Christianity's heart, and since the Church's complicity in the Holocaust has become so evident. To borrow from Fackenheim, if it is true that in the **kairos** which confronted the German Church in the 1930's the Holy Spirit was deeply wounded, then a healing and revitalization of the Spirit in the Christian Church today may very well depend not only upon repentance, but upon the cleansing of anti-Judaic sentiments from Christian teaching and practice. The freedom which, by all appearances, God entrusts to human beings means that the responsibility for this purging of Christian tradition lies snugly in Christian hands.

(d) The possibility of divine struggle, ambiguity and even darkness, particularly as raised by the kabbalists, serves as a reminder to Christians that God is **ruach,** the mysterious and potent Spirit whose ways are past finding out, and whose thoughts are not human thoughts. The Church has traditionally thought itself to possess an unambiguous revelation of divine character and intention through Jesus as the Christ, a belief which has tended to encourage the notion of a tame and predictable God. But closer examination tends to dissolve such triumphalism,[76] as do the Hebrew scriptures' strictures against an overly presumptuous claim to knowledge about God in God's own self. For this God, who creates both light and darkness (Is 45:7), is also reported more than once to have warned, "No one can see me and live."

(e) The impossibility of an unambiguous apprehension of God, and the corresponding necessity of human interpretation of God's activity in the world, points to the always mediated, ever elusive character of the Spirit's presence. This seems especially so in a post-Holocaust world.

Wandering in an exile on the edge between the "presence" of received tradition and the "absence" of a world which produced the **Einsatzgruppen** (Nazi "special action" [read "mass murder"] groups) and the death camps, the intentionally post-Holocaust theologian gropes uncertainly for hints and clues of God's presence as Spirit in the vagaries of history. Rabbinic tradition conceded that God, whose revelatory activity among the Jews was a daytime affair, occasionally visited and spoke to Gentiles under cover of night. But from the perspective of the kabbalists' hermeneutic of exile, newly revived and necessitated by the Holocaust, can anyone imagine that Jewish *or* Christian theology is done anywhere but in the dark? The image of groping and stumbling in the darkness is a graphic reminder of the inescapably ambiguous nature of the unavoidably necessary task of human interpretation of God's presence as Spirit.

NOTES

1. For a helpful presentation and critique of various Jewish theological responses to the Holocaust, see Steven Katz, *Post-Holocaust Dialogues* (New York University Press, 1983), pp. 94–317.

2. For a brief treatment of the significance of the anti-Judaic tradition in Christian teaching as far as the German Church struggle is concerned, see Littell, *The Crucifixion of the Jews,* esp. c. III, "The Church Struggle and the Jews." A more thorough treatment may be found in Richard Gutteridge, *Open Thy Mouth for the Dumb* (Oxford: Blackwell, 1976).

3. Henry P. van Dusen, *Spirit, Son and Father* (New York: Charles Scribner's Sons, 1958), pp. 19ff.

4. David Tracy, *The Analogical Imagination,* p. 361. The larger context of the quotation, Chapter 8 ("The Situation: The Emergence of the Uncanny"), is truly "must reading" for anyone concerned with a post-Holocaust theology of culture.

5. Martin Buber, *On Judaism* (New York: Schocken Books, 1967), pp. 224, 225.

6. Buber, *Two Types of Faith* (London: Routledge & Kegan Paul Ltd., 1951), p. 143.

7. See Buber, *The Prophetic Faith* (New York: Harper & Row, 1960), pp. 189ff.

8. The criticism began early, of course, with Gershom Scholem's well-known debate with Buber over the latter's existentialist eisegesis of Hasidic myth. See "Martin Buber's Interpretation of Hasidism" in Scholem's *The Messianic Idea in Judaism,* pp. 228–250. Steven Katz repeats Scholem's criticisms, and adds a few of his own, in the more recent "Martin Buber's Misuse of Hasidic Sources" in *Post-Holocaust Dialogues,* pp. 52–93.

9. Buber, *The Origin and Meaning of Hasidism* (New York: Horizon Press, 1960), p. 22.

10. Buber, *Hasidism and Modern Man* (New York: Horizon Press, 1958), pp. 36, 38.

11. *Ibid.,* p. 88.

12. *The Origin and Meaning of Hasidism,* pp. 104, 105.

13. *Ibid.,* p. 28.

14. *Ibid.*

15. Buber, *I and Thou,* trans. Walter Kaufmann (New York: Charles Scribner's Sons, 1970), p. 130. See also *The Origin and Meaning of Hasidism,* pp. 117, 134.

16. *Hasidism and Modern Man,* p. 242. This, of course, is a common theme in Buber's philosophy. See *I and Thou,* pp. 126–128, 143; and *Between Man and Man* (New York: The Macmillan Company, 1972), pp. 50–58.

17. *Hasidism and Modern Man,* p. 117.

18. *Ibid.,* p. 179.

19. *Ibid.,* p. 50.

20. *The Origin and Meaning of Hasidism,* p. 179.

21. *I and Thou,* p. 163.

22. *Hasidism and Modern Man,* p. 207.

23. *Ibid.,* p. 89.

24. Buber, *Eclipse of God* (New York: Harper & Row, Publishers, 1952), p. 129.

25. See *I and Thou,* pp. 106–107; and *Israel and the World* (New York: Schocken Books, 1963), pp. 19–21, which includes a moving passage about "turning" as "the revolution of the whole being . . . onto the way of God." Buber continues: "This [way of God], however, does not merely indicate a way which God enjoins man to follow; it indicates that he, God himself, walks in the person of his **Shekhinah,** his 'indwelling,' through the history of the world; he takes the way, the fate of the world upon himself. The man who turns finds himself standing in the traces of the living God" (p. 21).

26. *On Judaism,* p. 86.

27. Emil Fackenheim, *To Mend the World: Foundations of Future Jewish Thought* (New York: Schocken Books, 1982), p. 254.

28. Fackenheim, *God's Presence in History* (New York: Harper & Row, Publishers, 1972), pp. 11–14. It is noteworthy that, in this passage, Fackenheim draws heavily on a long quotation from Buber's *Moses.*

29. *God's Presence in History,* p. 15.

30. *Ibid.,* p. 19.

31. See Chapter 2 and Chapter 3 of this book.

32. *God's Presence in History,* pp. 29, 39, 40.

33. See Irving Rosenbaum, *The Holocaust and Halakhah* (New York: Ktav Publishing House, 1976), pp. 97–108.

34. Fackenheim, *God's Presence in History,* p. 14.

35. *Ibid.*, p. 88.

36. *Ibid.*, pp. 92, 93.

37. *Ibid.*, p. 77.

38. Fackenheim also notes the sense of hope with which Buber ended *Eclipse of God*, but closes his second chapter, "The Challenge of Modern Secularity," with an extended quotation from Buber, written late in his life, in which that optimism is significantly tempered. It is worth repeating here: "These last years in a great searching and questioning. . . . I have arrived no further than that I now distinguish a revelation through the hiding of the face, a speaking through the silence. The eclipse of God can be seen with one's eyes, it will be seen. He, however, who today knows nothing other to say than, 'See there, it grows lighter!' he leads into error" (*ibid.*, p. 61).

39. Fackenheim, *To Mend the World: Foundations of Future Jewish Thought* (New York: Schocken Books, 1982), pp. 254, 256.

40. *Ibid.*, p. 135.

41. *Ibid.*, pp. 217, 218.

42. Rabbi Isaac Nissenbaum, as quoted by Lucy S. Dawidowicz, *The War Against the Jews 1933-1945* (New York: Bantam Books, 1976), pp. 291, 292.

43. Fackenheim, *To Mend the World*, pp. 291, 292.

44. See Buber's "The Two Foci of the Jewish Soul" and "The Man of Today and the Jewish Bible," both of which essays are in *Israel and the World.*

45. Arthur Cohen, *The Tremendum: A Theological Interpretation of the Holocaust* (New York: The Crossroad Publishing Company, 1981), p. 5.

46. *Ibid.*, p. 80. Cohen also judges inadequate Buber's oblique response to the Holocaust in *Eclipse of God*. Cohen writes, "Buber . . . believed until the end of his life that God continued to speak but that no man heard. Moreover, he continued to believe that God's speech was his action and that not hearing that speech was, in effect, to destroy the efficacy of God. . . . Six million died and God's speech was not heard. Not enough. Moving rhetoric, but unfortunately not theology, not thinking. It has to be tougher than that. It has to be more than the eclipse of God. . . . Not enough. And we know that now" (p. 20).

I will anticipate my later argument enough to suggest that, for all of Cohen's eloquent criticisms, there is not a significantly substantial difference between Buber's idea of the eclipse of God and what Cohen finally offers in Chapter 4 of *The Tremendum.*

47. *Ibid.*, p. 54. See, of course, Chapter 3 of this study.

48. *Ibid.*, p. 21.

49. *Ibid.*, p. 50.

50. *Ibid.*, pp. 5, 24, 83.

51. *Ibid.*, p. 34.

52. *Ibid.*, pp. 78, 86.

53. *Ibid.*, p. 85.

54. *Ibid.*, pp. 89, 90.

55. *Ibid.*, p. 93.

56. *Ibid.*, p. 97.

57. *Ibid.*, p. 95.

58. *Ibid.*, pp. 95, 96.

59. *Ibid.*, p. 97.

60. *Ibid.*, pp. 98, 99.

61. *Ibid.*, p. 94.

62. See note 46 of this chapter.

63. *The Tremendum*, pp. 20, 96, 97.

64. *Ibid.*, pp. 20, 98.

65. *Ibid.*, p. 83.

66. Fackenheim, in a footnote passage in *To Mend the World*, rejects process theology as a viable option for Jewish reflection, writing, "A currently fashionable Jewish theological resort is to the Whiteheadian God who can only inspire and not save. It is doubtful whether to this God there can be any kind of Jewish speech. . . . More doubtful still is, if Jewish speech to this God there is and can be, whether this God can survive the Holocaust, for that catastrophe casts doubt into the divine power to inspire as well as that of saving" (p. 327).

This is truly a trivialization of the vision of God in process theologians. God's action is not simply, if at all, "inspiration," but the presentation of initial aims to concrescent occasions. In actuality, this understanding of divine action has much more in common with Fackenheim's "commanding Voice" than it does with some generalized notion of inspiration. It is difficult, in fact, to discern how Fackenheim's "commanding Presence" differs significantly from the process idea of a God who offers aims to the creatures in every moment of becoming, but who is "helpless' as far as guaranteeing a faithful response by the creature which would further the process of redemption. In other words, one might counter that the Holocaust casts doubt upon God's capability as the commanding Presence of which Fackenheim speaks. See Bernard Lee, "The Helplessness of God," *Encounter* Vol. 38, No. 4, pp. 325–336; reprinted as "Holocaust" in *When God and Man Failed*, ed. Harry James Cargas (New York: Macmillan, 1981).

67. Alfred North Whitehead, *Process and Reality*, corrected edition, eds. David Griffin and Donald Sherburne (New York: The Free Press, 1978), p. 346.

68. This essentially was the vision of the God-world relationship offered in Chapter 2, but read through the concerns of pneumatology. Stated in traditional terms, it was an attempt through process categories to emphasize the work of the Spirit in creation.

69. Grace Jantzen, *God's World, God's Body* (Philadelphia: The Westminster Press, 1984), p. 84.

70. Clark Williamson, "Things Do Go Wrong (And Right)," *Journal of Religion*, Vol. 63, No. 1 (Jan. 1983), p. 54.

71. See Williamson's *Has God Rejected His People?* (Nashville: Abingdon, 1982); "Anti-Judaism in Process Christologies?" *Process Studies* Vol. 10, Nos. 3–4 (Fall-Winter 1980); and "Process Hermeneutics and Christianity's Post-Holocaust Reinterpretation of Itself," *Process Studies* Vol. 12, No. 2 (Summer 1982).

72. A noteworthy exception is Jim Garrison's process approach to evil, with a heavily Jungian slant, in *The Darkness of God: Theology After Auschwitz* (Grand Rapids: Wm. B. Eerdmans Publishing Company, 1983).

Also, one finds a much deeper intuition and appreciation for the ambiguities of existence, and of God, in the "empirical" process-relational theologians who find inspiration especially in the writings of Bernard Meland and Bernard Loomer; a list of such theologians would include Larry Axel, William Dean, Nancy Frankenberry and Bernard Lee. See Dean, *American Religious Empiricism* and, as co-editor with Axel, *The Size of God*. See also Lee, "The Two Process Theologies," *Theological Studies* 45 (1984), pp. 308–319.

Frankenberry, in reflection upon the strengths of Lee's work, has offered three recommendations "for the development and correction of process theologies" which are operative, hopefully, in the present work: "(1) a profounder sense of ambiguity in theological language about 'the whole,' (2) a more dialectical incorporation of the sense of mystery as a qualification, finally, of the status assumed or claimed for the strictly metaphysical deployments of process thought, and (3) the retrieval of the Jewish roots of Christianity and greater attention to post-biblical, Jewish traditions on the part of Christian process theologians" (*The Size of God*, p. 83).

73. A dissatisfaction, perhaps, with having made such a flawed creation as human beings turned out to be—and leading to a tragic over-reaction?

74. Bernard Lee, "Loomer on Deity: A Long Night's Journey into Day," in *The Size of God*, p. 68.

75. Paul van Buren, *A Christian Theology of the People Israel* (New York: The Seabury Press, 1983), pp. 300, 301.

76. See Chapter 5 of this book, pp. 151ff, and also pp. 163 and 187.

III. THE SPIRIT OF GOD AND THE PROBLEM OF ESCHATOLOGY

The extrusion of the Jewish element
from Christianity means an extrusion
of the divine demand and concrete messianism. . . .
The true spirit of Israel is the divine demand
implanted in our hearts.

Martin Buber, *"The Spirit of Israel and
the World of Today"*

5. Toward a Shekhinah Christology

The fifth level of the hermeneutic of exile, proposed near the conclusion of Chapter 4, asserted the inevitability of human interpretation as a mediating act in discerning the presence and activity of God as Spirit in the world. This inevitability, which in principle denies the possibility of an unmediated, uninterpreted experience of Spirit, points to the necessity of a hermeneutical paradigm by which the theologian attempts to discern and interpret God's presence. To be sure, no paradigm can remove all ambiguity from either God, world, or the interpreting self; "exile" remains our site. Nonetheless, every interpreter labors from and within a particular starting point or paradigm for understanding. For Christian theologians, the predominant paradigm has been, and is, Jesus as the Christ.

But even the formulation "Jesus as the Christ" obviously bears within itself a particular interpretation of this Galilean Jew. This indicates that, while in the history of Christian thinking the primary hermeneutical principle for understanding God's character and activity has been Jesus, the figure of Jesus itself demands interpretation. The day is past when Christian theologians could confidently and triumphally claim that God definitively and unambiguously revealed God's own self in Jesus as the Christ. For Christology is neither an exact science nor a univocal art; it is an ongoing process of interpretation. David Tracy's alliterative but accurate characterization of the situation of contemporary Christology as one of "complexity, conflicts and confusions" serves as a reminder that the ambiguities inherent in the task of interpreting God are not put to rest by an appeal to Christology.[1]

Furthermore, it is today a Christological truism that the apostolic witnesses to Jesus, found in the writings of the Christian Testament, together represent a distinct sort of interpretation of him. The gospels are not purely or even primarily biographies, neither giving us insights into

Jesus' personality or character, nor offering little tidbits from his daily life with the disciples, nor showing even the slightest interest in such mundane matters as his physical appearance. They are, rather, preaching and teaching materials, kerygmatic witnesses intended to persuade or assure their readers and hearers of Jesus' saving significance. But even the methods and symbols by which his significance is grasped and communicated vary widely among the gospels, the end result of which is an appreciable pluralism of modes and manners of witness to Jesus within the Christian Testament itself.

Granted this pluralism in the apostolic witness to Jesus, it has been recognized by many that probably the earliest, and most typically Jewish, formulations of Christology were the Spirit Christologies evident in the synoptic narratives.[2] Particularly in Matthew and Luke, it is clear that the Spirit is the initiating and sustaining power in the life and ministry of Jesus. This pneumatological interpretation of Jesus' significance obviously draws heavily upon the Hebrew scriptures' portrayal of the Spirit's enabling work in the lives of Israel's prophets, judges, kings and artisans. Perhaps it is best summarized in an excerpt from what is presented in the book of Acts as the first Christian sermon ever preached to Gentiles: "You yourselves know . . . [of] Jesus of Nazareth, how God anointed Him with the Holy Spirit and with power, and how He went about doing good, and healing all who were oppressed by the devil; for God was with him" (10:38).

It is the controlling assumption of this chapter that the early Church's Spirit Christology deserves renewed attention and interpretation in our time. This is especially the case for those who are concerned about pursuing the Christian theological task within the properly primary context of Israel's scriptures and covenantal history. And particularly in this study, where the Jewish notions of **ruach, pneuma,** and **shekhinah** have functioned as paradigms for understanding God as Spirit, the question of a Spirit Christology becomes all the more pressing.

But the argument may seem now to be veering in a circle: I began the chapter by noting that Jesus as the Christ has been Christianity's predominant symbol for interpreting God the Spirit, and then, recognizing the ambiguity and plurality inherent even within the apostolic witnesses to Jesus, have suggested that the most fruitful approach to Christology today will be via pneumatology—the doctrine of God as Holy Spirit! Undoubtedly it *is* a circle—it is the hermeneutical circle in the midst of which all understanding occurs. But even in the circular movement of understanding, one must enter somewhere. In this study the controlling point for entry into the hermeneutical circle has been the presupposition that a serious consideration of Israel's history of interpretations of itself in covenantal relationship to God is vital to Christian theology. This is the particular reason why a Spirit Christology deserves special consideration in intentionally post-Holocaust theological formulations, for it very readily fits into, and takes seriously, the context of Israel's history with God. In the words of Philip Rosato, the Spirit Christology of the earliest witness

> was biblical to the core. The person of Jesus was set into a larger framework—that of the spiritual, federal, and political concept of the Spirit of Yahweh. . . . Jesus was rightly seen in the continuum of Spirit-filled figures of Judaism.[3]

Such an approach entails interpreting Jesus within the larger context of God the Spirit's activity among the people Israel and in their history, and then in the even more comprehensive context of the Spirit's active presence in creation.

To be sure, the pneumatological approach to Christology so prevalent in the synoptics is evident also in some of the writings of the apostolic fathers, most notably Ignatius, Second Clement, and Shepherd of Hermas, for all of whom it was the Spirit who became incarnate in Christ. But by the middle of the second century, the Logos Christology of John, being far more resonant with Hellenistic culture, had effectively usurped the more Hebraically grounded Spirit Christologies of earlier generations. In C. F. D. Moule's judgment, then, "It would appear that experience shows that a mere 'Spirit-Christology', for all its reasonableness, proves inadequate."[4] Yet the viability of a Spirit Christology remains an important issue, and should not be prematurely written off simply on the historical basis that the Johannine Logos paradigm early assumed, and has maintained, predominance. One must inquire into the reasons for that shift, the reasons why a pneumatological approach to Christology has been considered inadequate, and whether those reasons are themselves adequate. In this regard, two theologians who merit attention for having recently issued criticisms against Spirit Christologies are Rosato and Jürgen Moltmann.

Rosato, while recognizing what he calls the "promise" of Spirit Christologies, isolates their recurring weakness in "the heresy of adoptionism," asking rhetorically, "Can any attempt to go back to a pre-Chalcedonian Christology avoid the danger of adoptionism and thereby preserve the absolute uniqueness of Jesus as the God-Man?"[5] Besides the fact that there is abundant evidence in the Christian Testament to support an adoptionist Christology, it also appears that Rosato works with a rather restricted idea about a pneumatic approach to the problem. A Spirit Christology does not necessarily depend upon some semi-Pelagian notion of Jesus having been sufficiently impressive in God's sight to have merited the Spirit; rather, it most deeply affirms that the Spirit is the root, cause and empowerment of the event of Jesus as the Christ. It is authentically a Christology "from above." In fact, Rosato's fear that a modern Spirit Christology will almost automatically assume that Jesus was simply a human being, at some point in his meritorious life adopted by God through Spirit possession, is unfounded—*as long as Jesus is not cut off from the religio-historical context of the Spirit's work in Israel. For it is God's adoption of Israel, and the Shekhinah's faithful calling of the people Israel to godly sonship and daughterhood through Torah, which provide a context for Jesus as the Christ.* Perhaps Rosato would see this as a compromise of his concern for the "absolute uniqueness" of Jesus, but Christian theology's age-old determination to safeguard his "absolute uniqueness" has succeeded primarily in divorcing him from his social, religious and historical context and turning him into a Christ-cipher. A recognition of this problem is, indeed, part of the intention behind calling this chapter's theme a "Shekhinah Christology": it serves as a continual reminder of the essentially Jewish context and character of Jesus the Nazarene.

The fact is, the only route available for placing Christ back into Israel's context is, to borrow Rosato's term, pre-Chalcedonian, though without being necessarily, or wholly, *anti*-Chalcedonian.[6] The creeds have served as guides for Christological reflection for much too long simply to be dismissed. But it is worth remembering that the creeds of Chalcedon and Nicea gave no attention to the Jewish context of Jesus; it was his humanity, in tandem with deity, which was stressed. And even his humanity tended to become a general metaphysical category which blurred Jesus' particularity, not only as a man among women and men, but also as a Galilean Jew among Jews. Consequently, the classical Christologies of Chalcedon and Nicea, so crucial to the history of Christian thought, have also been, even if indirectly, so very *crucifying* of Jews by their suppression of Jesus' own Jewishness.[7] If a Spirit Christology, set firmly in Israel's context, can aid the Church in a renewed appropriation and appreciation of Jesus' particularity as a Jew grounded in the religious history of his people, then it is well worth the effort.

Conversely, what is for Rosato one of the strengths of Spirit Christologies is, to my mind, probably their most problematic aspect. Rosato rightly indicates that, in addition to, and indeed an aspect of, their amenability to Israel's context is the decidedly eschatological dimension they entail, since in a predominant strand of Jewish eschatological expectation the universal outpouring of the Holy Spirit was expected to accompany the end (Jl 2:28–32). So Jesus, interpreted as the Man of the Spirit, was proclaimed the harbinger of God's future; in the words of the Acts sermon quoted earlier, "[God] ordered us to preach to the people, and solemnly to testify that this is the One who has been appointed by God as Judge of the living and the dead" (10:42). This eschatological perspective of early Christology, soon virtually eclipsed by the static, timeless categories of the Logos paradigm, has re-emerged in our own century as a critical factor in the work of the "theologians of hope" and many political theologians. Without belittling its importance, and while appreciating the historical and political thrust it inspires, I believe that the eschatological dimension of Spirit Christologies presents some difficult problems which call for thoughtful reinterpretation. This is the other part of the intention behind naming this chapter a "Shekhinah Christology": to shift the focus of interpretation of Spirit Christology from an eschatological context, and into a creation/Israel context.

Moltmann, too, has found fault with the pneumatic interpretation of Jesus' significance. While he does admit the strength of Spirit Christologies in their emphasis upon the Spirit's enabling power in Jesus' life and ministry, he criticizes them because, "for the sake of the One God, they are unable to bring Jesus into any essential unity with the Father."[8] It is critical to inquire of Moltmann, at this point, precisely what sort of "essential unity" he finds lacking in Spirit Christologies. If he means by it something like the unity of substance or nature to which the classical creeds refer, then obviously he is correct: such a notion of "essential unity" of the Son with the Father, grounded in a Hellenic substance metaphysic, is not a specific concern of a Spirit Christology any more than it was of the synoptic witnesses. But it is difficult to see why this criticism is of real importance. There is no a priori reason to assume that an ontology of substance or essence is better suited to Christology than is, say, an ontology of dynamic relationality—which, it appears, would undergird quite effectively the project of a pneumatic Christology. It is my argument, in fact, that the latter ontology provides the preferable approach. If this is so, then the weak point which Moltmann finds in Spirit Christologies, i.e., their inability to bring Jesus into "essential unity" with the Father, should find its answer in the strong point he concedes: that they build upon the early witness that the Spirit was the enabling power and reality of God in Jesus' life and ministry. Particularly if the understanding of the Spirit presented in Chapter 2 is assumed—that the Spirit signifies none other than the intimate and active presence of Israel's God, the one Jesus called "Abba"—then it is possible in a Spirit Christology to speak of a personal, moral union of God and Jesus which does not collapse their subjectivity into an "essential unity" of nature, substance or identity. The same reply holds for Rosato's claim that Spirit Christologies deny the ontological significance of Jesus—it all depends upon what sort of ontology is presumed.[9]

But ontology is not the primary issue at this point. For while it would be naive to argue that there is no ontology undergirding the synoptic witnesses to Jesus, certainly their primitive Christologies are a far cry from the philosophical issues of substance and nature which framed subsequent creedal reflections. Rather, in the gospels the saving significance of Jesus is communicated through narrative. The stories of the gospels, as well as the letters of Paul and others which were circulated among the early Christians, share many of the characteristics of rabbinic midrash, in which God's continuing presence and activity were explicated through narrative embellishment and imaginative interpretation of the Hebrew scriptures. To renew the sense of God's living presence, one *told the story* again in the light of contemporary socio-historical exigencies. Van Buren reminds us that, like Jesus, nearly all of Jesus' earliest followers were Jews, and aptly describes their midrashic activity as

> a typically Jewish move. . . . These Jews retold the story in such a way as to include this last chapter [concerning Jesus]. . . . This too [they believed] must therefore have been implicit in the story of God's dealings with Israel.[10]

In the following section of this chapter, I intend to isolate certain key incidents in the life and ministry of Jesus, as presented in the gospel narratives of the Christian Testament, in which his significance, framed within "the story of God's dealings with Israel," is interpreted either implicitly or explicitly in terms of the Holy Spirit's activity in and through him. As noted earlier, these narratives are not biographies which present clear insights into Jesus' personal psyche and idiosyncracies, or afford a direct access to Jesus' awareness of God. Instead, they are quite clearly theological interpretations of the significance of his life and ministry. Thus my intention is not to attempt a specific description of the nature of

Jesus' personal experience of the Spirit—an impossible task for anyone. Rather it is to examine, and appropriate theologically, certain critical "pneumatic moments" in the Christian Testament's interpretation of Jesus which provide the narrative grist for a Spirit Christology.

There is no question that the primary pneumatic moment in the history of Jesus, as far as the apostolic witness is concerned, is Jesus' resurrection. The apostolic sermons as presented in Acts, as well as the apparently early creedal statement which Paul quotes in Romans 1:3–4, make that clear. It would be theologically proper, therefore, to begin with Jesus' resurrection as *the* act of the Spirit in the event of Jesus as the Christ. But in order to uphold the fundamental narrative sense of the received witness, I will appropriate theologically seven pneumatic moments in Jesus' history in their narrative sequence: (1) conception, (2) baptism, (3) the Nazareth sermon, (4) defeat of demons, (5) transfiguration, (6) crucifixion, and (7) resurrection, *attempting to read them imaginatively from within the context and concerns of the continuing history of the Jewish people and faith.* Following this retrieval of gospel narrative, I will in the second and final section of the chapter reflect upon the "point" of a Shekhinah Christology.

A. SEVEN PNEUMATIC MOMENTS IN THE APOSTOLIC WITNESS TO JESUS

1. Conception/Pre-Existence (Mt 1; Lk 1:26–55)

In their birth narratives of Jesus' conception through the creative act of the Holy Spirit in the womb of the Jewish maiden Mariam, Matthew and Luke express the conviction that the Spirit of God was the creative ground of Jesus' existence as far back as one can trace it—to the very embryonic origin of his existence.

Most contemporary scholars of the Christian Testament believe that, in the earliest Christian confessions, it was the Holy Spirit's bestowal of resurrection life upon the crucified and buried Jesus which originally prompted the Christological designation, "Son of God" (Rom 1:4; Acts 13:32–33). Later, the critical pneumatic moment was shifted to his baptism, when God's address, "Thou art My Son," was heard, and God's Spirit was bestowed. By moving the moment of the Spirit's bestowal back from resurrection to baptism, Jesus' entire ministry of healing, teaching, compassion and exorcism could be interpreted as the work of the life-giving Spirit in him. Thus the prevalent understanding of the earliest

Christians was that Jesus was primarily a man anointed of God's Spirit (Acts 10:38). But, as Tillich indicates, it soon became clear that the reverse Christological development could not stop with Jesus' baptism as a point of divine adoption; it must reach back yet further:

> [The] question arose as to how the divine Spirit could find a vessel in which to pour itself so fully, and the answer came in the form of the story of Jesus' procreation by the divine Spirit. The story was justified by the insight into the psychosomatic level at which the Spiritual Presence works and the legitimate conclusion that there must have been a teleological predisposition in Jesus to become the bearer of the Spirit without limit.[11]

Tillich proceeds to call the birth narrative a half-Docetic legend that deprives Jesus of his full humanity. To be sure, many have argued that the virginal conception tends to extract Jesus from the historical and progenitive procession of humanity, so making him less than the "true Man" upon which the creeds insist. That may be a legitimate point, but certainly Matthew and Luke did not see it that way, for their narratives reflect a deep concern to locate Jesus in a genealogical procession. Nonetheless, Matthew and Luke are most deeply concerned to show that, from the very beginning, Jesus is the unique result of the Spirit's activity—that his "teleological disposition" derives not only from his genealogical history, but from God's creative **ruach**.

The Christian Testament reflects a further continuation of this reverse development with the idea of the pre-existence of Christ (Col 1:15; Jn 1:1; 8:58; 17:5). In the prevalent notion of pre-existence, it actually makes no sense to speak of a pneumatic moment **per se** in the life of Jesus; in fact, it has been noted already in this study that the movement toward the pre-existent Christ as Logos of creation actually pre-empted the place of the Spirit as understood in Hebraic patterns of thought. Interestingly, while John's gospel does make a passing reference to the descent of the Spirit upon Jesus at his baptism (1:32), for the most part Jesus, as the Logos enfleshed, has in John taken the place of the Shekhinah of rabbinic imagery. Like the Shekhinah among her people, he dwelt (**eskenosen**) among his own, who beheld his glory (**doxa**; Heb., **kabod**). Quite possibly the words about those who received him (1:11–12) reflect a common rabbinic phrase, "he who receives the face of the Shekhinah." And in 1 John 1:1 the writer testifies to having seen and even touched "that which was from the beginning"—very possibly a veiled reference to the rabbinic notion of **gilluy Shekhinah** ("the revelation of the Shekhinah"), in which, said the rabbis, God manifested the glorious divine presence to human sight or to some other of the senses.[12] And, as noted in Chapter 1, when the Spirit is introduced more thoroughly in the final discourse of Chapters 14–16, it is functionally, if not actually, the very Spirit of the Christ that is described. On the whole, Johannine pneumatology reflects a situation where the pre-existent Logos become flesh is the predominant paradigm. The Spirit is almost an afterthought, and a Logos Christology has usurped the place which the synoptics hold for pneumatology.

This brief glance at John's gospel helps to illustrate the common argument that the accounts of the virginal conception clash with the Johannine and Pauline notion of Christ's pre-existence. The former approach, it is argued, posits an origin point of the Christ in the Spirit's creativity in Mariam's womb, so that Jesus is considered almost literally —though without sexual overtones—to be God's "son." The latter, on the other hand, was a result of Christians drawing upon (i) Hellenistic Jewish thought about the pre-existent Logos, (ii) the pre-existent Torah of rabbinic thought, (iii) the pre-existent **sophia** of biblical wisdom literature, or, most likely, (iv) any creative mix of these ideas as they circulated in contemporary religious speculation. Then, by a projection of Jesus' earthly persona onto those images of pre-existence, they arrived at a notion of the pre-existence of Christ. The general argument is that these are two different myths which, though actually in contrast or even contradiction with one another, served the early Church as dual means of affirming the salvific significance of Jesus as God's own act.

There is no question that the latter notion, the Christological development backward beyond the point of birth to a pre-existent center of consciousness, is problematic. It sunders the very psychosomatic union of which Tillich spoke, the close interrelation of the Hebraic ideas of body and soul. The idea of individual pre-existence assumes that there is some dimension of human being which can exist independently of, and even prior to, the body. Similarly, it posits some basis of continuity of memory and consciousness which can perdure from a pre-existent intelligence, and then through gestation, birth, childhood development and adult maturity. It has led to Christian theologians throughout the ages speculating upon such questions as how the second Person of the Trinity could exercise his cosmic functions and at the same time be the Babe of Bethlehem. At its crassest, the notion of Christ's pre-existence had led to the assumption that God is a council of three, one of whom consented to become flesh and dwell among humanity, a Son choosing Mariam to be his mother and "descending" into her womb. This worst-case example simply illustrates the real difficulty in attempting to ascribe true humanity to Christ when he is interpreted as the pre-existent Son incarnate.

The root problem with the popular notion of pre-existence is readily indicated by the simple question, "Precisely what was it that pre-existed in the pre-existence of Jesus?" Van Buren, reinterpreting the Johannine tradition, suggests that the pre-existent dynamic which grounded the fully human Jesus was God's eternal Word or activity.

> What is pre-existent, utterly one with God before the Creation of the world, is the divine resolve to . . . make room for a fully personal cooperation of God's creatures [in the project of completing Creation]. This eternal personal resolve of God's . . . is that which was enacted in the personal existence of the man Jesus of Nazareth.[13]

By drawing upon Johannine imagery for a notion of pre-existence or, as he prefers to call it, the "priority" of God's Torah/Wisdom/Word, van Buren reflects the conventional wisdom that the source for reinterpreting the idea of Christ's pre-existence is derived necessarily from the Johannine tradition. Though what he offers is a vast improvement upon the traditional notion of pre-existence, such a Christology still tends, despite van Buren's intentions, toward speculation and ahistoricity. Rather than the Logos prologue of John, it may be that those genealogical prologues of Matthew and Luke provide the most sensible resource for understanding pre-existence, for they force the reader to take seriously God's history with Israel. Particularly in Matthew's genealogy, it is clear that what "pre-existed" Jesus is none other than the God of Israel, and the history of God's people Israel. Matthew's narrative reflects a strong sense of Israel's history with God as the precursor and context of Jesus' birth. Here Jesus is the son of David, who received God's promise of an everlasting kingdom, and the son of Abraham, who received God's promise as one in whom all peoples (Gentiles) would be blessed (1:1). In Matthew's genealogy there is a sense of the corporate personality of the people Israel, issuing down through the generations of Matthew's messianic line God's love and promises, as well as Israel's wrestlings and struggles, joys and pains. For Matthew, the pre-existent Christ can be said to be none other than God with Israel and Israel with God—aptly symbolized in Mariam's conception by the Spirit.[14]

Raymond Brown rightly indicates that, in the birth of Jesus by the Spirit's creative action in the virgin's womb, Matthew is claiming that

God's presence "made itself felt in an eschatological way . . . [and that] Jesus is the final and once-for-all manifestation of God's presence with us."[15] Nonetheless, this proclamation of eschatological newness must be kept within the context of the continuity of God's activity in, through and for Israel. The best illustration of this continuity lies in the four women Matthew chooses to include in the genealogy: Tamar (1:3); Rahab (1:5); Ruth (1:5); and Bathsheba (1:6). Traditional theories for Matthew's inclusion of these figures stressed either their questionable moral reputations, or their Gentile connections—both of which would accentuate the gospel message of God's gracious activity toward, and through, the "outsider." While these ideas have much to commend them, Brown argues convincingly that Matthew includes these four women primarily because, in the narrative history of Israel, (i) there was something extraordinary, irregular or, in particular cases, immoral about their sexual union with their partners which, though scandalous to proper society, issued in the messianic lineage; and (ii) in each case they showed extraordinary initiative or played a significant role in God's work in Israel, "and so came to be considered the instrument of God's providence or of His Holy Spirit. . . . In post-biblical Jewish piety these extraordinary unions and initiatives were seen as the work of the Holy Spirit."[16] In sum, Matthew's genealogy begins to take on a vibrant life of its own: it is the "pre-existent" life of God interpreted as the Spirit's activity in and through the actions of the women and men of Israel.

If in Matthew it is the genealogy which affirms the Spirit's preexistent life in the people Israel, in Luke that affirmation is embodied in his portrayal of the Jewish virgin Mariam. A comparatively quiet, even obscure figure in Matthew, she becomes in the third gospel a representative daughter of Zion, joyously proclaiming the greatness of Israel's God (1:46–55). In her case, of course, the shadow of scandal is cast by the question of her son's social legitimacy. But she manifests her own sort of initiative in her willing response—"Behold the handmaid of the Lord; be it done to me according to your word"—to the divine address (1:38). God's promise to her is that the Holy Spirit would "overshadow" (**episkiazein**) her, just as the Shekhinah overshadowed the wilderness Tabernacle (Ex 40:35), Mount Zion (Is 4:5), and God's own people Israel (Ps 91:4). God's life-bestowing Spirit would brood over her womb, as the **ruach** brooding over and breathing upon chaos in creation, to initiate the seed of a new creative act of God's own doing. And as Moses' sister Miriam burst into song on the Red Sea's bank after God's mighty **ruach** brought salvation and renewed life to the people Israel (Ex 15:21), so too this Jewish maiden Mariam, daughter of Zion and mother of Jesus, sings God's praise:

> My soul exalts the Lord. . . .
> For the Mighty One has done great things for me;
> > and holy is His name.
> And His mercy is upon generation after generation
> > toward those who fear Him. . . .
> He has given help to Israel His servant,
> > in remembrance of His mercy,
> as He spoke to our fathers,
> > to Abraham and his offspring after him (Lk 1:46–55).

Too often modern theologians have passed off the virginal conception in the Matthean and Lukan narratives simply as docetic denials of Jesus' full humanity. But the very fact that those same two narratives include genealogies, stressing Jesus' solidarity with his people, tends to militate against such a simple reading. When these two facets of their narratives are held together, it becomes evident that Arnold Come is correct in his observation that the interest in Jesus' conception by the Holy Spirit "is not magical but messianic."[17] Matthew and Luke are no more interested in gynecology **per se** than is Genesis in geology. The combination of the genealogies with the conception accounts helps to indicate that, at base, the birth narratives are primarily profound affirmations that God the Spirit is the power and dynamic in the life and ministry of Jesus from his very beginning—and even before his beginning, from his "pre-existent" beginning or "roots" in God's creation of humanity in the divine image (Luke) and, more particularly, in the history of Israel as God's chosen people and the avenue of the Spirit's activity (Matthew).[18]

Such an understanding of the people of Israel as the pneumatic context for Jesus complements a process-relational view of God's activity in the world. The genealogies teach that Jesus is the fruition of a long historical tradition that has prepared the way for him through Israel's responsiveness to God's aims presented in Torah. The incarnation, in this view, is not an isolated, completed act in Jesus of Nazareth. Rather, Jesus represents the continuing "incarnation" of God's Shekhinah in and with the Jewish people, particularly through Torah. In the words of process theologian Norman Pittenger, "It is Jesus-in-the-midst-of-his-own—past, present, future—who constitutes the proper location of God's activity which Christians have come to denote by the word Incarnation."[19]

It has long been the tragedy of Christians to think of themselves exclusively as those who are "his own," that the history of Israel as the bearer and interpreter of divine presence ended with Jesus and passed over to the Church. It would appear that the apostle Paul in his most mature theological work, after having observed in his later years already the beginnings of this attitude toward the people of God and of Jesus, warned against such supersessionism (Rom 9:4–5; c. 11). Subsequent Christian thought, having disregarded Paul's warning, traditionally has had no interest in a Jewish genealogy beyond Jesus, because Jesus was interpreted as the fulfillment and end of the Jews' history and the beginning of a new, spiritualized genealogy, the Church's. In our hindsight, we now know that this Christian triumphalism provided the basis for an **adversus Judaeos** tradition which, in its turn, contributed significantly to a twentieth century pagan regime which *did* express an interest in Jewish genealogy—and implemented its interest in the Nuremberg Laws. But the continuing existence and vitality of the Jewish people and faith, particularly in spite of the Holocaust and in view of the state of Israel, presents a stark challenge to the traditional theory of Christian displacement. Is it not possible that, today, the genealogies of Jesus actually could not only remind Christians of the Shekhinah's pre-existent presence, but also point to her continuing "post-existent" presence, in the people Israel? If so, then "Jesus-in-the-midst-of-his-own" will not only refer to Jesus, by the graciousness of God toward the Gentiles, present in the Spirit to the Church. It will also mean Jesus, by the graciousness of God's corporeal election of the Jews, among his brothers and sisters "according to the flesh" (Rom 1:3; 9:5).[20]

2. *Baptism (Mk 1:1–12; Mt 3:13–18; Lk 3:21–38; Jn 1:29–34)*

All four gospels agree in making Jesus' baptism in the Jordan River the beginning point of his public ministry. All four gospels also stress a manifestation of the Holy Spirit as being an integral aspect of that experience, so that this anointing of the Spirit becomes identified as the impelling power of his life and ministry (Mk 1:12). In the simple terms of the sermon preached to the household of Cornelius, this pneumatic anointing is the sign that "God was with him" (Acts 10:38).

The basic details of the narratives are spectacular in their simplicity. Ascending out of the waters, Jesus sees the heavens open and the Spirit descend upon him "as a dove," and then hears a voice from heaven—a **bat kol**, to use the rabbinic phrase: "Thou art My Beloved Son, in Thee I am well pleased" (Mk 1:11). In the synoptic gospels, Jesus then is led or even "driven" (Mk 1:12) by the Holy Spirit into the wilderness for a time of testing.

The descending dove as a symbol of the Spirit, which has become predominant in the Church's art and liturgy, offers several possible, equally rich interpretations. One of the most obvious possibilities recalls the dove in the story of Noah (Gen 8), "the symbol of reconciliation and peace and the harbinger of another covenant."[21] In this interpretation, just as the ark which saved Noah and his family "emerges" from the waters of the flood to be greeted by the dove, so too Jesus, emerging from Jordan's waters, is greeted. It is noteworthy that Noah, after having offered a pleasing burnt sacrifice to God, is called to witness, and to partake of, a renewed covenant with creation—a covenant, in fact, which in subsequent Jewish religious thought would be considered the basis of God's covenantal relationship with the non-Jewish peoples (Gen 8:20–9:17). So perhaps the dove which descends upon Jesus prefigures the offering which he, too, would make to God—an offering which does indeed result in an ingathering of the Gentiles to Israel's God.

Another possible interpretation of the dove symbol invokes the rabbinic notion of the "wings of the Shekhinah" as it was used to explicate Genesis 1:2, where God's dynamic **ruach** broods over chaos. For rabbinic commentators, the Shekhinah was "brooding over the face of the water . . . as a dove broods over its nest" (T.B. Haggigah 12a). In the context of Jesus' baptism, this imagery suggests not only the Shekhinah's maternal overshadowing of Jesus, but also the initial inklings of a renewed creation. The shades of the Genesis account would then suggest that Jesus be interpreted as a new Adam, the re-creation of God's image in humanity by the in-breathing of the Spirit, the **ruach** of life (Gen 2:7). Certainly this fits well with Luke's genealogy, which is placed immediately after Jesus' baptism, and which traces Jesus' lineage backward to Adam, "the son of God" (Lk 3:38). By this renewed gift of the Spirit, Jesus represents all of humanity created in God's image to be God's "son," and so becomes, in the Church's doxology, "the image of the invisible God, *the firstborn of all creation*" (Col 1:15). The ensuing period of temptation, then, recapitulates the first Adam's temptations in the garden—particularly in Mark, for whom Jesus "was with the wild beasts" (1:13)—but this second Adam emerges victorious over the tempter.

Another interpretation of the baptism scene, specifically as it occurs in Mark's gospel, has been offered recently, and for the purposes of this study is the most fascinating and fruitful.[22] In this reading, Jesus' baptism is a retelling of the **Akedah**, Abraham's binding of Isaac (Gen 22). In the Genesis narrative, the emphasis is upon Abraham's faithful obedience to God's will, even when the request flies in the face of the covenant promise (17:19–21). But in later midrashic versions of the story, including the Aramaic paraphrases of scripture called the Targums, the sacrificial spirit of Isaac himself becomes an integral part of the narrative. Thus, while in Genesis Isaac appears to be a naive child, according to one Midrash he was 37 years old and fully aware of what awaited him on the mount of sacrifice. Historical evidence makes it clear that, while the Targums and Midrash were not solidified into organized written materials until well after the era of the gospels, many of the exegetical traditions and even written passages may be dated much earlier. There is good reason to believe that midrashic interpretations of Isaac's willing obedience in the **Akedah**, which are known to have existed in Jesus' time, provided the paradigm for Mark's baptismal narrative.

The Targums to Genesis 22:10 report that, as Isaac lay bound upon the sacrificial altar, he looked up and saw "the angels on high," which would suggest an "opening" of the heavenly vault above the world where God and the angels were believed to dwell. ("He saw the heavens opening"; Mk 1:10.) Then there was a glorious manifestation of the Shekhinah of the Lord (Targums to Gen 22:14; cf. Mk 1:10, "and the Spirit like a dove descending upon Him"). Finally, a heavenly voice: "Come, see two chosen individuals in the world; the one sacrificing and the other being sacrificed; the one sacrificing is not hesitating and the one being sacrificed stretches forth his neck." ("Thou art My beloved Son . . ."; Mk 1:11.) In Genesis 22:2 God, with painful clarity, demands that Abraham sacrifice "your only son, whom you love." In the same passage, the Septuagint explicitly refers to Isaac as "the beloved son."

Even the second part of Mark's heavenly message, "in Thee I am well pleased," could well draw on contemporary **Akedah** traditions. The Greek word for "pleased" in Mark's text is **eudokeo**, and carries a strong sense of choice or election. Likewise, in the Targums on the **Akedah**, the notion of election is evident in the **bat kol**'s use of the Aramaic term **yehida'in** ("men singled out [by God]") to describe both Isaac and his father. Indeed in the Targums to Leviticus 22:27, Isaac is a "lamb who has been chosen," so that in the cases of both Isaac and Jesus, God's election is an election to self-sacrifice.

The Spirit's descent in the form of a dove is also subject to interpretation through the **Akedah** paradigm. The dove, too, could offer itself for sacrifice. The Midrash Rabbah on Song of Songs 4:1, "Thine eyes are as doves," comments:

> As the dove is chaste, so Israel is chaste. As the dove puts forth her neck for slaughter, so does Israel, as it says, "For Thy sake we are killed all the day" (Psalm 44:23). As the dove atones for iniquities, so Israel atones for the other nations.

If the dove symbolizes Israel in its purity and self-offering, "putting forth its neck for slaughter," then Isaac is a worthy representative for Israel since, as the heavenly voice observes, "he stretches forth his neck." "The dove, a symbol for Israel, makes atonement and stretches forth the neck. Isaac, too, stretches forth his neck on the altar as he makes atonement for Israel."[23] This understanding of the **Akedah** has its own integrity in Jewish self-understanding, but it also sheds light on the baptism narrative if the association of the dove and Isaac, as found in later rabbinic reflection, was already occurring in the era of the gospels. It would then serve as an identification of Jesus' role as being in line with Isaac's willing self-sacrifice. A further theological point is made when Isaac's "stretching forth his neck" and his vision of the Shekhinah are interpreted mutually; it suggests that God's presence is most evident in the "hiddenness" of suffering and self-sacrifice. The glory of the Shekhinah shines in and through the lowliness and humility of Isaac's outstretched neck. The **Akedah** is thus interpreted as a moment of at-onement for God and the people Israel, as the Fragmentary Targum to Genesis 22:14, translated by Geza Vermes, indicates:

> Now I pray for mercy before you, O Lord God, that when the children of Isaac come to a time of distress, you may remember on their behalf the binding of Isaac their father, and loose and forgive them their sins and deliver them from all distress, so that the generations which follow him may say: In the mountain of the Temple of the Lord, Abraham offered Isaac his son. . . .[24]

The similarities to a theology of the cross are so obvious as almost not to need rehearsing. Jesus' baptism, understood through the **Akedah**, anticipates his death upon the cross for the sins of all people. As the outstretched Isaac is enveloped by the glory of the Shekhinah, so the Spirit is manifest in Jesus' voluntary suffering and death for the sake of others, symbolized at the outset of his ministry by his response to John's baptism unto repentance in identification with his people. Ironically, however, the very confluence of the binding of Isaac and the baptism of Jesus has been twisted and deformed by subsequent Church-Synagogue relations. To ask modern Jews to reflect upon Jesus' baptism as a further enactment of the **Akedah** is highly presumptuous, given the subsequent centuries of church history in which Christian baptism was a forced "option," affording Jews their one opportunity to live in a Christian society or, in many circumstances, *to live at all*. Baptism in the history of Western Christendom has not been predominantly a sign of following Jesus into the waters of humility and self-giving before God, but a means of privilege and even power. The Church's reply to Jesus' question, "Are you able to be baptized with the baptism with which I am baptized?" (Mk 10:39), has been all too clear.

Meanwhile, the **Akedah** has perdured through centuries of Jewish existence as a key paradigm for self-understanding.[25] Sacrifice and surrender of oneself or one's possessions was not a distant ideal, but a real possibility, and often a harsh reality, for the Jewish people in the world of Christendom. Pogroms, mob violence and vilification were interpreted as opportunities for "sacrifice" to the God of Israel, for **kiddush hashem**, the sanctifying of God's holy name. Generally, such persecution of the Jews would occur in fits and starts, so that after an intense period of suffering the situation would cool to a relative, but always uneasy, state of coexistence—not unlike receiving a son back again. Thus, the **Akedah** model could make sense of the Jews' tenuous place in Christian societies. Did not the Midrash Rabbah say that, as the dove atones for iniquities, so Israel atones for the sins of the nations?

It is evident that, in the Holocaust, "the sins of the nations" against the Jewish people were fulfilled in their deepest intentions. While it would be incorrect to say that the Jews in the ghettos and camps atoned for the Gentiles' sins, it is nonetheless evident that they suffered and died *for*—in the sense that they died *because of*—"the sins of the nations." That aspect of the **Akedah**'s dove motif has held true. And for precisely that reason, it is also true that, in the ghettos and camps, the **Akedah** finally failed the Jews as a paradigm for self-understanding, for the ideal of self-sacrifice for God's sake played directly into Nazi intentions to create a world "cleansed of Jews" (**Judenrein**)—frighteningly enough, almost a baptismal image. And this time, not even those Jews who had undergone Christian baptism, whether out of necessity or conviction, were spared.

And where was God? The Targums to Genesis would invite us to consider the possibility that, just as Isaac the willing sacrifice beheld the

Shekhinah's glory while bound upon the altar, so also was the Shekhinah mysteriously present "there on the gallows" (Wiesel), compassionately present in the Jewish people's experience of unspeakable suffering and horrible murder.

3. The Nazareth Sermon (Lk 4:14–30)

The synoptic gospels all agree in placing Jesus' decisive period of temptation in the wilderness immediately following his baptism by John. But only Luke places particular emphasis upon the Spirit's role in Jesus' time of testing; the third gospel states that Jesus was "full of the Holy Spirit" and was "led about by the Spirit in the wilderness" (4:1)—a considerable softening of Mark's account that he was "impelled" into the wilderness by the Spirit, and of Matthew's implication that the Spirit led him into the wilds *in order to* be tempted by Satan (Mt 4:1). Luke, more than either of his synoptic counterparts, presents Jesus as a **Christus victor** whose power and authority are directly attributable to the Holy Spirit's robust presence in him. Thus, following his victories over the wilderness temptations, Jesus returns to his home region of Galilee "in the power of the Spirit" (4:14) and quickly gains fame and a following in the synagogues (4:15).

Given his unique emphasis upon the Spirit's role in Jesus' ministry, it is not surprising that Luke includes a pericope, unique to his gospel, in which the pneumatic dynamic is again trumpeted: Jesus' sermon in the hometown synagogue of Nazareth. His text is Isaiah 61:1:

> The Spirit of the Lord is upon Me,
> Because He anointed Me to preach the gospel to the poor.
> He has sent Me to proclaim release to the captives,
> And recovery of sight to the blind,
> To set free those who are downtrodden,
> To proclaim the favorable year of the Lord (Lk 4:18–19a).

Somewhat surprisingly, by the end of his brief homily the hometown folk, apparently enraged by his references to God's merciful actions toward non-Jews, try to throw him off a cliff (4:29). This, for Luke, is a proleptic portrayal of the fate of Jesus' ministry, a turning point which provides a model for the Lukan understanding of the gospel's course: just as Jesus' message is rejected by the Nazareth synagogue, ostensibly for speaking of God's miracles in behalf of Zarephath of Sidon and Naaman the Syrian though there were "many in Israel" with similar needs (4:25–27), so in Acts 13 there occurs a pivotal turning from Jews to Gentiles. "It was necessary that the word of God be spoken to you first," Paul and Barnabas boldly proclaim to "the Jews" of Pisidian Antioch. "Since you repudiate it, and judge yourselves unworthy of eternal life, behold, we are turning to the Gentiles" (vv. 45–46).

Jesus begins his sermon with a quotation from Isaiah 61, identifying himself with the messianic figure anointed of God's Spirit, and ends by indicating that God's compassion and concerns extend beyond the borders of Israel. Jesus is announcing that God's new age, the eschatological era of freedom and healing, has arrived through the presence and power of the Holy Spirit who fills and directs him. Luke's narrative, however, suggests that his people could not see him as other than the boy who had grown up in their midst, as one of "theirs": "Is this not Joseph's son?" (4:22). Their familiarity with him hinders their perception of his significance, and they violently reject him and his claim to fulfill Isaiah's prophecy.

It therefore appears that this narrative fulfills three functions for Luke: (i) it once again underscores that the significance of Jesus' mission of compassion, healing and liberation lies fundamentally in an experience of the Spirit's anointing and empowerment; (ii) it attempts to explain the Jewish rejection of Jesus as the Spirit-bearing herald of God's new age as being a result of their knowing him too well as one of their own and so, ironically, not really knowing him at all; and so (iii) it offers the first glimpse at what will become a Lukan pattern of Jewish rejection of the gospel in order that the Gentiles might hear it gladly (Acts 13:48; 18:6; 28:28), and that God might take "from among the Gentiles a people for His name" (Acts 15:14). Hence the Nazareth sermon offers Zarephath and Naaman from the synagogue's scriptures as examples demonstrating that God's mercy toward the Gentiles is already established in Israel's narrative history.

It is interesting to compare this Isaian quotation in Luke's gospel to a similar one in Matthew 12:18–21, which is actually placed in a roughly correspondent setting. Jesus has just had two separate confrontations with the Pharisees on the subject of Sabbath laws, the second of which occurs in a synagogue. The controversy is concluded with the Pharisees plotting Jesus' death and Matthew's simple comment, "But Jesus, aware of this, withdrew from there" (12:15). After his withdrawal from the synagogue, it is reported that Jesus healed all those who came to him but "warned them not to make Him known" (v. 16). Then, in accordance with his prominent "fulfillment of the prophets" theme, Matthew offers a quotation from Isaiah 42:1–4, the first of the "servant songs":

> Behold, My Servant whom I have chosen;
> My Beloved in whom My soul is well-pleased;
> I will put My Spirit upon Him,
> And He shall proclaim justice to the Gentiles.
> He will not quarrel, nor cry out;
> Nor will anyone hear His voice in the streets.
> A battered reed He will not break off,
> And a smoldering wick He will not put out,
> Until He leads justice to victory.
> And in His name the Gentiles will hope.

It is evident that Matthew's primary, and perhaps sole, reason for including the quotation is to explain the silence Jesus requires of those whom he heals. The quotation speaks of a humble, gentle, suffering servant, and so functions for Matthew as a context for the "messianic secret" theme so prominent in Mark. Yet it is interesting that this quotation also underscores the impetus of the Spirit in Jesus' ministry; indeed, C. K. Barrett suggests the possibility that, just as "he will not quarrel, nor cry out" refers back to "He warned them not to make Him known" (v. 16), so "I will put My Spirit upon Him" corresponds with "many followed Him, and He healed them all" (v. 15). "If this is so," he continues,

> his endowment, as the Servant with the Spirit, is given as the explanation of his power to work miracles; and it may be inferred that the miracles point back, through Jesus' character as a "pneumatic" person, his possession of the Spirit, to his peculiar nature as Servant or Messiah of God.[26]

But it is not simply that Jesus, through the anointing of the Spirit, is interpreted as God's Servant-Messiah. Even more significant is the *purpose* of that pneumatic anointing for Isaiah: *justice and hope for the Gentiles!* Abelson notes that the Targum rendered Isaiah 42:1, "Behold my servant the Messiah," showing that the messianic character of the passage was recognized within Judaism. He observes that "the infusion of the Spirit of God into him is the first condition of his Messianic-prophetic mission," and then, more importantly, indicates the nature of that mission:

> And the evident and widespread results of the spirit-imbued servant are
> that 'he shall bring forth judgment (**'Mishpat'**) to the nations.' By this
> phrase **'Mishpat'** is meant . . . the popularisation of religion throughout
> the world. Thus, the permanent abiding of the Spirit in an individual,
> brings about its permanent continuance in all men; and this involves a
> religious and ethical regeneration.[27]

Though his phrase "popularisation of religion throughout the world"
reflects an inadequate liberal reading of **mishpat**, a closer look at Isaiah
reveals that Abelson is, nonetheless, not far wrong. In Isaiah 42:1–4, including a portion which Matthew's version omits, the word **mishpat** is
used three times to describe the servant's task: he will bring forth **mishpat**
to the nations, or Gentiles (v. 1); he will faithfully bring forth **mishpat** (v.
3); and he will persevere until he has established **mishpat** in the earth, or
abroad (v. 4). Thus it is clear that this **mishpat** or "justice" which the
servant "brings forth" or "establishes" has a clear reference to the non-
Jewish peoples. Without belittling the simple and obvious meaning of
justice as an element of the servant's mission to the Gentiles, it is evident
that, in Isaiah, **mishpat** in connection with the Gentiles has a specific
content. In the divine summons to court of the nations and their deities
(41:1–5, 21–29), to which they are called for **mishpat** (41:1), the issue
revolves around the affirmation of Israel's God as **the** God of, and for, all
peoples: " 'I, the Lord, am the first, and with the last. I am He. . . . Present
your case,' the Lord says. . . . 'Behold, all of [their gods] are nothing; their
works are worthless, their molten images are wind and emptiness' " (41:4,
21, 29). Thus, the mission of the Spirit-anointed servant is to bring forth
mishpat to the Gentiles by bringing them knowledge of the God of Israel
—and, presumably, of the justice this God requires.

All of this would suggest that Matthew, quoting from Isaiah's servant
passage, understands Jesus as the Spirit-anointed messianic figure who
brings **mishpat**, or knowledge of the God of Israel, to the non-Jewish
peoples. However, Matthew's overall intentions appear, at least on the
surface, to be the inverse: only his gospel has Jesus sharply restricting the
disciples' first preaching mission to "the lost sheep of the house of Israel"
(10:5–6), and defining himself as having been sent "to the lost sheep of the
house of Israel" (15:24).

If Matthew understood Jesus as having been sent to Israel, then is the
mention of Gentiles in the Isaian quotation simply a detail which has no
significance for him, the quotation itself having more to do with Jesus'
demand of silence upon those he healed, and, possibly, with his character

as God's Spirit-anointed servant? Perhaps not, if Claus Westermann's comment on the "servant songs" is correct:

> We must . . . say that these [servant songs] lend no support to the idea that the servant was to go as a missionary to the Gentiles. . . . Instead, they suggest the other possibility, that because of his **via dolorosa** among his own nation, the servant was to bring God's **mishpat** to the Gentiles in an indirect way, so becoming their light.[28]

This "way of sorrow" and suffering in the servant's ministry is suggested by 42:4, "He will not be disheartened or crushed, until He has established justice in the earth," as well as in other songs. And in his suffering and rejection, he becomes, as Westermann says, *indirectly* "a light of the nations" (Is 49:6; cf. Lk 2:32).

This perspective affords a view different from the traditional Christian notion that the Jews' rejection of Jesus as God's messianic-yet-suffering servant led to their forfeiture of covenant with God, with Christians having assumed their stead. Rather, it suggests that, in order for Jesus to *be* a "light to the Gentiles," to bring **mishpat** to the nations, it was necessary that he be "thrust out of the synagogue," so to speak (cf. Rom 11:15, 25). However one interprets the prophecy-fulfillment theme of the Christian Testament, and of Matthew particularly, it is an inescapable fact that Isaiah's **mishpat**, or salvific knowledge of the God of Israel, has indeed reached inestimable numbers of people from among "the nations" through the apostolic witness to Jesus of Nazareth. History has shown that, from the perspective of those Gentiles who were at one time "far off" but who have been "brought near" to the God and commonwealth of Israel (Eph 2:12, 13), Jesus is the Spirit-anointed, suffering Jewish servant through whom Israel's God has brought them near. For many who were once "without hope and without God in the world" (Eph 2:12), Jesus indeed has become the one in whose name the Gentiles find hope (Mt 11:21). In an historical and concretely realistic way, he "fulfills" the role of which Isaiah spoke.

If the suffering servant role, which has been such an important Christological category in the history of Christian thinking, could begin to be interpreted along these lines as having been directed toward the Gentiles who "wait expectantly for His teaching" (Is 42:4)—a teaching which the Jews have already received in a particular form and fashion in Torah—it would have a revolutionary effect upon the Church's attitude toward the Jews. It would mean that God's mercy toward, and acceptance of, non-

Jewish peoples through the Christ[29] does not entail God's rejection of the covenantal people Israel—a truth upon which Paul insisted explicitly in Romans 11:1—but that Jesus, one of Israel's own, is God the Spirit's anointed agent through whom God takes "from among the Gentiles a people for His name" (Acts 15:14). If the Church could effect such a revolution in its history of thought and attitude, perhaps Jesus could truly fulfill Simeon's Spirit-inspired blessing which, according to Luke, took place during the child's dedication in the Jerusalem Temple in accordance with Mosaic law: Jesus could become not only a light of revelation to the Gentiles, but also the glory of God's people Israel (Lk 2:32). But as long as the Church continues to interpret Jesus' suffering servanthood in an essentially anti-Judaic manner, he will necessarily remain an outcast, exiled from his own people.

4. Defeat of Demons (Mt 12:28; Lk 11:20)

In Matthew's gospel, the quotation from Isaiah 42:1–4 is immediately followed by an account of an exorcism which sparks more controversy with the Pharisees. The fact that, in their heated encounter, Matthew has Jesus claim that he casts out demons "by the Spirit of God" is a strong indication that the mention of the pneumatic anointing of God's servant in the Isaian quotation is, indeed, significant to the author. It would suggest that Matthew is advocating a recognition that the Holy Spirit is active not only in Jesus' exorcisms, but in his healing and possibly even teaching as well (cf. Mt 10:20)—so that the Holy Spirit is understood to be the animating power of the whole of Jesus' life and ministry.

It is noteworthy that Luke, in his parallel passage (11:20), has "finger of God" rather than Matthew's "Spirit of God," especially considering Luke's propensity to accentuate heavily the pneumatic character of Jesus' ministry. It may be that Luke's physical metaphor is meant to stir a memory of "the finger of God" which the Pharaoh's magicians reluctantly recognized in the plagues (Ex 8:19), in which case those who refused to recognize "the finger of God" active in Jesus—Luke does not refer specifically to Pharisees, writing instead of an indefinite "some" who object—come off looking worse than the minions of Pharaoh. Finally, though, the phrases are not essentially different; both are ways of referring to the active presence of God's own self in Jesus' ministry or, in Barrett's words, "the personal activity of God . . . whether described by his 'finger' or his 'spirit' matter[ing] little, since both these terms denote his immediate, immanent power."[30]

The more critical point, at which Matthew and Luke agree, is that the Spirit's empowering presence in Jesus' ministry is an eschatological sign: "if I cast out demons by the Spirit of God, then the kingdom of God has come upon you" (Mt 12:28). Jesus' miraculous activity, which is the work of God's own Spirit, is a decisive indication of the imminent fulfillment of God's salvation promises. This is most evident in the exorcisms, which manifest the Kingdom's coming in triumph over the dark forces of hell. The passage does not aver that only Jesus performed exorcisms at this time; Matthew 12:27, in fact, has Jesus referring explicitly to other Jews who cast out demons. Nonetheless, there is a unique claim made for Jesus' pneumatic works. In Barrett's words,

> The unique element in the exorcisms of Jesus is that they are special signs of God's power and of his Kingdom. . . . They may be signs that the Kingdom has come, or proleptic manifestations of it; or, perhaps, not exactly either of these things; but certainly it is meant that the exorcisms are taking place in virtue of the divine Kingdom. They are not magic or thaumaturgy; they are not occasional miracles granted in answer to the prayer of a sage or holy man; they are a particular and unique event in God's fulfilment of his promise or redemption in his Kingdom.[31]

In the biblical passages before us, then, God's Spirit and God's Kingdom are closely linked as eschatological terms which find their proper context, meaning and fulfillment in the ministry of Jesus. It is important to be reminded that this conclusion does not suggest anything about what Jesus himself thought or taught about his ministry or works, but how he is interpreted and presented in the gospel accounts. Yet Jesus' own religio-historical context was one filled with eschatological hopes, often of an apocalyptic hue, and there is every reason to believe that he shared in those expectations. In his masterful *Jesus and Judaism*, E. P. Sanders locates Jesus in a "Jewish restoration eschatology," prevalent in his time, whose main themes included the redemption of Israel (whether politically or in a new world), a new or renewed temple, repentance, judgment, and admission of Gentiles.[32] His followers shared that expectation and, in light of Jesus' resurrection, believed that he would occupy a central, kingly role in the already-arriving eschaton. "The Christian movement was differentiated from the rest of Judaism by the conviction that the Lord would soon return," Sanders writes, "and this is to be seen as a transformation of Jesus' view that the kingdom of God was near."[33]

Meanwhile, the gift of the Spirit to the Church was a present experience of the eschatological era soon to arrive in its fullness, a "down-payment" on the coming Kingdom of God (Rom 8:11; 2 Cor 1:22; Eph 1:13–14).

This points to a problem for pneumatology: the Christian doctrine of the Holy Spirit has a decidedly eschatological context, so that the Spirit, on the basis of the Christian Testament, can be characterized rightfully as the presence of the resurrected and coming Lord already in his people's midst. This problem has already been touched upon briefly in this study,[34] and will demand fuller attention in Chapter 6. For now it must be recognized that the Church's claim on the presence of the eschatological Spirit provided a logical basis for an exclusivist orientation: because the Holy Spirit manifested God's soon-coming Kingdom in the ministry of Jesus, and because the resurrected and glorified Jesus has bestowed that same Spirit upon the Church, making it God's eschatological community, it is in the Church that God is present, and God's Kingdom already rules, through the Holy Spirit.

If one insists on an eschatological perspective for a Christian doctrine of the Holy Spirit, then the obvious question is whether the considerable delay of the eschaton—and it is safe to say that not only Paul, but even Jesus himself, along with probably the great majority of first-century Jews, were wrong about its imminence—will make any difference in the way the Holy Spirit is interpreted. The traditional Christian response to the **parousia**'s delay has been to spiritualize Jesus' messiahship, interiorize the Spirit's presence into a notion of personal salvation, and individualize the eschatological hope into the expectation of eternal life in heaven. This critical shift has made it possible for the Church to maintain an (empirically indefensible) exclusivist claim upon God the Spirit's presence as a foretaste of the messianic age, or even to interpret itself as the manifestation of God's Kingdom on earth. Meanwhile, on the whole Jews have rejected this individualizing of the messianic age, maintaining that a simple glance out one's window is evidence enough that the Messiah has not come. Obviously, in the history of the Church-Synagogue relationship, not to mention the Church's broader history of effects, there has been far too little testimony in Christian behavior to indicate otherwise.

The whole direction of this study, to be sure, has been to argue from a point opposite the eschatological perspective, attempting to interpret the Spirit in the contexts of creation and of Israel's covenant history with God. This beginning point allows for a pneumatology which claims a unique, Christomorphic experience of God's Spirit in the Church, but not one which claims that the Church is the exclusive bearer and only legitimate interpreter of divine presence. This does not solve all the problems raised by eschatology or by the Church's corresponding doctrine of the eschatological Spirit; for the moment, it is enough to indicate the tensions inherent in that doctrine, and to concede the correctness of the Jewish observation that, judging by the full-bodied expectations of the Hebrew scriptures, the days of the Messiah have yet to come.

5. *Transfiguration (Mk 9:2–13; Mt 17:1–13; Lk 9:28–36)*

One of the most fascinating synoptic narratives is that of Jesus' transfiguration in the presence of his inner circle of disciples, Peter, James and John, on a lonely mountain top. It casts a glance both backward and fore, sharing with the earlier baptism narrative the account of a heavenly voice proclaiming his sonship, and with the later Gethsemane narrative an intimate glimpse into Jesus' filial relationship to God from the perspective of the three disciples nearest him. Indeed, the sense of past and future being brought into dynamic relation in the Transfiguration can be extended even further: the appearance of Moses and Elijah "in glory" (Lk 9:31), conversing with the transfigured Jesus, bespeaks both Israel's history and Israel's eschatological hope, for it was a common apocalyptic expectation that the coming of the Messiah would signal also the appearance of the ancient heroes and saints.[35] Past and future converge in a present filled with God's glorious presence, but as with the baptism and Gethsemane narratives, that presence itself will become hidden, and so transformed and transfigured, under the shadow and sign of Jesus' cross.

The similarities between the Transfiguration episode and the Sinai account of Exodus are both obvious and significant. The gospels mention that a period of six days had transpired since Jesus had spoken of his death and issued a call to cross-carrying discipleship. Likewise, Moses and his "disciple" Joshua, having left the elders below, were on Mount Sinai in the midst of God's glory for six days before, on the seventh day, God called to Moses from the midst of the cloud (Ex 24:14–16). The gospels report that, on that seventh day on "a high mountain by themselves" (Mk 9:2), Peter, James and John saw Jesus transfigured (**metemorphothei**) before them. Similarly, when Moses descended the mountain with God's gracious gift of Torah, "behold, the skin of his face shone, and [the children of Israel] were afraid to come near him" (Ex 34:30). Terrien writes, "Not unlike the man who spoke with Yahweh face to face, Jesus was 'transfigured' by the proximity of the divine."[36] As the narrative indicates subsequently, the glory of this metamorphosis is none other than the glory of the Shekhinah, God's presence, manifest in Jesus. For just as God called to Moses out of the cloud of glory "like a consuming fire on the mountain top," reducing the people in the camp to trembling (Ex 24:16–17; 19:16), so in the Transfiguration a bright cloud thunders with a voice of command, "This is My beloved Son, with whom I am well-pleased; listen to Him," driving the disciples' faces to the ground in fear (Mt 17:5–6). Furthermore, all three synoptics report that the cloud "overshadowed" (**episkiazein**) them, using the same verb by which Luke described the creative brooding of the Spirit over the virgin Mariam, and thereby recalling not only the Shekhinah's presence settling upon and within the wilderness Tabernacle (Ex 33:9; 40:35), but also the continuous empowering presence of God as Spirit in Jesus' whole history.

The explicit mention of Moses, then, in company with Elijah, only serves to accentuate the numinous presence of Sinai as the background narrative for the Transfiguration account. But why is Moses accompanied by Elijah? The traditional interpretation has been that Moses represented the law and Elijah the prophets, so that together they embody the testimony of the law and prophets to the messiahship of Jesus. More convincing is the reading of Ernst Lohmeyer, offered and expanded upon by Arthur Ramsey in the 1949 work *The Glory of God and the Transfiguration of Christ*. For them, the significance of Moses and Elijah, as well as Peter's interjection about building three tabernacles for the glorious conversants, is decidedly *eschatological:*

> The coming of Moses and Elijah portends the nearness of the end of the age, and the reference to tabernacles has as its background the eschatological associations of the Feast of Tabernacles in connection with the idea of the tabernacling of God with his people. . . . Saint Mark regarded the Transfiguration as a foretaste of the glory of Jesus at the Parousia.[37]

The mystery surrounding the ends of the earthly lives of Moses and Elijah contributed to a considerable amount of Jewish speculation concerning their importance in heaven and in future events. Elijah "went up by a whirlwind to heaven" (2 Kgs 2:11) and was expected to return as a forerunner of the Day of the Lord (Mal 4:5–6); Moses' death was unseen and his grave unknown (Deut 34:6), leading, in the first-century work "The Assumption of Moses," to speculation concerning its protagonist's pre-existence and present role as intercessor in the unseen world.[38] Midrash such as Deuteronomy Rabbah 9:5, which has God saying to Moses,

"In this age thou didst lead my sons, and into the age to come I will lead them by thee," illustrates also the continuing preeminence of Moses in Jewish hopes for the future. Thus there is support for Lohmeyer's claim that "the entry of Moses and Elijah indicates that the end of time, the day of deliverance and establishment of an everlasting reign of God is imminent."[39]

This interpretation makes sense of Peter's blurting suggestion about building tabernacles for Jesus, Moses and Elijah. It has been suggested that the setting for the Transfiguration account was the Feast of Tabernacles, during which messianic hopes were especially high. The eschatological flavor of the Feast is explicit, for example, in Zechariah 14:16–19, in which the Day of the Lord includes an annual celebration in Jerusalem of the Feast of Booths by the nations who had once opposed Jerusalem and its people. The messianic age would be characterized by God's tabernacling with God's own people and with "the nations." Even the cloud of God's glorious presence, from which God's voice is about to interrupt Peter's proposal, was expected to reappear in the end time (2 Mac 2:8). The entire glorious manifestation on the mount of transfigured presence bathes the disciples in an eschatological aura. So interpreted, Peter's statement means, "Here and now let the tabernacling begin, with the Messiah and Moses and Elijah dwelling in glory."[40]

The narrative immediately replies, instead, with one of the classic deconstructive moments in the gospels. Peter longs to prolong this "mountain-top experience" of pure and unambiguous divine presence so powerfully symbolized in eschatological hope. Even the sudden manifestation of the Shekhinah as a bright cloud initially appears to confirm that hope. But then issues a voice, directing attention to Jesus as God's beloved Son and spokesman, and immediately all the trappings of eschatological glory—Moses, Elijah, the cloud, even the brightness of Jesus' transfiguration—are gone. "And all at once they looked around and saw no one with them anymore, except Jesus alone" (Mk 9:8). In a glance the glory of the transfigurative presence is already vanished, and all that remains is a de-glorified man and the **bat kol** ringing in their ears. The messianic dream has been interrupted, the eschatological glory displaced, by the simple command to heed Jesus' words (Mk 9:7).

This sudden, deconstructive transformation of transfiguration even works backward into the narrative to suggest another meaning for the appearance of Moses and Elijah. Both of them had, in their earthly lives, encountered God on God's holy mountain. But neither of them, despite their yearnings, had been granted the moment of full and unambiguous presence. Moses prayed to see God's glory, but received only a glimpse of a fleeting backside—and that from within the narrow cleft of a rock! (Ex 33:18ff). A despairing Elijah perhaps hoped to witness a display of God's mighty power and presence in a wind, earthquake and fire reminiscent of Sinai, but perceived God's presence only in a voice, "a sound of a gentle blowing" (1 Kgs 19:9ff). In both situations, a desire for pure presence is met with the commanding Voice. Remembering that, for Derrida, the word "face" is a metaphor for presence, his observation that "the face of God which commands while hiding itself is at once more and less a face than all faces"[41] is eminently apropos.

However, traditional Christian interpretation of the Transfiguration has tended to become fixated upon the eschatological dream of pure presence exemplified in Peter. Accordingly, Kittel writes that "His Transfiguration is the anticipation of His Eschatology," and Ramsey that "the Transfiguration does indicate that the messianic age is already being realized: Jesus *is* the Messiah, the Kingdom of God *is* here, the age to come *is* breaking into this world."[42] But the narrative in its entirety, finding its surprising denouement in a de-glorified Jesus leading his undoubtedly puzzled disciples back into the valley of human suffering and sorrow (Mk 9:14–29), is far less triumphal. Can it not then be interpreted as a reversal of the Christian claim of eschatological inbreaking in Jesus? Rather than pure presence, does not the Transfiguration narrative leave us finally only with the command to "listen to him"?

On this reading, God's presence as Spirit is not the pure, unambiguous presence of the eschatological age breaking in upon the world through the Church. Rather, the Spirit directs Jesus' disciples back to heeding and following the Nazarene in compassionate ministry; back into the valley of history and human responsibility for its course; back to tracking God's presence through hearing, and continually interpreting, the words of him we confess to be the Christ. In short, this interpretation of the Transfiguration directs us onto the way of the cross (Mk 8:31–34; Lk 9:31).

6. Crucifixion (Mk 15:22–38; Heb 12:4; 9:14)

In the art museum at Yad Vashem, the Holocaust Martyrs' and Heroes' Remembrance Authority in Jerusalem, there is displayed a series of black-and-white prints whose stark images portray some of the Holocaust's horrors and truths. One of the most striking prints shows a seemingly endless line of human figures, backs to the viewer, trudging away

toward a distant vanishing point on the horizon. They are hemmed in on
either side by insurmountable black walls. In the foreground, blocking off
escape from behind, is an armed Nazi soldier. But he is doing more than
preventing escape; his back to the viewer, he is pulling down another
human figure, skinny and bleeding, from a cross. And more than pulling,
he is tugging on him, nearly tearing him off to force him to join in the
death march. The crossbar of the crucifix points toward the deathly vanishing point on the horizon, indicating the **via dolorosa** not only for this
pathetic figure but for all those marching before him. The head of this
crucified one is turned toward the viewer: his blank but weary expression
and imploring eyes seem to ask, "How many more times must this
happen?"

Is there a better way than this to answer Emil Fackenheim's simple
question, "Where would Jesus of Nazareth have been in Nazi-occupied
Europe?"[43] The question is rhetorical, but it points out the fundamental
truth that the best context for understanding Jesus' crucifixion is found in
history's repeated attempts at "the crucifixion of the Jews" (Littell). For it
is in this uniquely chosen people's suffering for the sake of Torah and
covenant, singled out because they unavoidably represent God's presence
in a God-hating world, that Jesus' own suffering finds its first meaning. It
is always instructive to recall that, during the Roman occupation of the
land and people of Israel, Jesus was but one of many thousands of Jews
who were murdered on crosses and by other means. Indeed, another Jew,
whose death for God's sake is considered by Jews a model of **kiddush
hashem**, and who could equally come to remind the Gentiles of the many
Jews who have died on common ground with Jesus, is Rabbi Akiva, killed
about a century later. He is remembered for having died with the **Sh'ma**
on his lips, his skin raked from his body with hot iron combs by the
Romans, counting himself blessed for the opportunity to love God with
heart, soul and strength. " 'When shall I have the opportunity of fulfilling
this [commandment]? Now that I have the opportunity shall I not fulfill
it?' He prolonged the word 'One' until he expired while saying it" (T.B.
Berakhot 61b).[44]

Thus, as Paul van Buren has indicated, the cross of Jesus should
remind Christians of God's conflict with a recalcitrant world—a conflict
in which Israel, called to God's side, is forever involved.[45] If this is so, then
by the same token the suffering and murder of millions of God's people
Israel in the Holocaust may remind Christians of the intimate connection
between the attempted genocide of the Jews in our own time and Jesus'
passion twenty centuries ago, indeed of God's own eternally suffering

presence in a God-forsaking world. Traditional Christian theories of the cross have tended, however, to obscure such continuities, fixating instead upon Jesus' cross as the sole and exclusive site of divine suffering. This is particularly the case in so-called "substitutionary" theories of atonement, in which Jesus' passion is isolated as the only suffering that truly matters, thus tending to numb Christians both to the suffering of others, and to the gospel's call to a suffering discipleship in following Jesus (Mk 8:34).

It is the assumption of this chapter, however, that Jesus' suffering in solidarity with the covenant people Israel is the first meaning of his cross.[46] Beyond this primary consideration, it must be asked whether this study's pneumatological perspective on Christology contributes anything more. In other words, how does Jesus' death qualify as a pneumatic moment? Admittedly, there is very little by way of explicit scriptural reference to the Spirit in connection with the crucifixion. But if it is not inappropriate to read the whole of Jesus' life and ministry as being grounded in and empowered by the Spirit of God, then his cross certainly may also be so interpreted. This would seem to be the perspective offered in Hebrews 9:14, which says that "Christ . . . through the eternal Spirit offered Himself without blemish to God." In a Spirit-filled life of compassion and servanthood, the humility and self-sacrifice of the cross is, in fact, the zenith of Jesus' anointed ministry. As Alisdair Heron has written,

> [The Holy Spirit] is the motive and power of his dedication to the Father, which culminates and is sealed upon the cross. . . . The decisive actualisation of the presence of God's Spirit in human life and history is encompassed in his offering of himself.[47]

If Jesus' entire life of self-giving—finally exemplified in his death on the cross—was empowered and motivated by the Spirit, then the name "Suffering Servant" first and best describes the Holy Spirit of God, or God's own presence in relationship to creation and human history. God's presence as Spirit *is* a suffering servant in the world, manifested in Israel's entire history, but re-presented for the Church in Jesus' own history and summed up in his cross. In words reminiscent of Kierkegaard, Arnold Come writes, "The Spirit of God, as manifested and related to men in and through Jesus . . . comes with all his creative power in the **incognito**, which is yet a revelation of his true being, in the form of the Suffering Servant."[48] Here we arrive at the heart of a Christian response to the problem of evil—the problem which, in reality, has tracked us from Chapter Three down to this moment. That response is that, in the cross of

Jesus as the Spirit-filled, Spirit-led man, God's own suffering at the hands of God's world is revealed; God bears the pain of a world gone awry. In that cross is revealed to the Church a divine love which calls creation into existence as an "other" distinct from God the Creator, a love which calls human beings and communities into partnership with God the Redeemer, and a love which suffers under humanity's repeated rejections of those covenantal overtures in creation and redemption. In the poetic words of Charles Allen Dinsmore, "There was a cross in the heart of God before there was one planted on the green hill outside Jerusalem."[49] The understanding of the Spirit's alluring activity in creation as presented in Chapter 2, and the profound sense of divine vulnerability symbolized in the Shekhinah's exile as explored in Chapters 3 and 4, find confirmation in a pneumatology of the cross in which God the Spirit is revealed in the suffering and death of Jesus. For in this process-relational interpretation of Shekhinah/Spirit, God's presence is given in the aim which God presents to every occasion of creation, and both God and creation suffer when the divine vision of **shalom** is rejected or compromised by the creatures. God, then, in patience and longsuffering, *creates a world of freedom, and bears the sin and suffering that freedom inevitably entails,* throughout history. God bears sin precisely by "bearing with" this free "other" which God calls into existence and into partnership, continually calling humanity to a turning toward covenantal responsibility. Contrary to one traditional interpretation, the cross of Jesus does not effect a change in God's orientation toward humanity and creation; rather, it is an exemplification of God's eternal commitment to lead creation noncoercively toward the vision of **shalom**.

> Listen to Me, O house of Jacob,
>   and all the remnant of the house of Israel,
> You who have been borne by Me from birth,
>   and have been carried from the womb;
> Even to your old age, I shall be the same,
>   and even to your graying years I shall bear you!
> I have done it, and I shall carry you;
>   and I shall bear you, and I shall deliver you (Is 46:3–4).

The "exile of the Shekhinah" has narrated for Jews this intuition of God as a suffering servant, just as surely as Christ's cross has for Christians.

Tragically, this interpretation of the God-world relationship means, too, that those who respond faithfully to God's call also will suffer, for such a response places them in a position of conflict with most of the rest of the world. Such is one meaning of Jesus' cross, as well as of the martyrs of both Jewish and Christian traditions. But the ironic twist is that, in much of Christendom's history, this is a meaning most deeply felt by the Jewish people, who have suffered so much in the shadow of the cross. It cannot be surprising if most Jews today yet experience a tinge of revulsion at the sight of a crucifix, since it has been for centuries a symbol of their *own* suffering under Christian vilification, crusades, inquisitions, pogroms and apathy. And in fact the Jewish people have most often been persecuted for refusing, out of faithfulness to the covenant founded upon Torah, to conform. So it has been that, because of a commitment to respond to God's aims mediated through their tradition, the Jewish people often have suffered greatly. Robert Willis said it well:

> What is presented [in the Holocaust] is the dreadful irony of a community, long accused of the crime of deicide, embodying totally the image of crucifixion claimed by the church as the most potent symbol of God's love and the meaning of discipleship.[50]

We have, in a sense, come full circle: from the suffering of the Jewish people in history as the primary context for understanding Jesus' own death, to the ironic fact that the people of Israel have more effectively, if unwillingly, embodied the meaning of the cross than has the Church which marches "as to war, with the cross of Jesus going on before." The Jewish people have historically, and understandably, preferred to comprehend their sufferings through the paradigm of the **Akedah**, but as indicated earlier in this chapter, the cross itself can also be interpreted effectively through that same paradigm. Either image still points to a God present in suffering: to the Shekhinah manifest in Abraham's and Isaac's sacrifice, or to the Spirit most fully present in the human experience of deepest absence. It is appropriate, then, that the only words which Mark's gospel attributes to Jesus on the cross are a quotation from the scriptures of his people, spoken countless times by other Jews both before him and after: "My God, my God, why have you forsaken me?" (Ps 22:1; Mk 15:34).

7. Resurrection (Mk 16; Acts 2:32–33; Rom 1:4, 8:11)

"My God, my God . . ."

The despair of Jesus upon the cross should not be taken lightly nor passed over too quickly. If he could tell his inner circle of disciples in Gethsemane's garden the night before, "My soul is deeply grieved to the point of death" (Mk 14:34), how much deeper was his despair on the cross, having been forsaken by those same disciples and apparently by God as well? This consideration should provide a reply to yet another of Fackenheim's imaginative questions addressed to the Christian theologian: "Could Jesus of Nazareth have been made into a **Muselman**?"[51] Could a Christ of the Nazi death camps finally be reduced to a walking dead man, dehumanized to a point of virtual non-identity? It is a troubling question. Fackenheim suggests that a negative response to this question makes a mockery of the Christian concern to affirm the full humanity of Jesus, but that a positive response would deny either his deity or the efficacy of God's sustaining, empowering presence in him. Thus he writes, "However the Christian theologian seeks to understand the Good News that is his heritage, it is ruptured by the Holocaust. One ponders this awesome fact and is shaken."[52]

What Fackenheim fails to see is that the gospel or "good news" does not rest on any premise concerning the immunity of Jesus from the destructive forces in the world, whether on the cross or in the dehumanizing processes of the Nazi camps. *Of course Jesus could have been made into a Muselman!* The gospel lies precisely in the faith and proclamation of *resurrection*—God's mysterious "raising up" of *precisely* this crucified, debased, even despairing man on the cross, Jesus of Nazareth. It is the faith that God's animating Spirit can breathe upon the dead, dry bones of history's waste and re-create dehumanized human beings in God's image. It is the faith that Jesus' cry of dereliction, "My God . . . ?" was answered "on the third day," and that God's resurrecting power provides the ground for hope even yet for the **Muselmanner** and burning children, the gassed and the hanged, for all the victims of the camps—and for every other nameless victim, forgotten by history but remembered by God. This is the gospel, a gospel of resurrection, a gospel which, as Pinchas Lapide has shown, is essentially Jewish.[53]

It is clear that, in the apostolic proclamation of the gospel, the resurrection of Jesus is *the* eschatological act of God, vindicating Jesus' life and ministry as God's own cause and announcing the dawning of the eschatological age, which in Jewish hope had been characterized by the pouring out of God's Spirit and the general resurrection of the dead. This hope, for the early, predominantly Jewish Church, was focused and proleptically fulfilled in Jesus of Nazareth. The first Christian sermon, as presented in

Acts 2, exemplifies this eschatologically focused emphasis upon resurrection and the Holy Spirit:

> Men of Israel, listen to these words: Jesus the Nazarene, a man attested to you by God with miracles and wonders and signs which God performed through Him in your midst, just as you yourselves know— . . . This Jesus God raised up again, to which we are all witnesses. Therefore having been exalted to the right hand of God, and having received from the Father the promise of the Holy Spirit, He has poured forth this which you both see and hear (Acts 2:22, 32–33).

Paul, too, evidently quoting an early creedal hymn, states that Jesus "was declared the Son of God with power by the resurrection from the dead, according to the Spirit of holiness" (Rom 1:4), and reminds the church at Rome that their own resurrection hope is based upon the indwelling of "the Spirit of Him who raised Jesus from the dead" (8:11). Thus Jesus' own resurrection, which provides the hope and basis for the resurrection of those who believe in him, is understood in eschatological terms as the act of God's outpoured Spirit. Jesus, having received the Spirit promised in Joel, has become transformed into a "spiritual body," a "life-giving spirit" (1 Cor 15:44–45), "a creature fully in the dimension of God,"[54] and is now the one who bestows that Spirit upon the eschatological community of Christian believers.

It is this faith in God's resurrection of Jesus through the creative power of God's own Spirit which enabled his early followers to interpret his life and ministry retrospectively as the work of the Holy Spirit, and so provided the basis for the early Spirit Christologies. This is particularly so in the case of his life's end in crucifixion. The Spirit who transformed the crucified Jesus into "a life-giving spirit," who transformed the disciples' own despair at Jesus' death into joy and wonderment at his mysterious living presence in their midst, now also transformed their apprehension of the cross. It first had been the unspeakable murder of an innocent man by the representatives of a politics of power on "the wooden instrument of a dreamer's death"; it now became God's own act by which human beings are confronted by the love and grace of God, "the supreme altar of the Christian faith."[55] So now the cross, comprehended through the prism of resurrection, was understood to have been no unexpected tragedy for God but rather the culminating point of an entire history of the Spirit's continual activity in and through Jesus—back all the way to his very conception and, as suggested earlier in this chapter, even prior to his conception in the pre-existence of the Spirit in the history of Israel. Likewise in forward trajectory, the transformative Spirit of resurrection bespoke the fact that God, not despair and death, has the final word, for this God could be characterized as the One "who gives life to the dead and calls into being that which does not exist," the One who has "raised Jesus our Lord from the dead" (Rom 4:17, 24).

Such has been the admittedly triumphalist reply of Christian faith to the cross and, by implication, to every human experience of abandonment or ambiguity, despair or death. Jesus' cry, "My God, my God," has been readily forgotten in favor of eschatological presence, the absence of God displaced by the resurrected Christ. But while Christian faith rightly holds, and holds tightly, to the answer of resurrection, it cannot be glibly bandied about as though it represents the unambiguous manifestation of divine presence, or the irresistible inbreaking of the eschatological fulfillment. Belief in Jesus' resurrection inevitably went hand-in-hand with faith in his soon return, but the obvious fact is that the end of history in the **parousia**, and the accompanying general resurrection of the dead, did not occur as the early Church expected. Instead, Christians have lived and died for nearly twenty centuries: through the political intrigue of ecclesiastical power brokerage; through the bloody Crusades; through a long-standing tradition of anti-Judaism; through inquisitions, pogroms and witch hunts; and in this century through perhaps the Church's worst failure ever of nerve and compassion, its relative silence during Hitler's attempted genocide of the Jewish people. Thus Lapide's observation, "The resurrection of Jesus was ambiguous as an event, but unambiguous in the history of its effect,"[56] is indefensible and particularly incomprehensible when offered by a Jew. To put it mildly, God's presence in this presumably eschatological age of the Church has been, at best, ambiguous.

I suggest that, just as Jesus' resurrection provided his disciples with a hermeneutic lens by which to read his life and ministry, so now the past twenty centuries of the Church's history in the world might provide a lens by which to read Jesus' resurrection. When such a hermeneutic of ambiguity, even of exile, is practiced, it becomes apparent that the triumphalist claim of eschatological presence is overblown. For in the gospel's resurrection accounts there is no full and given "presence" of Christ. Rather, there are various fleeting and conflicting sketches whose one point of unanimity seems to be an empty tomb—which hints only indirectly and inversely at divine presence. It is but a trace of God, a presence denoted by absence. The earliest manuscripts of Mark's gospel end with the women fleeing the tomb in trembling astonishment, afraid to say anything (16:8). Matthew narrates that, when the resurrected Jesus appeared among his disciples in the hills of Galilee, "some were doubtful" (28:17). There are no eyewitnesses of this mysterious event which, in accordance with Jewish tradition, was called resurrection—only an often unrecognized stranger who, at the very instant of recognition, vanishes (Lk 24:31). Even in John's gospel, with all its emphasis upon divine presence inhering in Jesus the Word incarnate, the risen Christ does not allow Mary to touch or cling to him (20:17). There is something fleeting and mysterious about this risen One which resists the theological attempt, too, to grasp him and place him firmly in the center of a secured, logocentric system of divine presence. Terrien observes,

> While the stories represent Jesus as "being seen" in bodily form, they all agree in implying the elusiveness of his presence in time and space. In addition, all of them lead to the spoken word. An appearance is never a mere "sighting." It is the channel of an exhortation, a command, or a commission. The presence of the risen Lord was "presence as the Word."[57]

And "the Word," we could add to Terrien, demands interpretation, as well as obedience, ever anew. Jesus' resurrection did not erase the ambiguities of history and human interpretation in the first century, and if not then, it certainly does not do so now, nearly two millennia later.

Such a reading of Jesus' resurrection should serve to chasten the triumphalist eschatology which has undergirded so much of the history of Christian thought. It entails interpreting the resurrection not so much as the proleptically experienced end of history, ushering in the eschatological age, but more as a mysterious new beginning in history, opening a way for the Gentile peoples to enter into covenantal faith in the God of Israel through the risen Jew of Nazareth. It understands the fundamentally Pharisaic faith in "the God of the living," before whom, and to whom, Abraham, Isaac and Jacob live (Lk 20:37–38), as having now been delivered also to Gentiles who believe the gospel, for whom Jesus, as the Christ, "lives to God" (Rom 6:10). In this respect Lapide is correct:

> Without the Sinai experience—no Judaism; without the Easter experience—no Christianity. Both were Jewish faith experiences whose radiating power, in a different way, was meant for the world of nations.

> For inscrutable reasons the resurrection faith of Golgotha was necessary in order to carry the message of Sinai into the world.[58]

Whether and how this movement of resurrection faith into the Gentile world can be interpreted from an eschatological perspective is the burden of Chapter 6. For now, it must be said that Jesus' resurrection by God's Spirit is a mysterious, flickering hope in the midst of human history's long catalogue of atrocities, suffering and death—but not an unambiguous guarantee of a victorious future.

B. THE POINT OF A SHEKHINAH CHRISTOLOGY

The heading of this brief concluding section of the chapter may hint at an acceptance of Schubert Ogden's argument in *The Point of Christology*. That argument, in scantest summary, is that the point of Christology is *existential:* its question is not solely or even primarily who Jesus was, in and of himself, but rather what Jesus' meaning is *for us,* which is at the same time the question of the meaning of what Ogden calls "ultimate reality" for us, and so, finally, the question of how we ought authentically to understand ourselves in the light of that ultimate reality.[59]

It should be clear that notions such as "ultimate reality," or an "authentic self-understanding" which pertains to all human beings, are quite foreign to this study. Ogden's generalized, philosophical approach to the question of Christology misses the emphases upon particularity, ambiguity and narrative which have been germane here. Even so, he has made his "point," and it remains for us to consider briefly what difference the pneumatic approach to Christology actually makes for a Christian apprehension of God, Jesus as the Christ, and particular human communities. Four summary observations will suffice:

(a) A Spirit Christology can only be understood within the context of what "Spirit" means within the history of Jewish interpretations of **ruach** and **pneuma**, and even of **shekhinah**—which task was undertaken in Chapters 2 and 3 of this study. This, then, places not only the category of "Spirit," but Jesus himself, within Jewish history, culture and religious tradition, for pneumatic influence or activity is an interpretation of Jesus' life and ministry which he shares with other significant figures in the history of Israel. This, in turn, emphasizes the utterly simple truth—so simple that it is often overlooked—that Jesus was, and is, a Jew. Ogden, for example, is so anxious to downplay whatever might be discerned about the "empirical-historical Jesus," in favor of the "existential-historical Jesus," that he misses the distinct possibility that the simple fact of Jesus' Jewishness may indeed be of existential import *for us*—particularly when the "us" in question refers to Gentiles.

The problem is that existentialist anthropology can only concern itself with generalizations about the meaning of the human condition, while the whole argument of this chapter is that Jesus' meaning is *not* univocal; the event of Jesus as the Christ, on the basis of both the Hebrew scriptures and the Christian Testament, can be interpreted as bearing different meanings for Jews and for non-Jews. Such a dual significance can be found in the "suffering servant" songs, is hinted at in Simeon's blessing of Jesus as a light of revelation to the Gentiles *and* the glory of God's people Israel (Lk 2:32), and becomes most explicit in Paul's assertion that "Christ has become a servant to the circumcision (the Jews) on behalf of the truth of God to confirm the promises given to the fathers, *and* for the Gentiles to glorify God for His mercy." (Rom 15:8–9).

Thus, at its barest level of affirmation, a Shekhinah Christology avers that Jesus in himself, as a Jew, bears existential significance: he is *the Jew*—in solidarity with his people the Jews—*for us Gentiles!* The traditional Christological concern to apply the category of "uniqueness" to Jesus should begin precisely here: Jesus is *the* Jew through whom the God of Israel has uniquely and mercifully gathered many peoples to God's own self, the "suffering servant" through whom God has delivered **mishpat** to the nations. If this seems too meek an assertion of uniqueness, it is because the Church has come to take this salvation for granted; it is no longer surprised, as the writer of Ephesians was, by the gracious outreaching of the God of Abraham, Isaac and Jacob to the non-Jewish peoples "by the blood of Christ" (2:11–13).

(b) This emphasis upon the particularity of Jesus as a Jew among Jews only makes sense within the particular context of God's covenantal relationship to the people Israel. Ogden speaks often of the category of "ultimate reality," which for him designates that upon which we are dependent for our being and meaning as human beings. This presumes an unmistakably philosophical context, but it is equally clear that, for him, this "ultimate reality" is what we mean when we say "God." Regrettably, he has divorced his "God-talk" from the only context in which it makes any sense to speak of Jesus' meaning for us: from God as the God known in and through covenant with Israel. Van Buren's point is apropos to the "point of Christology" when he deems it senseless to ask, "Israel apart, what do we mean by *God?*"[60] We Gentiles who have come to believe, through Jesus as the Christ, in the God of Israel have no other legitimate context for theology, and thus necessarily no other for Christology. Rather than using Christology as the paradigm for apprehending God or "ultimate reality," the more fruitful approach is to adopt Israel's interpreted covenantal history before God as the paradigm for understanding and reconstructing Christology. A Shekhinah Christology, drawing upon Jewish interpretations of divine presence, is an attempt to do precisely that.

(c) The pneumatic emphasis of a Shekhinah Christology means that the accent is placed upon God's activity in and through this human figure Jesus of Nazareth as interpreted by his followers, rather than upon the figure of Jesus itself. This Christology does not encourage "Jesusology" or a Jesus-cult. Rather, it emphasizes the priority of the Spirit, or God's own active, dynamic presence in creation and particularly in the people Israel, and so underscores the common observation that to talk about Jesus as the Christ is, and must be, primarily and finally to talk about God. This is supremely exemplified in Paul's understanding of Jesus' resurrection, for it is first a proclamation about who God is (One "who gives life to the dead," Rom 4:17), and what God has done ("raised Jesus our Lord from the dead," 4:24)—and only secondarily a proclamation about Jesus himself. To place the decisive accent upon the priority of the Spirit's presence in, and salvific activity through, Jesus of Nazareth is to respond sympathetically to the Church's creedal concern that he is "truly God" without succumbing to the substance metaphysic underlying Nicean and Chalcedonean Christologies.

Not that the identity of Jesus is unimportant; rather, the fact that God's recreative Spirit raised him from death is, for Spirit Christologies, an evidence of that same Spirit's activity in and through his entire life and ministry. Yet this still means that the primary actor in the gospels is not Jesus, but the Spirit of the God of Israel; in the words of Colossians 1:19, "it was *the Father's good pleasure* for all the fullness to dwell in [Christ]." This "good pleasure" bespeaks that sense of election which has been such an important factor in the history of Israel's self-understanding before God, and which is also expressed decisively in the synoptic accounts of Jesus' baptism and transfiguration. Both the priority of God, and the particularity of God's election, are safeguarded in the pneumatic interpretation of Jesus' significance.

Nonetheless, the notion of election also presumes a response on the part of the elect. This is particularly necessary in the process-relational perspective of this study, in which the fulfillment of God's aims depends upon the faithful responses of the creatures. Thus, if this Shekhinah Christology is itself to fulfill its aim, it must be free to consider Jesus' own receptivity and responsiveness to God's presence in the aims provided him. God's priority must be complemented by Jesus' faithfulness, and this *is* an integral aspect of the witness of the Christian Testament (Acts 10:38; Heb 5:7–9). This moral and relational dynamic, surprisingly enough, may find its highest expression in John's gospel, which so often seems to emphasize a static indwelling of the **logos** in Jesus. But when it has Jesus say, "He who sent Me is with Me; He has not left Me alone, for I always do the things that are pleasing to Him" (Jn 8:29), John's gospel is pointing toward something very much like the dynamic relationality of the Shekhinah in relationship to human beings of which the rabbis spoke, and which was reappropriated from a process perspective in Chapter 2.[61] It bespeaks a moral, personal union between God and Jesus, in which both God the Spirit's priority and Jesus' own response-ability are upheld. On this point it would be difficult to improve upon Lampe:

> A Spirit Christology . . . enables us to say that Jesus is authentically human. . . . On the other side, it makes it possible for us to acknowledge that through this personal union of God with man in Jesus we are encountered by God himself. In that union God is truly God and man is authentically man, for when we speak of God as Spirit we are not referring to a divine mediator. . . . It is God himself . . . who meets us through Jesus and can make us Christlike.[62]

What the process-relational approach adds to the understanding of Jesus' faithfulness is an appreciation for the historico-religious context in which that response occurred; Jesus' obedience to God's aims for him are predicated upon a "prevenient" history in which occurred a high measure of responsiveness to the Torah among God's people Israel, symbolized in Luke by his mother Mariam's faithful reply, "Be it done to me according to your word" (1:38). Hence, this chapter's emphasis upon the Matthean genealogy as the proper context for understanding the Spirit of God's work in Jesus the Anointed. This upholds the creedal concern that he is "fully human," but complements that concern with the further reflection that, as a faithful Jew, he responded obediently to the priority of the Spirit's "Christ-creating" activity in and through him.

(d) Finally, the label "Shekhinah Christology" reflects this chapter's concern to appropriate the fore-mentioned strengths of Spirit Christologies, while attempting to de-emphasize their eschatological dimension. The motivations for this de-emphasis lie in the demonstrated relationship between the Church's self-understanding as the eschatological community of the Spirit and the exclusivist claim upon God's effective presence, and in the self-evident fact that the Church's eschatological hope is in dire need of reinterpretation. The word "Shekhinah," denoting divine presence or indwelling in creation and in Israel, does not carry the heavily eschatological connotations which are associated in Christian faith with the phrase "Holy Spirit," and thus serves the purposes of this chapter well.

But the eschatological dynamic of Christian faith, and of Christian pneumatology in particular, cannot be ignored. Thus, while the readings of seven pneumatic moments in the apostolic witness to Jesus as the Christ, offered in this chapter, are attempts to interpret Christology from a Shekhinah or de-eschatologized perspective, the following, final chapter will offer an interpretation of eschatological hope in an intentionally post-Holocaust theology.

NOTES

1. Tracy, *The Analogical Imagination,* p. 235. It is this obvious and inevitable pluralism in Christology which renders problematic Tracy's own claim that "for Christianity . . . of course, the event of Jesus Christ as self-manifestation of God" is "the central exception" to his own argument that the best we can hope for in our religious expressions is relative adequacy (*ibid.,* p. 192, n. 86). Whatever God may manifest in Jesus Christ is still subject to interpretations, some more adequate than others but all, at best, only relatively adequate.

2. See, for example, Walter Kasper, *Jesus the Christ* (New York: Paulist Press, 1977); Heron, *The Holy Spirit,* pp. 126–130; Tillich, *Systematic Theology* Vol. III, pp. 144–148. A particularly helpful overview of the issues involved in a Spirit Christology can be found in Philip J. Rosato's "Spirit Christology: Ambiguity and Promise" (*Theological Studies* No. 38 [1977], pp. 423–449).

Only recently a book has come to my attention which engages the issues of a Spirit Christology in ways similar to those suggested in this chapter, but far more thoroughly: Paul W. Newman's *A Spirit Christology* (Lanham, MD: University Press of America, 1987).

3. Rosato, "Spirit Christology," p. 436.

4. Moule, *The Holy Spirit,* p. 60.

5. Rosato, p. 429.

6. On this point see van Buren, *Christ in Context,* "Chapter X. The Incarnate Word."

7. The obvious relationship between suppressing Jesus' Jewishness and Jew-hatred has been explored in Robert T. Osborn's "The Christian Blasphemy," *Journal of the American Academy of Religion* LIII/3 (Fall 1985), pp. 339–363.

8. Moltmann, *The Trinity and the Kingdom,* p. 132.

9. Rosato, p. 435. Though in *Christ in Context* van Buren is concerned specifi-

cally with developing a covenantal Christology, the following passage certainly is appropriate in defending a dynamic, relational Spirit Christology:

"It might be objected that this concept of unity, in contrast to that of the hypostatic union of classical christology, is not ontological. That is true only in so far as the metaphysical question is begged. What metaphysics is to govern the discussion of union? . . . If . . . reality is analysed in personal terms, with the relationship of love between human beings taken as the highest possible form, if reality consists primarily of relationships of love and trust and forgiveness, and then, on a lower level, of material relationships, then it could be said that the covenantal model of unity is indeed ontological by its own metaphysical presuppositions. . . . That is a real unity, but, being personal, it is always of two distinct subjects, of two partners in the one covenant" (p. 257).

10. van Buren, *Discerning the Way*, p. 80.

11. Tillich, *Systematic Theology* Vol. III, pp. 144, 145. In regard to the "psychosomatic level" at which God as Spirit works in human life, it would be difficult to express it better, or more graphically, than does the Babylonian Talmud, Niddah 31a:

"The father sows the whiteness from which come bones, sinews, nails, brains, and the white of the eye. The mother sows the redness from which comes skin, flesh, blood, hair, and the black of the eye. And the Holy One, blessed be He, puts into the person spirit [**ruach**], soul [**neshama**], the form of the face, the seeing-ness of the eye, the hearing-ness of the ear, the speech of the mouth, the walking of the feet, knowledge, understanding, and intelligence. When the time comes to leave the world, the Holy One, blessed be He, takes back His share and leaves behind that of the father and mother."

12. See Abelson, *The Immanence of God in Rabbinic Literature*, p. 80; and Kadushin, *The Rabbinic Mind*, pp. 228ff.

13. van Buren, *A Christian Theology of the People Israel*, p. 83.

14. Though Raymond Brown does not make an explicit connection between the synoptic genealogies and the idea of pre-existence, his magnificent work *The Birth of the Messiah* (Garden City: Doubleday & Company, Inc., 1977) has been a rich resource in these reflections.

15. *Ibid.*, p. 153.

16. *Ibid.*, p. 73. Brown points out that, much later in Midrash Rabbah II 1, it is written that "the Holy Spirit rested on Rahab before the Israelites arrived in the Promised Land" (*ibid.*, n. 31).

17. Arnold B. Come, *Human Spirit and Holy Spirit*, p. 130.

18. More could be said about the different intentions of the two genealogies— and more will, in the following subsection on baptism. For it is after Jesus' baptism that Luke inserts the genealogy that traces Jesus' lineage all the way back to Adam as God's son.

19. Norman Pittenger, *Christology Reconsidered* (London: SCM Press, 1968), p. 68.

20. See Michael Wyschogrod, *The Body of Faith* (Minneapolis: Winston Press,

1983); and van Buren, *Christ in Context,* esp. c. III, "The Context of Jesus Christ: Israel."

21. Marie Isaacs, *The Concept of Spirit,* p. 116.

22. See William Stegner, "The Baptism of Jesus: A Story Modeled on the Binding of Isaac," *Bible Review,* Fall 1985, pp. 36–46.

23. *Ibid.,* p. 45.

24. Quoted in Stegner, p. 46. The atoning significance of the **Akedah** is carried forward as a central motif in the Rosh ha-Shana liturgy of the Synagogue. At that time the prayer is offered:

"Our God and God of our fathers, let us be remembered by thee for good: grant us a judgment of salvation and mercy from thy heavens, the heavens of old; and remember unto us, O Lord our God, the covenant and the lovingkindness and the oath which thou didst swear unto Abraham our father on Mount Moriah: and consider the binding with which Abraham our father bound his son Isaac on the altar, how he suppressed his compassion in order to perform thy will with a perfect heart. So may thy compassion overbear thine anger against us; in thy great goodness may thy great wrath turn aside from thy people, thy city and thine inheritance. . . . O remember the binding of Isaac this day in mercy unto his seed. Blessed art thou, O Lord, who rememberest the covenant."

25. See Shalom Spiegel's history of Jewish interpretations of the **Akedah** in *The Last Trial* (Philadelphia: The Jewish Publication Society of America, 1967). I am also indebted in what follows to William Kostelec's reflections upon the **Akedah** in his hitherto unpublished paper "Abraham, Father of Faith: Rethinking the Abraham Model after the Holocaust."

26. C. K. Barrett, *The Holy Spirit and the Gospel Tradition* (London: SPCK, 1958), p. 100.

27. J. Abelson, *The Immanence of God in Rabbinic Literature,* p. 186.

28. Claus Westermann, *Isaiah 40–66* (Philadelphia: The Westminster Press, 1969; Old Testament Library series), pp. 95, 96.

29. It has already been suggested in Chapter 2 that, once the Church can reinterpret its tradition to say that the Torah is God's primary way for the Jewish people and Jesus as the Christ is God's primary way for the Church of the Gentiles, it raises a possibility that God has other salvific means at God's disposal. More will be said on this in Chapter 6.

30. Barrett, p. 87.

31. *Ibid.,* p. 62.

32. E. P. Sanders, *Jesus and Judaism* (Philadelphia: Fortress Press, 1985), p. 335.

33. *Ibid.,* p. 152.

34. See Chapter 1, pp. 24–27.

35. See Arthur M. Ramsey, *The Glory of God and the Transfiguration of Christ* (London: Longmans, Green and Co., 1949), pp. 109ff.

36. Samuel Terrien, *The Elusive Presence* (San Francisco: Harper & Row, Publishers, 1978), p. 424.

37. Ramsey, p. 103.

38. *Ibid.,* p. 110.

39. *Ibid.*

40. *Ibid.,* p. 115.

41. Jacques Derrida, "Violence and Metaphysics," as printed in *Writing and Difference,* trans. Alan Bass (University of Chicago Press, 1978), p. 108.

Maimonides, in Part I, Chapter 37 of *The Guide of the Perplexed* (trans., intro. and notes by Shlomo Pines, The University of Chicago Press, 1963), offers an interesting reflection in this regard upon the biblical notion of "face" (**panim**). The Rambam states that biblical references to "face to face" relationships denote "presence to presence." Thus, the "hiding of God's face" is a hiding of divine presence. The biblical phrase "My face shall not be seen," he writes, refers to the ungraspability of the "true reality of [God's] existence" (p. 86).

42. Ramsey, pp. 118, 119.

43. Fackenheim, *To Mend the World,* p. 280.

44. See Eugene Borowitz, *Contemporary Christologies: A Jewish Response* (New York: Paulist Press, 1980), p. 80.

45. Paul van Buren, *Christ in Context,* pp. 126–128.

46. On this see also Ellis Rivkin, *What Crucified Jesus?* (Nashville: Abingdon Press, 1984).

47. Alisdair Heron, *The Holy Spirit,* p. 58.

48. Arnold B. Come, *Human Spirit and Holy Spirit,* p. 131.

49. Charles Allen Dinsmore, as quoted by D. M. Baillie, *God Was in Christ* (New York: Charles Scribner's Sons, 1948), p. 194. Chapter VIII of Baillie's book, from which the quotation is taken, is helpful on this idea of God's everlasting bearing of sins.

50. Robert E. Willis, "Auschwitz and the Nurturing of Conscience," in *When God and Man Failed,* ed. Harry James Cargas (New York: Macmillan, 1981), p. 158.

51. Fackenheim, *To Mend the World,* p. 286.

52. *Ibid.,* p. 288. See the entire discussion, pp. 280–288.

53. See Pinchas Lapide, *The Resurrection of Jesus: A Jewish Perspective* (Minneapolis: Augsburg Publishing House, 1983).

54. Rosato, p. 439.

55. H. Wheeler Robinson, *The Christian Experience of the Holy Spirit* (New York and London: Harper & Brothers, 1928), p. 78.

56. Lapide, p. 144.

57. Terrien, p. 428.

58. Lapide, p. 92.

59. Schubert M. Ogden, *The Point of Christology* (San Francisco: Harper & Row, Publishers, 1982).

60. van Buren, *Discerning the Way,* p. 35.

61. See Chapter 2, pp. 58ff.

62. Lampe, *God as Spirit,* p. 144.

6. Eschatological Spirit in Creation, Covenant and History

We have had occasion repeatedly in this study to recognize the eschatological milieu in which Christian faith, identity and teaching were shaped during the early, formative decades of the Church's existence. The significance of eschatology for Christian reflection has become prominent in the work of "theologians of hope" such as Jürgen Moltmann and Carl Braaten, who, among others, have retrieved the Christian Testament's eschatological dynamic and made it a central issue in theological conversation during the past two decades.[1] What they have shown to be true of Christian faith in general is true particularly of Christian pneumatology: the Christian doctrine of the Holy Spirit has a thoroughly eschatological thrust. This is especially, though not exclusively, the case for the apostle Paul, in whose thought the Holy Spirit is the Spirit of the new creation, the Spirit of God whose eschatological reign has already begun in the life, death and resurrection of Jesus, and will come to fulfillment in the imminent return of "this same Jesus" (Acts 1:11; cf. Rom 6:8–11). In his insightful little study *The Holy Spirit and Eschatology in Paul,* Neil Q. Hamilton captures well the eschatological flavor of Pauline pneumatology:

> By linking the Spirit with the resurrected, exalted Lord, Paul automatically links the Spirit with the future . . . [so that] what we witness of the post-resurrection action of the Spirit can be understood only when viewed as a breaking-in of the future into the present. In other words, on the basis of the work of Christ, the power of the redeemed future has been released to act in the present in the person of the Holy Spirit.[2]

To be sure, the eschatological fervor underlying the early Christian claims concerning Jesus, the Holy Spirit and the Church was of a piece

196

with Jewish eschatological expectations of the time. Jewish hope for "the day of the Lord" included both the resurrection of the dead and the belief that God's renewing **ruach** would be poured out upon all flesh (Is 44:3; Jl 2:28–32). The Church interpreted Jesus to be the primary heir of those promises through his resurrection and glorification, and itself to be the exclusive recipient of God's eschatological Spirit, "fellow heirs" through faith in Jesus (Acts 2:32–33; Rom 8:16–17). Possibly drawing particularly from the self-understanding of the Qumran covenanters, those early Christians understood themselves to be the eschatological community of the Spirit, a remnant people who, in the Spirit, already experienced a foretaste of future glory (Rom 8:11–17).[3]

The eschatological hopes of first-century Jews, and consequently also of the Church, often were framed in the setting of apocalyptic imagery; it is instructive that both the Hebrew scriptures, with Daniel, and the Christian Testament, with Revelation, contain books which are almost wholly of that genre. The predominant themes of apocalyptic literature include: final and irresistible divine victory over those human kingdoms which resist God and persecute the chosen people; the resurrection of all people, the evil and the righteous, to receive either God's hellish judgment or heavenly rewards; a denigration of present existence in favor of God's imminent kingdom; a fatalistic view of human history as nearing its inevitable closure by the Creator and Lord; and a return to an idyllic existence promised to those who have remained faithful in the time of intense persecution, or who have died in their faithfulness. The book of Revelation is replete with imagery intended to remind the reader of a return to the Garden of Eden, to instill hopes of the advent of a blissfully unambiguous reign of God over the faithful remnant. Apocalyptic hope might be represented, then, as a closed circle, the return of history to its origins in the Creator, a "longing for totality, for total presence."[4]

It is noteworthy that in the past few decades there has been a renewal of apocalyptic themes in modern literature, film and philosophy, as well as in religious thought. One prominent factor in this revival of apocalyptic is the relatively recent realization that human technological "progress" is steadily turning our planet into an uninhabitable void. Another is the beginning of space exploration, with its extensive expansion of human knowledge, its potent reminders of human finitude and apparent insignificance in the universe, and the inevitable popular speculations concerning intelligent life, possibly malevolent, on other planets. But undoubtedly the most important factor was the manufacture and utilization of atomic weapons to end the war with Japan almost five decades ago. Since

Hiroshima and Nagasaki, humanity has lived under the ominous shadow of a self-destruction caused simply by the pressing of a few buttons. The stockpiling of atomic weapons by the Soviet Union and the United States, a suicidal competition which just recently has begun, hopefully, to be reversed, has been for many inhabitants of our planet a particularly dreadful foretaste of an inevitable, universal holocaust. The recent deeper comprehension of the indirect environmental effects of a large-scale nuclear war—not to mention the potential of such a war for direct killing power—in concert with the legitimate fear that some terrorist group is bound to secure nuclear weapons sooner or later, has led in our time to a certain fatalism about our planet's chances to survive another century. Such a fatalistic outlook—that there is virtually nothing we can do to avoid the mass destruction of planet Earth in a nuclear holocaust—shares a great deal with the fatalism of the apocalyptic mood, and appears to have led to a renewed, if decidedly secularized, appreciation of apocalyptic themes in our time.

Indeed, traditional eschatology *does* represent a particular sort of fatalism about the project of human history. Even when it does not share the extreme negation of the present state of existence in favor of an imminent inbreaking of God's powerful rule as found in apocalyptic literature, it still envisions an "end," a fulfillment, a completed goal. It may reflect a more positive sense of a new beginning, a sign of hope for history rather than its annulment, but even then eschatology, traditionally interpreted, reflects the sense of a closure to history, an end brought about by the Creator and Lord of history. It looks for, and faithfully expects, the day when, in Paul's words, "all things will be subjected . . . to Him, that God may be all in all" (1 Cor 15:28).

The whole tenor of the pneumatological doctrine proposed herein—formulated as it is within a process-relational framework which envisions the divine activity and presence in terms of the persuasive offering of initial aims to creation's every occasion, and understanding this interpretation of God's dynamic presence to be a viable metaphysical foundation for a covenantal understanding of God's relationship to creation and history—is obviously in tension with the sense of unilateral closure assumed in traditional eschatologies. Process theology affirms a radical openness to the course of history, a contingency finally dependent upon the free responses of every occasion, but especially upon the decisions of those complex series of occasions called human beings. Thus, from the process perspective, nothing is predetermined except that creation, the "other" which God continues to call into existence, actually determines its own course through the responses of the creatures to God's guiding aims. In John Cobb's words,

> God offers possibilities that would lead us into the new life we need. God lures, urges, and persuades. We decide. If we decide to enter into the reality into which God calls us, we choose life. If we decide to refuse it, we choose death, a continual dying throughout life and a contribution to the planetary death.[5]

To be sure, it is not only process theology which provides a more open-ended view of history than is allowed by traditional eschatologies. Indeed, Cobb's statement, which draws from the alternative offered between life and death in Deuteronomy 30:19, suggests that the Bible itself might offer the seeds of a different approach to eschatological themes. It is my belief that it does, and that the biblical categories of creation and covenant both can be legitimately interpreted in such a way as to create a tension between them and the traditional eschatological idea of God's unilateral completion of creation and closure of history. Furthermore, the ongoing processes of history, particularly as disclosed in this century by both the Holocaust and the establishment of the state of Israel (as I hope to show), also suggest the need for a reinterpretation of eschatological hope.

Yet the fact that God's transforming presence as Spirit in the Church has an eschatological significance in Christian Testament and tradition cannot be lightly dismissed. Admittedly, through the first five chapters of this study, I have attempted consistently to interpret the Spirit of God as denoting God's animating, commanding presence in creation and history, and particularly in Israel's history, thus shifting the focus of pneumatology away from traditional eschatological concerns and toward a more "worldly" or historical mode. But it has been noted several times, particularly in the reading of Christology offered in Chapter 5, that the eschatological problem continually comes to the fore. It is the purpose of this chapter to engage the problem directly. In what follows, then, I intend to reflect upon the significance of the Christian understanding of the eschatological Spirit from the particular "creation/Israel" perspective of this book, hoping thereby to offer an interpretation of eschatology as a divine impulse occurring *within,* rather than as a divine fulfillment which brings closure to, the interrelated processes of creation, covenant and history.

A. ESCHATOLOGY AND CREATION

From the process perspective, creation is God's ongoing activity. The word of "letting be" which echoes throughout Genesis 1 is a word which God, intending to direct creation toward the divine vision of **shalom,** continually speaks in the presentation of initial aims to new occasions. And just as Genesis speaks of God's **ruach** hovering over the chaotic waters, and just as the rabbis spoke of the Shekhinah brooding over the creation as a bird upon its nest, so in this study the notion of God as Spirit, or God as intimately present to creation, has been central. God's presence to creation is discovered primarily in the aims God provides, and since the Church uses the phrase "the Holy Spirit" to refer to God's presence, it was the argument of Chapter 2 that, from the process perspective, the Holy Spirit is the Church's name for God's "call" in the presentation of initial aims, particularly as that call is mediated to Christians through the figure of Jesus as the Christ.[6]

The fact that God's dynamic presence in the offering of initial aims can be rejected, distorted or only partially fulfilled by the concrescent occasion indicates another key theme in this study: while creation is God's project, it is nonetheless fundamentally "other" than the Creator. Especially with the appearance on this planet of human beings, created in the **imago dei** with capacities for reflection, relationality, self-transcendence and freedom, God labors within a creation which does not automatically offer faithful response to the divine aims. Creation is God's activity and God's possession, but on a deeper level it is equally God's risk: the calling into existence of that which is "other," that which can and most often does resist easy compliance with God's ideal aims. It was suggested in Chapter 2 that this resonates rather well with the rabbinic notion of the human capacity to attract God's presence as Shekhinah through righteous living, and to "press against the feet" of the Shekhinah through disobedience. God's persuasive calling into existence of a creation which is "other" means that God wills to be vulnerable, to create and to redeem through the self-limitation of internal relation to the other, indeed to live and even to suffer in that other's presence.

Creation, then, in this perspective already carries within itself a movement toward covenantal relationship. What is called "history" is precisely that creation as it is shaped, directed and interpreted by human beings.

Process theology rejects a sharp distinction between nature and history because human beings, though created in the divine image and through the divine **ruach** afforded a unique relationship to God, are nonetheless also internally and organically related to their ecological environment. That environment, quite apart from human beings, is of inherent value to God, and itself is rudimentarily "addressed" by the Creator in the presentation of initial aims, thus sharing in a covenantal relationship, broadly speaking, with God.

Within this understanding of the dynamic presence of God in the presentation of initial aims, or God as Spirit in creation, is there any way to maintain the notion of the Spirit's eschatological significance? I believe there is, as long as the "end" which **eschaton** implies can be interpreted to refer to a final aim or goal toward which God acts in the offer of initial aims, rather than to a predetermined closure or completion of history. For while process theology conceives of creation as an ongoing, open process, it also posits that God has a vision for creation which determines the aims that God provides to the creatures. Thus, the aims God provides reflect God's vision for the creation as it can best be suited to the particular context of the moment. God's vision for creation, then, is operative in every moment of becoming as the goal or end which God intends; it is, in this sense, an eschatological vision.

The creation narratives in Genesis, in fact, lend some insight into the nature of God's eschatological vision for creation, and for human beings particularly. God creates the human as male and female, in God's image, in order to rule over the other creatures. They are given sovereignty, so that in responsibility and partnership they care for the world. That they are created in God's image strongly suggests that they are to be God's representatives, to *re-present* the Creator in creation. The creation is an open process, and the human as male and female is given responsibility for tending and directing it. The human, in fact, is called upon to contribute to the very process of creation. This is particularly evident when one recalls the significance of names and naming for the Hebraic mind: in the naming of the animals in Genesis 2 the man actually is continuing the process of creation, ordering the world and assigning its constituents their meaning and place in it. "And whatever the man called a living creature, that was its name" (2:19). Creation of humanity in the divine image suggests that God is committed to a partnership in creation—obviously not a partnership of equals, but a partnership nonetheless.

But is the divine calling to humanity to partnership with God in creation negated, perhaps even destroyed by sin and rebellion, as narrated

so powerfully in Genesis 3? The stories of Babel and the Flood would
suggest that it nearly is, and many interpretations of the Christian doctrine of original sin have tended toward such a pessimistic conclusion. Yet
even after the flood, Genesis portrays a God who remains committed to
the task of a "partnered" creation. Soothed by the aroma of sacrifice—
perhaps experiencing for the first time the pleasurable urges which
prompt human beings to evil?—the Lord establishes a covenant to sustain
creation ("I will never again destroy every living thing," Gen 8:21) and
calls upon the renewed human community to respect and to protect the
lives of human beings, for they are created in God's image (9:6). The
Noahide covenant, then, re-establishes both God's faithfulness to creation, and God's demand of responsibility upon humanity to contribute
to a sense of safety and well-being in that creation. God will not do it all.

In the opening chapters of Genesis, then, the presence of God as
eschatological Spirit is actually a presence who calls forth the "other," and
gives to that other a significant measure of responsibility for the world's
course. This means that, on the barest level of affirmation, God desires a
creation whose history is radically open and undetermined, contingent
upon the degree of faithfulness with which the creatures, particularly human beings, respond to the divine call. Eschatology from within this perspective, then, points to an "end" which lies not in a predetermined and
certain conclusion, but precisely in the open-endedness of human partnership with God in creation and history.

B. ESCHATOLOGY AND COVENANT

The themes discerned in reflection upon the Genesis narratives—
those of divine self-limitation in the very act of creation, and the offer of
partnership to an "other," suggesting an indeterminate history—become
even more evident in the biblical notion of covenant. In the Hebrew
scriptures God makes covenant with the people Israel, graciously giving
Torah to them, so that they become to God "a kingdom of priests and a
holy nation," uniquely representing God in God's own creation (Ex 19:5–
6). Through Torah, God renews the call to human beings to "stand in" for
the Creator, electing this particular people to be a special possession,
partner and representative.

But one must be careful not to harden the category of covenant into a
static, once-for-all entity. Our own experience teaches us that personal
relationships undergo changes and even radical transformations, and it is
clear from the witness of the Hebrew scriptures that God makes many

covenants, and looks forward to more in the future (e.g., Jer 31:31–34). And as David Hartman argues so forcefully in his book *A Living Covenant,* God's covenants with Israel have assumed many contours, shaped by the exigencies of history. Following the destruction of the Temple in 70 CE, for example, the rabbinic transformation and interiorization of the covenant, which to that point had depended significantly upon the Temple cultus, was truly a remarkable feat. The people Israel, stripped of those sure outward signs of the covenant, nonetheless believed that God continued in covenantal relationship. This example from Israel's history might teach us that, rather than taking an overly rigid approach to the notion of covenant, it may be preferable simply to say that God's orientation toward, or approach to, creation is *covenantal,* signifying that God, while remaining God, desires to take the other seriously *as other,* to work in and through "partnered" relationships. At the same time, this would mean that God relates covenantally to the other in its particularity; that is, it is not enough to say that God adopts a covenantal approach toward creation as a whole, if this affirmation is not grounded in the evidences for God's preference for partnership in particular covenants with particular peoples.

For Christian faith, evidence of God's covenantal orientation is found first of all in the Hebrew scriptural witness to God's promises to Abraham, Isaac and Jacob, and then to the Exodus-Sinai experience of the people Israel. It is in the midst of this people that Christians may first learn of the workings of this covenantal God who has drawn near to Israel through Torah. Thus, in order to attempt to discern the presence of the eschatological Spirit at work in covenant, it is best to begin there.

1. In Israel

It is essential to keep in mind that, in the history of Jewish religious thought, there is no one simple meaning for, or theology of, covenant. Furthermore, it is hardly the responsibility of a Christian theologian to offer one. Rather, the very plurality of interpretations of covenant within Jewish thought again serves as a warning against an excessively rigid or structured framework for understanding this category. In this regard, one of the most impressive and helpful works, mentioned earlier in this chapter and elsewhere in this volume, is Hartman's *A Living Covenant,* which might be characterized as a relational theology of covenant. The sense of flexibility, plurality and fluidity of Hartman's covenantal model is revealed in his use of "a" rather than "the" in his title: it is "*a* living covenant." He writes,

> One can claim, I believe, in the spirit of the rabbinic tradition that so long as the centrality of **mitzvah** and the eternity of the covenant are not undermined, there is enormous room for building multiple images of God and of His relationship to the community, nature, and history, a multiplicity that enables the covenant to remain a living option.[7]

Hartman's deep sense of openness in understanding covenant, and the emphasis upon human creativity and autonomy which his interpretation of covenant encourages, suggest that God values highly the human community's contribution to the processes of creation. Thus, while God has initiated the covenant through the obligations of the gift of Torah, and remains at every step the Lord of Israel and of all creation, the very fact that God issues commands to the people Israel means that God considers their decisions and behavior to be of real significance. Furthermore, there is in rabbinic Judaism a profound recognition that God's covenantal will must be continually reinterpreted for a changing community in its ever-shifting settings, for the Torah "is not in heaven" (Deut 30:12; cf. Talmud, Bava Metzia 59b). Perhaps this intuition is no better illustrated than in the midrashic account of God's chuckling admission of defeat at the hands of the talmudic sages: "He laughed, saying: 'My sons have defeated Me, My sons have defeated Me.' "[8] It was argued in Chapter 2 that, in this dynamic halakhic process which is grounded in the divine gift of Torah but equally dependent upon the creative readings of subsequent generations, God's own presence draws near to the Jewish people: "It is not in heaven. . . . But the word is very near you, *in your mouth and in your heart, that you may observe it*" (Deut 30:12, 14). It is in and through the particular interpretive structure of **halakha** that God's aims for the people Israel are most clearly mediated to them, drawing them toward a share in the divine image of holiness (Lev 19:1).

Is there an eschatological impulse at work within the Jewish experience of divine presence offered in Torah? One might offer an affirmative answer to this question on several levels:

(a) Insofar as God's initiation of covenant with the people Israel is a reaffirmation of the partnership implied already in creation, there is an "end" which God envisions for the covenant relationship: that it will be open-ended, fully involving the people Israel in the never-ending process of completing creation. In covenant, God re-calls specifically this people to the place of representation, responsibility and partnership to which God, according to the creation narratives, has called all of humanity. Thus, God "raises up" the people Israel to be the model of covenantal partnership for the world, a "light to the nations." On this level of affirmation, the eschatological thrust is simply that God's envisioned "end" for creation is that a truly covenantal partnership with God's creatures, particularly those fashioned in the divine image, will be developed and nurtured. In the biblical testimony, this work which embodies God's "end" has its beginning in and with Israel.

(b) Yet there is in the gift of Torah a deeper, more recognizably eschatological thrust, in that God shares with this people something of the vision which God has for the whole of creation. Several times in this study the rich Hebrew word-concept **shalom** has been used to describe this vision. It is beyond the scope of this work to examine this word-concept more deeply, but it is noteworthy that the Hebrew scriptures, particularly in the prophetic literature, use other vibrant images for that eschatological aim which **shalom** embodies: the lion lying down with the lamb; every person resting, unthreatened, in the shade of his or her own fig tree; swords being beaten into plowshares; or justice rolling down like waters. In short, the eschatological impulse of the Torah-structured community impels Israel, rooted in love for both the neighbor and the stranger, toward justice and compassion to all people (Lev 19).

(c) The eschatological impulse of Israel's Torah-shaped life is also evident in the prophetic hope that, one day, all nations would stream to Jerusalem to learn of God's covenantal mercies and judgments (Is 2:60; Zech 8:21–23), that justice and compassion would rule even beyond Israel's borders, that the earth would "be filled with the knowledge of the glory of the Lord" (Hab 2:14). In that day Israel's faith would be vindicated, for all peoples would worship and obey the God of Israel. This, as we have seen, was at the heart of the mission of Isaiah's "suffering servant," who brings **mishpat** to the Gentiles awaiting his instruction (Is 42:4). Here, then, is envisioned something of an eschatological fulfillment, in that through the people Israel God brings all peoples into the relationship of covenantal partnership. Yet this fulfillment obviously does not issue in an end to the historical process; indeed, it more thoroughly involves the nations in God's partnership, in the divine commitment to a creation which pursues its course in covenantal freedom—even when that freedom entails the risk of rejection or distortion of God's vision of **shalom** for creation.

These are three aspects of the eschatological impulse at work in the logic of Israel's covenant with God. No doubt there are others, but the point here is to show that the Spirit of God, or Shekhinah, at work in and among the people Israel through the gift of Torah does indeed lure them in the direction of an eschatological vision. God has drawn near to this people, and called them to holiness, through Torah. This gift is the mediating structure—and a pliable, dynamic, ever re-interpretable structure it is—through which God's initial aims, rooted in the divine eschatological vision for all of creation and for every people, are offered to this particular people Israel.

2. In the Church

While the covenant established through Torah has undergone many twists, turns and transformations throughout the history of Israel's self-interpretation, there is no good reason for Christians to imagine that God is finished with the specific covenantal relationship with that people. Yet for nearly two millennia they have imagined precisely this, believing that the "new covenant" initiated through the blood of Jesus has displaced God's covenantal relationship with the Jewish people (Heb 9:11ff). The Roman destruction of the second Temple and ransacking of Jerusalem clearly contributed to this belief, but it is more deeply rooted, as has been argued at several points in this study, in the early Church's message that the eschatological age had dawned in the ministry, death and resurrection of Jesus of Nazareth. It was he who received the promise of the Holy Spirit from God, and who had in turn poured out this Spirit upon the Church (Acts 2:17–33). The early Christians understood themselves to be God's eschatological community, in whose fellowship the risen and victorious Christ dwelt through the Spirit.

The Christ-centered hermeneutical paradigm of early Christians, then, provided them a structure of interpretation of scripture and experience in which God's presence as Spirit was mediated through the figure of Jesus as the Christ. The Spirit inevitably and rightfully became Christomorphic in the Church's experience and thought, so that the Spirit could be called "the Spirit of Christ" (Rom 8:9; 1 Pet 1:11), "the Spirit of Jesus Christ" (Phil 1:19), and "the Spirit of His Son" (Gal 4:6). The last reference is particularly significant, for in that passage the Spirit is said to create within Christians the subjective experience of intimate yet obedient sonship exemplified in Jesus' own prayer in Gethsemane. Just as Jesus in his time of testing cried out, "Abba! Father!" (Mk 14:36), so, writes Paul, "God has sent forth the Spirit of His Son into our hearts, crying, 'Abba! Father!'" Similarly, just as Luke can describe his gospel as an "account . . . about all that Jesus began to do and teach" (Acts 1:1), so his Acts sequel could be characterized as a further account of the resurrected

Jesus' doings, for the Holy Spirit who fills and directs the apostles can be called by Luke, in the same breath, "the Spirit of Jesus" (Acts 16:6, 7). This identification, writes Moule, "appropriately signalises the close connection between the Jesus of history and the Spirit of God as experienced through him in the period after the first Easter."[9] Thus, within the interpretive structure of the Church's preaching of Jesus as the Christ, it is inevitable and proper that for Christian believers to be indwelt by, and to respond to, God's Spirit is to be brought into increasing conformity with the interpreted figure of Jesus; in Lampe's formulation, for the Church "the phrases 'God as Spirit' and 'presence of Christ' are two alternative interchangeable forms of words referring to the same experienced reality."[10]

But is it also inevitable and proper for the Church to claim that it is *only* by hearing with faith the message of Jesus as the Christ that the Spirit, or God's active presence, is experienced among human beings? Or that the Spirit may be equated with, or reduced to, the Spirit or presence of the resurrected Jesus? What factors lay behind this exclusivist claim? Again, it is my argument that the primary factor for the early Church was its eschatological interpretation of Jesus, the Spirit, and of course itself. For if the "new age" of God's Spirit has indeed dawned, the reasoning went, then all else will fade in its escalating glory (2 Cor 3). And it was Jesus, the Second Adam and Head of the Church, who was the sign and figure of God's already inrushing eschatological age. "And so," writes James Dunn,

> the character of Jesus became as it were the archetype which the eschatological Spirit filled, the "shape" which the Spirit took on as a mould, the shape which the Spirit in turn stamps upon believers. . . . In brief, the dynamic of the relationship between the Spirit and Jesus can be expressed epigrammatically thus: as the Spirit was the "divinity" of Jesus, so Jesus became the personality of the Spirit.[11]

The mediation of God's presence as Spirit through the figure of Jesus, as interpreted in the apostolic proclamation of his ministry, cross and resurrection, provided the early Christians an experiential basis for their eschatologically motivated exclusivism. At the center of the Church's preaching, as the Acts sermons make clear, was the death and resurrection of Jesus, "and there is salvation in no one else; for there is no other name under heaven that has been given among men, by which we must be saved" (4:12; cf. v 10). And, as mentioned earlier, the destruction of the Jerusalem Temple in 70 CE only seemed to confirm the early Church's conviction that God's new age, initiated in the crucified and risen Jesus, was on the brink of fulfillment.

Since the earliest Christian communities were almost exclusively Jewish, it was inevitable that they should interpret their Spirit-filled life and fellowship as a harbinger of the imminent fulfillment of Jewish eschatological expectations. This led these Jewish followers of Jesus to their new, Christocentric reading of the scriptures; the resurrected Jesus became their hermeneutical paradigm, since everything was rushing to fulfillment in him. Though there are countless examples of such readings in the pages of the Christian Testament, there is one that is particularly appropriate to the concerns of this chapter, for its context represents the apostle Paul's lengthiest, and most profound, extant wrestling with the question of the people Israel's relationship to Jesus as the Christ: Romans 9–11. In the midst of this impassioned struggle, Paul draws upon what was seen in Section B.1 of this chapter to have been a central biblical passage for rabbinic Judaism, Deuteronomy 30:11–14:

> . . . For Christ is the end of the law for righteousness to everyone who believes. For Moses writes that the man who practices the righteousness which is based on law shall live by that righteousness.

> But the righteousness based on faith speaks thus,

> "*Do not say in your heart, 'Who will ascend into heaven?'* (that is, to bring Christ down),

> or, '*Who will descend into the abyss?'* (that is, to bring Christ up from the dead)."

> But what does it say? "*The word is near you, in your mouth and in your heart*"—that is, the word of faith which we are preaching, that if you confess with your mouth Jesus as Lord, and believe in your heart that God raised Him from the dead, you shall be saved. . . .

> So faith comes from hearing, and hearing by the word of Christ (Rom 10:4–9, 17).

To be sure, Paul may be readily criticized for ripping these verses from Deuteronomy, with no regard for their original intent, and making them mean something quite different from what they meant in historical and literary context. But that would hardly be a charge that would make sense to, let alone bother, the apostle or anyone else in the first century. Paul has offered here a typically rabbinic reading of sacred text, in which highly creative and even imaginative interpretation yields a radically new message. In short, he is writing Christian midrash on this classic Deuteronomic text, thereby showing that the word through which God draws near in salvation "to Jew and Greek" (v. 12) is the word of the gospel, the apostolic preaching of Christ. If in rabbinic literature the Holy Spirit was "really almost synonymous with God as he addresses men through the scriptures,"[12] or God's presence experienced through Torah engagement, for Paul and most of the other writers of the Christian Testament the Holy Spirit was, as we have seen, none other than the Spirit of Christ. Hence, the value of those same scriptures lay in their amenability to Christocentric interpretation, i.e., in their capacity for pointing toward "the sufferings of Christ and the glories to follow" (1 Pet 1:10–11). This is precisely the hermeneutic by which Paul reads the Deuteronomy text in Romans 10.

It is crucial to remember that the rabbis also utilized this passage from Deuteronomy, though with a rather different reading and intention. For them, it is the word of Torah which "is not in the heavens," for God has entrusted this word of instruction to the people Israel to interpret and apply to the concrete issues and ethical questions confronting them. The biblical text expresses a basic confidence that the word of Torah is not too difficult or out of reach; it is eminently *do-able:* "But the word is very near you, in your mouth and in your heart, that you may observe it" (Deut 30:14). For both the Deuteronomist and rabbinic Judaism, the Torah is not burden but gift, a pathway of instruction, the means by which God draws near in love to Israel, and offers them aims which lead to life (30:15–20).

A critical question in Jewish-Christian conversation today is: can the Church affirm the rabbis' reading as well as Paul's? Conversely, can it with integrity still stake an exclusivist claim upon the salvific, active presence of God in the world, considering the evidence that the eschatological expectation which provided the basis for this claim apparently was a misinterpretation of God's intentions, and considering also the destructive and even genocidal impact this claim has wreaked upon Jews? Is it not possible for Christians to recognize the gracious intent of God's gift of Torah to Israel, as affirmed in Deuteronomy 30:11–14 and reaffirmed in the rabbinic recognition that this gift "is not in the heavens," but entrusted to God's chosen people to study and to obey? Or, in the process terms of this study, that this is the structure of meaning and interpretation through which the Shekhinah, God's presence as "initial aim" or lure to holiness, addresses Torah-centered Jews? Such recognitions, radically transforming though they would be of the Church's traditional reading of Jews and Judaism, do not necessitate a denial of Paul's reading, for it is the Church's confession and experience that *God has also drawn near to human beings through the apostolic interpretation and preaching of Jesus as the Christ.* The Church's perennial mistake has been to assume that its Christomorphic experience of God's presence as Spirit is the *only* and *exclusive* "word" or interpretive structure through which God addresses human beings, and it could make this mistake only by ignoring or violently reinterpreting for two millennia much of the Hebrew scriptures which it includes in its canon. The suggestion here is that, while Paul has taught the Church to read the gospel of Jesus as the Christ into, or out of, Deuteronomy 30, it is time for the Church to recognize also the validity of what is obviously an alternative reading, a reading which John Wesley would call the "plain meaning" of the passage: the one which has helped to provide grounds for the rabbinic renewals of the Jewish people's covenantal relationship with God—the Sinaitic meaning.

This proposal, to be sure, calls for Christian faith to reinterpret itself with particular attention to the problem of its traditional eschatology. Would it be possible, given such a reinterpretation, to say that God's Spirit at work in the Church, for so long understood eschatologically, can still be rightly considered the *eschatological* Spirit? Could there yet be recognized an eschatological impulse in a Christianity which does not claim exclusive rights to God as Spirit? These questions can once again be answered affirmatively, and on several different levels:

(a) It should first be recalled that a predominant Jewish eschatological hope envisioned the spreading of **mishpat,** or true knowledge of the God of Israel, to the Gentile nations. Often in the prophetic literature this awakening among the nations was portrayed as their "streaming up to Jerusalem" to worship the Lord and to receive the instruction of Torah (Is 2). It is evident that the apostle Paul himself saw his mission of preaching the gospel to the Gentiles precisely along these lines: that he was an (or perhaps *the*) eschatological spokesman of Israel, sent to the Gentiles; and that this ingathering of Gentiles through God's mercy, extended to them in Christ, was a sign of the eschatological age which was already dawning (Rom 11:25–26).

From such a perspective, it is the activity of the eschatological Spirit to call and gather the Gentile peoples through Jesus, the Anointed of the Spirit, to the God of Israel. Essentially, this would mean that the age of the Church *is indeed* the eschatological age—but that this **eschaton** does not signify the annulment of covenantal partnership through a closure of history. Rather, God's eschatological "end" or aim for the Church is that it join the people Israel in open-ended covenantal relationship to Israel's God. Even so, this does not mean that Gentile believers in Jesus become Jews; that was, to be sure, an issue which the Church in its first generation had to settle (Acts 15:1–29). For the eschatological Spirit draws Christian believers into covenantal relationship not primarily through the word of Torah, but through the word of the proclaimed gospel of Jesus as the Christ. Nevertheless, the Church is called to walk and worship alongside the people Israel, as even the apostle Paul, after having wrestled exhaustively with the question in Romans 9–11, seems to suggest in 15:8–12:

> For I say that Christ has become a servant to the circumcision on behalf of the truth of God to confirm the promises to the fathers, and for the Gentiles to glorify God for His mercy; as it is written . . .
>
> *"Rejoice, O Gentiles, with His people."* . . .
>
> And again Isaiah says,
>
> "There shall come the root of Jesse, and He who arises to rule over the Gentiles. *In Him shall the Gentiles hope."*

The eschatological Spirit of God who addresses the nations through Jesus as the Christ calls them to acknowledge, and respond to, the gift and demand of partnership for history already implicit in God's ongoing, never-completed act of creation—the creation of a responsible "other"— and made explicit in God's initiation of covenant with Israel. Thus the Church, gathered by God's Spirit through Jesus as the Christ, is called not only to sing God's praises in concert with God's people Israel, but to learn from that people the dynamics of responsible, covenantal relationship to the Creator.

Several related issues arise when, as is the case in this chapter, the Church is understood to be an essentially Gentile phenomenon, a gathering of the nations to the God of Israel, through Jesus as the Christ, to worship and serve *alongside* the people Israel: (i) It is quite true that the Church in its origin was essentially, and virtually completely, Jewish. But from the biblical perspective, this was inevitable, since the Jewish people are a uniquely selected—though not the exclusive—vehicle of God's activity and presence. Paul and his fellow preachers to the Gentiles could legitimately consider themselves to be an eschatological "remnant," in that they were those Jews who were carrying out this eschatological mission to the Gentiles. What eventually became an essentially Gentile mode of hearing God's address was, of necessity, in its origins a Jewish interpretation of God's activity in the world, for "salvation is from the Jews" (Jn 4:24). (ii) As argued in Chapter 5, the general Jewish "rejection" of Jesus provided the occasion for the word of the gospel to reach its divinely intended audience, "the nations." In fact, Paul's statement that the people Israel are "from the standpoint of the gospel . . . enemies for your sake, but from the standpoint of election . . . are beloved for the sake of the fathers" (Rom 11:28) might well be extended in this way: what is from the finite perspective of the Church interpreted as a "blindness" or "hardening" of the Jewish people to the gospel, is from the perspective of God a faithfulness to the covenant relationship established through the gift of Torah. (iii) Nonetheless, this does not mean that the Church should not welcome Jewish believers in Jesus, nor think it strange that there should be such people. Jewish Christians serve as an essential reminder and affirmation of Christianity's rootedness in the faith, scriptures and practices of the people Israel. Additionally, they, like non-Jews who join in the worship and practice of the Synagogue, are testimonies to the unpredictability and open-endedness of God the Spirit's covenantal activity among human beings. They remind us, once again, that the covenantal approach of God toward creation should not be forced into wooden, inflexible categories that rob God of the freedom to do a new thing, or deny humans the freedom to respond faithfully to the Spirit's mysterious activity in new ways.

(b) The Holy Spirit's work in the Church also conveys the eschatological impulse in the sense that God's aims, offered to Christians through the apostolic preaching of Jesus as the Christ, reflect God's ideal vision for creation. It might be suggested that, while it is through the apostolic preaching of Jesus' death and resurrection that the Spirit gathers the Christian community, it is primarily through this proclaimed Jesus' *teaching* that God's aims for Christians are actually given concreteness. God's presence as Spirit in the Church, then, is experienced in the address and demand of Jesus' recorded words and actions.

In this regard it is significant that, for the synoptic gospels, the fine point of God's call through Jesus' teachings is narrowed to the demand for full-fledged love of God as called for in the **Sh'ma,** and in an accompanying demand for love of one's neighbor (Mk 12:28–31). This means that the Church, when it listens to the words of its Master Teacher, hears a divine address already offered to the people Israel through Mosaic legislation (Deut 6:4–5; Lev 19:18). To both the Church and the people Israel, God's eschatological vision for creation has at its center an all-encompassing love, which issues in compassion, mercy and the struggle for justice to all peoples.

The gift of Torah has been given to the people Israel for specific instruction as to how the command of love for God and neighbor might be carried out in the particularities of existence. But that gift itself is in need of ever-evolving interpretations for new socio-historical situations, necessitating creative Jewish interpretation and responsible Jewish implementation of the divine address; "it is not in the heavens." Similarly the Church, drawn to God by God's own Spirit not primarily through the gift of Torah but through the gift of Jesus, looks to the Nazarene as its model of love but must continually work at how best to interpret, and to express concretely, this love manifest in him—which is a way of saying that *Christology* is not in the heavens, either! Love is a covenantal gift and demand, open-ended in its possibilities, so that the divine call upon the Church to love God and neighbor allows considerable room for freedom and creativity concerning love's most adequate expressions in particular situations. This is the nature of covenantal partnership, and in the freedom which that partnership bestows, a measure of ambiguity is inevitable. But this seems also to be the nature of the eschatological adventure upon which God continually embarks in the acts of creation and covenant.

(c) Beyond the surprising ingathering of Gentile peoples to the God of Israel through Jesus of Nazareth, and beyond the presentation of initial aims which reflect God's vision of a creation governed by love, there is a third mode in which the Church has experienced the Spirit's presence as an eschatological reality: God's presence as Spirit wields a transforming and sanctifying power in the lives of those open to the divine call through Jesus of Nazareth. That is, beyond the command of love by which Christians are addressed in the teaching and actions of Jesus, there is, at times, an awareness both of *being loved* and even *being "loved through"*; in Paul's words, "the love of God has been poured out within our hearts through the Holy Spirit who was given to us" (Rom 5:8). So, as Dunn has written, "The first Christians' experience of an inner power that transformed and made new was such that they could only conclude: This is the power of the new age, this is the eschatological Spirit."[13] This awareness and claim seems most vibrant in the Church today in the Wesleyan-holiness, charismatic and pentecostal movements which, for all their diversity and differences, place a high premium upon the ecstatically transformative power of the Spirit in human life.

Several words of qualification, even warning, are crucial in a theological consideration of this claim: (i) Christians must honestly reckon with

the all-too-apparent shortcomings, sin, and ambiguities in their own lives
and in the history of the Church; there is, in reality, little in the way of
convincing testimony to the Spirit's transforming power. We remain
quite human, quite frail, quite prone to moral failure. Indeed, it is often in
those movements of the Church where the Spirit's presence and power are
loudly and triumphally trumpeted that Christians can, through an illusion of sanctity, most easily deceive themselves. Again, the typically Jewish response to the Church's claims to have experienced, and been transformed by, the eschatological Spirit is so simple but so very appropriate:
Where in the world is the evidence? (ii) This suggests that the Christian
claim to have experienced the transforming power of the Spirit must be
tempered by, and framed within, a theology of the cross. Indeed, the very
notion of "power" must come under suspicion, due to the Church's misuse of it throughout its history. If in the Church the Spirit truly is apprehended as the Spirit of Christ, then the power of the Spirit will be the
"power" of the Cross—the power of suffering and sacrificial love. (iii)
Claims for the transforming power of the eschatological Spirit go too far if
they bypass or undermine the scriptural witness to the deeply covenantal
mode of God's activity in creation. In the argument of this chapter, God is
seeking partnership and representation in creation. Covenant means that
God takes seriously the "other" as a partner in history, and if the Spirit's
transforming presence is understood actually to delegitimate or control
the other, then it is critically *mis*understood. Thus, rather than negating
the mutuality and relationality of the covenant image, the eschatological
power of transformation, available to the Church through openness to
God's presence mediated through Jesus as the Christ, lures Christians to
higher capacities for responsibility to the Creator for creation, to mature
relationship with others, and to covenantal love toward God, neighbor
and stranger (Gal 5:22–23). In short, God's eschatological Spirit calls human beings and communities, and specifically the Church through Jesus
as the Christ, toward **shalom**.[14]

C. ESCHATOLOGY AND HISTORY

It is a fundamental concept of process thought that history is radically open. While past occasions contribute significantly to the range of
possibilities open to the present, God's dynamic presence in the offering
of initial aims is the basis for novelty, freedom, and contingency in history's course. God, then, is not the guarantor of an assured outcome;

rather, God the Spirit's labor in history is continually to draw human beings and communities toward greater covenantal responsibility for history's course through the address and command mediated by specific traditions of interpretation and experience.

In this study the traditions which have engaged us are Judaism and Christianity, though it must be remembered that neither of these is, properly considered, a monolithic entity. Indeed, the very plurality inherent in both of these traditions suggests, again, a deconstruction of the tendency to rigidify the category of "covenant," and also poses the distinct possibility that God draws near in address and command through many other religious and cultural traditions. As van Buren has written, "And if [God is] the God of Israel and the church, then why not also the God of all his creatures? God's continuity may be able to contain far more novelty than either Israel or the church has dared to imagine."[15] The fact that the histories of both the Synagogue and the Church are filled with novelties, factions, disagreements and a plurality of self-interpretations certainly would suggest as much.

It would be beyond the bounds of this study to attempt to address the specifics of God's presence as Spirit in other traditions of interpretation and experience. Yet a word is surely due that other family of nations in Abraham's patrimony, the Moslems. For if God has indeed drawn near in covenantal relationship to the people Israel in the word of Torah (Deut 30:11–14), and to the Church in the word of the gospel (Rom 10:5–10), there is reason to believe that the eschatological Spirit may be addressing Moslems through the Qu'ran. It may be that such a new, covenantal movement arose out of a failure of the Christian faith among these peoples who have been apprehended by Allah through the prophet's message. But regardless of how one answers the question of Islam's origins, it is clear that neither Jews nor Christians have yet taken seriously enough the tremendous power, the explosive **dunamis,** of the Islamic peoples in the present moment of history. In the Hebrew book of beginnings, there is the tantalizing hint that God's eyes and benevolence are upon Abraham's son Ishmael and his descendants, to make a great nation of him (Gen 21:13–21). It is significant that this promise, made to Ishmael's mother Hagar, is given after the two have been exiled from Abraham's covenantal family due to the sibling struggle between Ishmael and Isaac. The continuing Middle East conflicts seem to suggest that this struggle may be with us always. And no current issue can more clearly remind both Christians and Jews that their theologies must necessarily maintain a conscious recognition of their this-worldly, historical context, and must take up responsibility for seeking a just peace among the many peoples, faiths and cultures of our planet.

Such concerns are not usually considered within the purview of Christian pneumatology, but in this reinterpretation of the eschatological Spirit at work in history they are germane indeed. For the Spirit's activity is precisely to bring us into a covenantal consciousness, into a deeper sense of responsibility for the world. In Marjorie Suchocki's words,

> God's aim is always oriented toward well-being in the world—there is a worldward thrust to God's aim for us, so that we are pushed in obedience to that aim, not necessarily to an awareness of God but to a deeper awareness of the world.[16]

Admittedly, this has not been Christianity's characteristic approach to the world for most of its history. It has largely devalued creation and history, since often it was thought that creation's value had been irrevocably lost through human disobedience, and that history was essentially meaningless since Christ had come to redeem believing souls out of the world. Anything that happened after Jesus' death and resurrection was really only an afterthought, a postscript, to God's eschatological act. The eschatological finality of Jesus as the Christ was interpreted to mean that God would do nothing new or different in history—only that God would end it with the imminent return of Christ. Essentially, the apocalyptic framework of the Church's first-century eschatological expectations has held dominant sway, even if usually only implicitly, throughout much of Christian life and thought.

But Christian faith has been confronted again and again with the fact that history did not, and has not, come to an end. Meanwhile, the Jewish theologian Irving Greenberg and the Christian theologian van Buren have forcefully argued that, because in the Bible history is interpreted as God's avenue of activity, revelation has not ended either. For them both, the events of this century—particularly those awesome events at whose heart the Jewish people have stood, the Holocaust and the establishment of the state of Israel—bear a potentially revelatory significance. In *Discerning the Way,* van Buren has suggested that the revelatory truth of those events, simply stated, is that we human beings are entrusted with the course and outcome of history. In the Holocaust, the message of human responsibility is communicated negatively in the Nazis' genocidal atrocities; in the re-establishment of the Jewish homeland in Israel, that message is a confirmation of Zionism's emphasis upon the place of Jewish efforts in lieu of the Messiah's arrival.

For Greenberg, similarly, the divine silence of the Holocaust reveals that "God is calling humans to take full responsibility for the achievement of the covenant. . . . But the theological consequence is that without taking power, without getting involved in history, one is religiously irresponsible."[17] The countless prayers and cries to God from the camps, imploring divine justice, were not answered with the Messiah's coming as the pious hoped. Instead, the Holocaust, a technicized mass murder of human beings (primarily the Jews) by other human beings (namely the Nazis and their helpers), was finally stopped by other human beings (the Allied Armies)—and even then, much later than it need have been. The point of putting it this way is to show that the Holocaust is an ugly reminder of the covenantal responsibility for creation which is entrusted to humanity.

So, too, the establishment of Israel, so closely following the Holocaust and after centuries of Jewish homelessness, underscores the responsibility of human beings to assume political power in the divine calling to shape history's course. The Jews' return to power in their ruggedly beautiful land has about it something of the character of a resurrection, and serves the people Israel as a sign of hope not unlike the Church's Easter faith. But it was and is, at the same time, a human achievement, and like all human achievements partakes of the ambiguities of history and politics. From the eschatological perspective of the many orthodox Jews who criticized the Zionists for wanting to build a Jewish homeland apart from the Messiah's intervention in history, Israel's mundane character was, and for some still is, a perversion of divine will. But from the eschatological perspective of this study, the Israeli state is an embodiment of God's eschatological vision of a covenantal, open-ended history. As Hartman has indicated, the state of Israel provides the Jewish people with a societal context in which its covenantal obligations and opportunities can truly be exercised, a context which bespeaks the concreteness of nature and history, of land and people. There are, indeed, concrete and insuperably difficult challenges facing Israeli society today, the greatest of which is the Palestinian issue, or how the people Israel will best demonstrate love and justice to the "stranger in their midst." The fact that this issue appears so stubbornly insoluble only underscores the weighty responsibility God has entrusted to human communities to care for the creation. And if the image of the covenant properly reflects God's way of relating to the world, then it is precisely toward the "mundane" matters of land, political power and justice for human communities that God's eschatological aim is directing us. Greenberg writes,

If you want to know if there is a God in the world and is there still hope, if you want to know whether there is still a promise of redemption—the Bible says one goes back to Israel and makes the streets of Jerusalem resound with the laughter of children and the sounds of bride and groom dancing. . . . The flaws, the tragic conflicts with Arabs, the difficulties, all these are part of the fundamental proof that here we have the hidden Presence. This moment of revelation is fully human; this moment of redemption is humanly fully responsible in the presence of God.[18]

D. ESCHATOLOGY AND THE SPIRIT

There is no question that the interpretation of God's presence as eschatological Spirit offered here is radically other than that derived from traditional Jewish and Christian messianic expectations, particularly as those were shaped by apocalypticism. But if the interpretations of this chapter are valid, then the apocalyptic expection was, and is, in direct conflict with the eschatological aims of God as revealed first in the movement of creation, and then as specified in particular covenants, and finally as evidenced in decisive historical events in our own century. Van Buren writes in this regard, "For Christians there is revealed [in the Holocaust and the State of Israel] a relationship between God and His creatures more nearly in line with Jewish Halachic faithfulness than with our idea that all that happens does so solely by God's action."[19] The difference, however, is originally not so much between Christians and Jews; it is between an apocalyptic expectation of God's *sole action*—and corresponding devaluation of meaning in human history—and a more covenantal understanding of the relationship between the Creator and humanity, God's partner, within the unfinished, open-ended processes of history.

The apocalypticism in which the early Church was rooted, to be sure, had a different idea. It tended toward a fierce denial of the world and of history. It anticipated a vengeful, supra-historical messianic figure who would strike down the enemies of the righteous and unilaterally establish justice and righteousness upon the earth. Such hopes die slowly. Indeed, it is ironic that for centuries the Church has criticized Israel's refusal to believe in a suffering servant-messiah when, in reality, it has also refused to believe that God's Anointed might best be perceived in the revelation of the cross. The Church has, on the whole, preferred what it has read in the Revelation of St. John, expecting a return of the Messiah in more lordly fashion: head and hair "white like white wool, like snow," eyes "like a flame of fire," feet like "burnished bronze, when it has been caused to glow in a furnace," and a voice "like the sound of many waters" (Rev 1:14, 15).

Such an expectation was justified from within the purview of the apocalyptic tradition, for the resurrection of Jesus was interpreted within that context as the beginning of the end, the universal resurrection, the final judgment. But if indeed Jesus was and is the Anointed One of the Spirit, the Christ, then his ministry and ignoble death provide a different, more faithful revelation of God as the Creator who calls into existence the "other" of creation, and who in covenantal relationship willingly suffers the evils and sins of human history, sharing deeply in the world's pains and persistently alluring humanity to deeper responsibility and care for that world. The apocalyptic longing was, and is, that God would put an end to history; perhaps, in Jesus as the Christ, God reassigns to this lowly "eschatological Adam"—and through him to the Church and all human beings—responsibility for the creation and for history's course. If this is so, then God's resurrection of Jesus is not a spur to apocalyptic expectation, but a negation of it, even a judgment upon it, for the resurrection vindicates a suffering and crucified Messiah. Jesus' "messiahship," if it can be so called, was and is a repudiation of typically apocalyptic hopes.

There are, to be sure, many variations of messianism within the eschatological hopes of both the Jewish and Christian traditions which themselves conflict with the apocalyptic orientation. Yet certainly as far as much of Christian theology is concerned, it is indisputable that the apocalyptic genre continues to hold considerable sway in the formulation of eschatology. And it is clear that, in both Jewish and Christian apocalyptic expectation, the distinctive element is the unilateral, irresistible action of God in ushering in God's Kingdom. Thus, in Arthur Cohen's words, much of "eschatological teaching is formally a repostulation of a divine fiat that acknowledges no human opposition or human contrast, [and so] reaffirms at the end what was present before the beginning of creation."[20] The argument of this chapter is that God's commitment to a covenantal partnership with creation, and particularly with human beings in their communities and histories, is far deeper than allowed by such a traditional eschatological perspective. Indeed, God's covenantal commitment to work in, with and through human beings and communities actually becomes more evident when Jesus is seriously interpreted as a messianic figure, for the Spirit-anointed ministry and death of this "messiah" appears actually to upend the apocalyptic hope of a unilaterally accomplished end to history by God.

The eschatological Spirit, then, rather than being the "down pay-ment" on a soon-coming, unilaterally established Kingdom of God, might be interpreted to be drawing the Church into covenantal responsi-bility for history through Jesus as the Christ, just as the Spirit has the people Israel through Torah. History did not come to an end with Jesus' death and resurrection; indeed, it has not even become less ambiguous since his coming. There is much in our own century which would discour-age a hopefulness for the future and, from this perspective, there are no guarantees of a glorious outcome. Such hopes, in fact, seem rather slim, with the **Muselmanner** and the burning children—not to mention the mushroom cloud—ever haunting our attempts to affirm a hope for, or discern God's active presence in, history.

And yet, for Christians, there remains that strange and solitary note of hopefulness: the mystery of the eschatological Spirit's resurrection of Jesus. It is through this act and its proclamation that the Gentile peoples have been addressed by God's own Spirit and so drawn into covenantal relationship and responsibility for creation. It also inspires a hopefulness in our own resurrection, however understood, of reward to the righteous, of justice for the oppressed and for the innocent sufferers, and perhaps even of judgment upon those who have ignored the demands of justice, thereby threatening and even destroying God's creation. Yet for all of this, the Christian hope of Jesus' resurrection cannot be turned into a trium-phalist guarantee; as van Buren has written, "Easter invites us to trust that God is persistent, not that he is victorious."[21] It is a celebration, after all, of the admittedly mysterious resurrection of one Jew within the ambigui-ties of history—and yet it is also a sign of God's presence in history.

And for the people Israel, there remains a different, but no less strange or solitary note of hopefulness: the mystery of the re-establish-ment of the state of Israel. It is through this act, argue Greenberg and Hartman, that a truly renewed affirmation of the people Israel's covenant with God is occurring, particularly in Eretz Israel but also in the diaspora. And it is in this act that the Jewish people have been drawn more deeply into a sense of responsibility for creation and history. Yet it cannot either be turned into a triumphalist guarantee of messianic proportions; Israel continues to live, somehow, with the ominous threats of extinction from its neighbors and the closely related struggle with how truly to love the Palestinian "stranger." It too represents, after all, a strange and surprising twist in the ambiguities of history and politics—but is also no less a sign of God's presence in history.

Extremely difficult as it is to affirm God's presence as Spirit after the

Holocaust, it is these two strange and solitary notes of hopefulness to which the Church and Israel must hold tightly—and perhaps learn to share with one another more deeply—precisely for the sake of the **Muselmanner** and the burning children.

NOTES

1. See Moltmann, *Theology of Hope* (New York: Harper & Row, Publishers, 1967); Braaten, *The Future of God* (New York: Harper & Row, Publishers, 1969); and relevant works by Johannes Metz, Wolfhart Pannenberg and Douglas Meeks.

2. Neil Q. Hamilton, *The Holy Spirit and Eschatology in Paul* (Edinburgh: Oliver and Boyd Ltd., 1957), pp. 17, 26.

3. See Marie Isaacs, *The Concept of Spirit,* p. 86.

4. Will Beardslee, *A House for Hope* (Philadelphia: The Westminster Press, 1972), p. 100.

5. John Cobb and David Griffin, *Process Theology: An Introductory Exposition,* p. 158.

6. See Chapter 2, pp. 65ff of this study.

7. David Hartman, *A Living Covenant,* p. 200.

8. *Ibid.,* pp. 32ff.

9. C. F. D. Moule, *The Holy Spirit,* p. 34.

10. Geoffrey Lampe, *God as Spirit,* p. 62. For an insightful suggestion concerning the mode or nature of the Church's apprehension of Christ's presence as Spirit, see Arnold Come, *Human Spirit and Holy Spirit,* pp. 116–118.

11. James Dunn, *Jesus and the Spirit* (Philadelphia: The Westminster Press, 1975), p. 325.

12. Lampe, p. 60; cf. Chapter 2, pp. 55–56 of this study.

13. Dunn, p. 311.

14. On this matter, there is a rather interesting tension evident between the works of Hartman and van Buren. In several instances in *A Living Covenant,* Hartman downplays or even denies the validity of the eschatological promises of Jeremiah 31:30-32 and Ezekiel 36:25-27 which speak of a "new heart" in the Jewish people which would apparently act as a safeguard against lapses in covenantal faithfulness or morality (pp. 41, 213–214, 263–265). Such a vision, Hartman argues, does not take seriously God's covenantal commitment to work with the Jewish people within the framework of their actual finitude.

Van Buren, in *Christ in Context,* is obviously attempting to write Christology and ecclesiology from a covenantal perspective that is heavily influenced by Hartman, his friend and theological partner. And he does so quite thoroughly, for the most part. The real tension arises in Chapter XI, Section 3.iii., "Covenantal fruit" (pp. 275–278). Here van Buren espouses a strong doctrine of sanctification that would appear to conflict with Hartman's lowly estimations of Jeremiah and Ezekiel. Both of those prophetic passages have, of course, been important in the

Church's history of self-interpretation, for they have often been claimed to have been fulfilled in the Church's appropriation of the eschatological Spirit.

It would be an interesting study, but beyond our present scope, to attempt to discover whether their difference at this crucial point is due more to theological tradition, with van Buren the Christian theologian possessing a deeper sense of God's presence as eschatological than Hartman the rabbinic philosopher, or to differing philosophical understandings of the human potential for radical transformation.

15. van Buren, *Christ in Context,* p. 195.

16. Marjorie Suchocki, *God, Christ, Church,* p. 193.

17. Irving Greenberg, "The Relationship of Judaism and Christianity: Toward a New Organic Model," *Quarterly Review,* Vol. 4, No. 4, p. 20.

18. *Ibid.,* p. 21.

19. van Buren, *Discerning the Way,* p. 183.

20. Arthur Cohen, "Eschatology," in *Contemporary Jewish Religious Thought,* eds. Cohen and Paul Mendes-Flohr (New York: Charles Scribner's Sons, 1987), p. 185.

21. van Buren, *Christ in Context,* p. 122.

Bibliography

Abelson, J. *The Immanence of God in Rabbinic Literature.* New York: Hermon Press, 1969.

Axel, Larry. "Process and Religion: The History of a Tradition at Chicago." *Process Studies* Vol. 8, No. 4 (Winter 1978), pp. 231–239.

Baillie, D. M. *God Was in Christ.* New York: Charles Scribner's Sons, 1948.

Barrett, C. K. *The Holy Spirit and the Gospel Tradition.* London: SPCK, 1958.

Basinger, David. "Divine Persuasion: Could the Process God Do More?" *Journal of Religion* Vol. 64 (July 1984), pp. 332–347.

Beardslee, William. *A House for Hope: A Study in Biblical and Process Thought.* Philadelphia: The Westminster Press, 1972.

Berkhof, Hendrikus. *The Doctrine of the Holy Spirit.* Richmond: John Knox Press, 1964.

Bianchi, Eugene. "A Holistic and Dynamic Development of Doctrinal Symbols." *Anglican Theological Review* Vol. LV, No. 2 (April 1973), pp. 148–169.

Blau, Joseph. *The Christian Interpretation of the Cabala in the Renaissance.* New York: Columbia University Press, 1944.

Bloom, Harold. *Kabbalah and Criticism.* New York: The Continuum Publishing Company, 1983.

Blumenthal, David, ed. *Understanding Jewish Mysticism: A Source Reader,* Vols. I and II. New York: Ktav Publishing House, Inc., 1978 and 1982.

Borowitz, Eugene. *Contemporary Christologies: A Jewish Response.* New York: Paulist Press, 1980.

Bracken, Joseph. *The Triune Symbol: Persons, Process and Community.* Lanham: University Press of America, 1985.

Brown, Delwin. *To Set at Liberty.* Maryknoll: Orbis Books, 1981.

Brown, Raymond. *The Birth of the Messiah.* Garden City: Doubleday & Company, Inc., 1977.

Buber, Martin. *Between Man and Man.* New York: The Macmillan Co., 1965.

———— *Eclipse of God.* New York: Harper & Row, Publishers, 1952.

———— *Hasidism and Modern Man.* New York: Horizon Press, 1958.

———— *I and Thou.* New York: Charles Scribner's Sons, 1970.

———— *Israel and the World.* New York: Schocken Books, 1948.

———— *On Judaism.* New York: Schocken Books, 1967.

———— *The Origin and Meaning of Hasidism.* New York: Horizon Press, 1960.

———— *The Prophetic Faith.* New York: Harper & Row, 1960.

———— *Two Types of Faith.* London: Routledge & Kegan Paul Ltd., 1951.

Cargas, Harry James and Lee, Bernard, eds. *Religious Experience and Process Theology.* New York: Paulist Press, 1976.

Carr, Wesley. "Towards a Contemporary Theology of the Holy Spirit." *Scottish Journal of Theology* Vol. 28, pp. 501–516.

Cobb, Jr., John. *Beyond Dialogue.* Philadelphia: Fortress Press, 1982.

———— *Christ in a Pluralistic Age.* Philadelphia: The Westminster Press, 1975.

———— *God and the World.* Philadelphia: The Westminster Press, 1969.

———— *Process Theology as Political Theology.* Philadelphia: The Westminster Press, 1982.

———— and Griffin, David. *Process Theology: An Introductory Exposition.* Philadelphia: The Westminster Press, 1976.

Coffey, David. "The 'Incarnation' of the Holy Spirit in Christ." *Theological Studies* 45 (1984), pp. 466–480.

Cohen, Arthur and Mendes-Flohr, Paul, eds. *Contemporary Jewish Religious Thought.* New York: Charles Scribner's Sons, 1987.

———— *The Tremendum.* New York: The Crossroad Publishing Company, 1981.

Cohen, Norman. "Shekhinta Ba-Galuta: A Midrashic Response to Destruction and Persecution." *Journal for the Study of Judaism,* Vol. XIII, No. 1–2, pp. 148–159.

Come, Arnold. *Human Spirit and Holy Spirit.* Philadelphia: The Westminster Press, 1959.

Congar, Yves. *I Believe in the Holy Spirit,* Vols. I–III. New York: The Seabury Press, 1983.

Davies, Alan T., eds. *Anti-Semitism and the Foundations of Christianity.* New York: Paulist Press, 1979.

Davies, W. D. *Jewish and Pauline Studies.* Philadelphia: Fortress Press, 1984.

Dawidowicz, Lucy. *The War Against the Jews 1933–1945.* New York: Bantam Books, 1975.

Dean, William. *American Religious Empiricism.* Albany: State University of New York Press, 1986.

———— "An American Theology." *Process Studies,* Vol. 12, No. 2 (Summer 1982), pp. 111–128.

———— "The Challenge of the New Historicism." *Journal of Religion,* Vol. 66, No. 3 (July 1986), pp. 261–281.

———— "Deconstruction and Process Theology." *Journal of Religion,* Vol. 64 (Jan 1984), pp.1–19.

———— and Axel, Larry, eds. *The Size of God: The Theology of Bernard Loomer in Context.* Macon: Mercer University Press, 1987.

Derrida, Jacques. *Writing and Difference.* Chicago: The University of Chicago Press, 1978.

Dunn, James. *Jesus and the Spirit.* London: SCM Press, 1975.

Eckardt, A. Roy. "**Ha'Shoah** as Christian Revolution: Toward a Liberation of the Divine Righteousness." *Quarterly Review,* Winter 1982, pp. 52–67.

Fackenheim, Emil. *God's Presence in History.* New York: Harper & Row, Publishers, 1972.

———— *To Mend the World.* New York: Shocken Books, 1982.

Fasching, Darrell. "Can Christian Faith Survive Auschwitz?" *Horizons* 12/1 (1985), pp. 7–26.

Ford, Lewis. "Can Trinitarian Reflection Provide a Theological Bridge Between Christians and Jews?" Unpublished paper, 1986.

———— *The Lure of God.* Philadelphia: Fortress Press, 1978.

Fossum, Jarl. "Jewish-Christian Christology and Jewish Mysticism." *Vigilae Christianae* 37 (1983), pp. 260–287.

Frankenberry Nancy. "Some Problems in Process Theodicy." *Religious Studies* 17 (June 1981), pp. 179–197.

Garrison, Jim. *The Darkness of God: Theology After Hiroshima.* Grand Rapids: Wm. B. Eerdmans Pub. Co., 1982.

Greenberg, Irving. "Cloud of Smoke, Pillar of Fire: Judaism, Christianity, and Modernity after the Holocaust." In Eva Fleischner, ed., *Auschwitz: Beginning of a New Era?* New York: Ktav Publishing Co., Inc., 1977.

———— "The Relationship of Judaism and Christianity: Toward a New Organic Model." *Quarterly Review,* Vol. 4, No. 4, pp. 4–22.

Griffin, David. *God, Power and Evil: A Process Theodicy.* Philadelphia: The Westminster Press, 1976.

———— *A Process Christology.* Philadelphia: The Westminster Press, 1973.

Hamilton, Neill Q. *The Holy Spirit and Eschatology in Paul.* Edinburgh: Oliver and Boyd Ltd., 1957.

Handelman, Susan. "Jacques Derrida and the Heretic Hermeneutic." In Krupnick, Mark, ed., *Displacement: Derrida and After.* Bloomington: Indiana University Press, 1983.

Haroutunian, Joseph. *God With Us: A Theology of Transpersonal Life.* Philadelphia: The Westminster Press, 1965.

Hartman, David. *A Living Covenant.* New York: The Free Press, 1985.

Hayman, A. P. "Rabbinic Judaism and the Problem of Evil." *Scottish Journal of Theology,* Vol. 29, pp. 461–476.

Hendry, George. *The Holy Spirit in Christian Theology.* London: SCM Press Ltd., 1965.

Heron, Alasdair. *The Holy Spirit.* Philadelphia: The Westminster Press, 1983.

Isaacs, Marie. *The Concept of Spirit: A Study of Pneuma in Hellenistic Judaism and its Bearing on the New Testament.* Heythrop Monographs 1. London: Heythrop College, 1976.

Kadushin, Max. *Organic Thinking.* Philadelphia: Jewish Publication Society, 1938.

———— *The Rabbinic Mind.* New York: Blaisdell Publishing Co., 1965.

Katz, Stephen. *Post-Holocaust Dialogues.* New York University Press, 1983.

Kauffman, Gordon. *Theology for a Nuclear Age.* Manchester: University of Manchester Press, 1985.

Kaufman, William. "Judaism and Process Philosophy." *Judaism,* Vol. 32 (Winter 1983), pp. 34–39.

Killough, Richard. "A Reexamination of the Concept of Spirit in Christian Theology." *American Journal of Theology and Philosophy,* Vol. 6, Nos. 2 & 3 (May & Sept. 1985), pp. 140–146.

Koenig, John. *Jews and Christians in Dialogue: New Testament Foundations.* Philadelphia: The Westminster Press, 1979.

Küng, Hans and Moltmann, Jürgen, eds. *Conflicts About the Holy Spirit.* New York: The Seabury Press, 1979.

Lacocque, Andre. *But as for Me: The Question of Election for God's People.* Atlanta: John Knox Press, 1979.

Lampe, Geoffrey. *God as Spirit.* London: SCM Press Ltd., 1977.

Lapide, Pinchas. *The Resurrection of Jesus: A Jewish Perspective.* Minneapolis: Augsburg Publishing House, 1983.

———— and Moltmann, Jürgen. *Jewish Monotheism and Christian Trinitarian Doctrine.* Philadelphia: Fortress Press, 1981.

Lee, Bernard. *The Becoming of the Church.* New York: Paulist Press, 1974.

———— "An 'Other' Trinity." Unpublished manuscript, 1986.

———— "The Two Process Theologies." *Theological Studies* 45 (1984), pp. 308–319.

Lewis, Arthur. "The New Birth Under the Old Covenant." *The Evangelical Quarterly,* Vol. 56, pp. 35–44.

Loomer, Bernard. "The Holocaust and Theology." Unpublished manuscript, 1975.

McDonnell, Kilian. "A Trinitarian Theology of the Holy Spirit?" *Theological Studies* 46 (1985), pp. 191–227.

McFague, Sallie. *Metaphorical Theology.* Philadelphia: Fortress Press, 1982.

McGarry, Michael. *Christology after Auschwitz.* New York: Paulist Press, 1977.

McGill, Arthur. *Suffering: A Test of Theological Method.* Philadelphia: The Westminster Press, 1968.

Mackey, Louis. "Slouching Toward Bethlehem: Deconstructive Strategies in Theology." *Anglican Theological Review,* Vol. LXV (July 1983), pp. 255–272.

Magliola, Robert. *Derrida on the Mend.* West Lafayette: Purdue University Press, 1984.

Mathews, Shailer. *The Atonement and the Social Process.* New York: The Macmillan Company, 1930.

Matt, Daniel Chanan, trans. and intro. *Zohar: The Book of Enlightenment.* ("Classics of Western Spirituality" series.) New York: Paulist Press, 1983.

Meland, Bernard, *Fallible Forms and Symbols.* Philadelphia: Fortress Press, 1976.

————, ed. *The Future of Empirical Theology.* Chicago: The University of Chicago Press, 1969.

———— "Interpreting the Christian Faith within a Philosophical Framework." *The Journal of Religion,* Vol. XXXIII, No. 2 (April 1953), pp. 87–102.

Meyendorff, John. "The Holy Spirit, as God." In Dow Kirkpatrick, ed., *The Holy Spirit* (Nashville: Tidings, 1974), pp. 76–89.

Meynell, Hugo. "Two Directions for Pneumatology." *Religious Studies Bulletin* Vol. 2, No. 3 (Sept 1982), pp. 101–117.

Milbank, John. "The Second Difference: For a Trinitarianism without Reserve." *Modern Theology,* Vol. 2, No. 3 (Sept 1982), pp. 213–234.

Miller, Randolph Crump. *The American Spirit in Theology.* Philadelphia: United Church Press, 1974.

Moltmann, Jürgen. *The Crucified God.* New York: Harper & Row, Publishers, 1974.

––––––– *God in Creation: A New Theology of Creation and the Spirit of God.* San Francisco: Harper & Row, Publishers, 1985.

––––––– *The Trinity and the Kingdom.* San Francisco: Harper & Row, Publishers, 1981.

Moule, C. F. D. *The Holy Spirit.* Grand Rapids: Wm. B. Eerdmans Publishing Co., 1978.

Neville, Robert. "The Holy Spirit as God." In Axel Steuer and James McClendon, Jr., eds., *Is God GOD?* (Nashville: Abingdon, 1981), pp. 235–264.

Niebuhr, H. Richard. *The Meaning of Revelation.* New York: The Macmillan Company, 1941.

Novak, David. "A Jewish Response to a New Christian Theology." *Judaism,* Vol. 31 (Winter 1982), pp. 112–120.

Ogden, Schubert. *Faith and Freedom.* Nashville: Abingdon, 1979.

––––––– "On the Trinity." *Theology,* Vol. LXXXIII, No. 692 (March 1980), pp. 97–102.

––––––– *The Point of Christology.* San Francisco: Harper & Row, Publishers, 1982.

––––––– *The Reality of God and Other Essays.* San Francisco: Harper & Row, Publishers, 1977.

O'Leary, Joseph S. *Questioning Back.* Minneapolis: Winston Press, 1985.

Osborn, Robert T. "The Christian Blasphemy." *Journal of the American Academy of Religion* Vol. LIII, No. 3 (Fall 1985), pp. 339–363.

Pannenberg, Wolfhart. "The Doctrine of the Spirit and the Task of a Theology of Nature." *Theology,* Vol. LXXV, No. 619 (Jan. 1972), pp. 8–21.

Pittinger, Norman. *Christology Reconsidered.* London: SCM Press, 1968.

––––––– *The Holy Spirit.* Philadelphia: United Church Press, 1974.

Pregeant, Russell. *Christology Beyond Dogma: Matthew's Christ in Process Hermeneutic.* Missoula: Scholars Press, 1978.

Ramsey, Arthur M. *The Glory of God and the Transfiguration of Christ.* London: Longmans, Green and Co., 1949.

Richardson, Cyril. *The Doctrine of the Trinity.* Nashville: Abingdon Press, 1958.

Ricoeur, Paul. *The Symbolism of Evil.* Boston: Beacon Press, 1969.

Rivkin, Ellis. *What Crucified Jesus?* Nashville: Abingdon Press, 1984.

Robinson, H. Wheeler. *The Christian Experience of the Holy Spirit.* New York & London: Harper & Brothers, 1928.

Rosato, Philip. "Spirit Christology: Ambiguity and Promise." *Theological Studies* 38 (1977), pp. 423–449.

Rosenbaum, Irving. *The Holocaust and Halakhah.* New York: Ktav Publishing House, 1976.

Ruether, Rosemary Radford. *Faith and Fratricide.* New York: The Seabury Press, Inc., 1974.

Samartha, S. J. "The Holy Spirit and People of Various Faiths, Cultures, and Ideologies." In Dow Kirkpatrick, ed., *The Holy Spirit* (Nashville: Tidings, 1974), pp. 20–39.

Sanders, E. P. *Jesus and Judaism.* Philadelphia: Fortress Press, 1985.

Scholem, Gershom. *Kabbalah.* Jerusalem: Keter Publishing House, 1974.

——— *Major Trends in Jewish Mysticism.* New York: Schocken Books, 1941.

——— *On the Kabbalah and its Symbolism.* New York: Schocken Books, 1969.

Shapiro, Susan. "Hearing the Testimony of Radical Negation." In Elisabeth Schüssler-Fiorenza and David Tracy, eds., *The Holocaust as Interruption* (Concilium 175, Oct. 1984), pp. 3–10.

——— "Post-Holocaust Writing and the Discourse of Post-modernism." Pre-publication manuscript for *Semeia: Text and Textuality.*

Slingerland, Dixon. " 'The Jews' in the Pauline Portion of Acts." *Journal of American Academy of Religion,* Vol. LIV, No. 2 (Summer 1986), pp. 305–321.

Smith, Wilfred Cantwell. *Towards a World Theology.* Philadelphia: The Westminster Press, 1981.

Soloveitchik, Joseph B. *Halakhic Man.* Philadelphia: The Jewish Publication Society of America, 5743:1983.

Spiegel, Shalom. *The Last Trial.* Philadelphia: The Jewish Publication Society of America, 1967.

Stegner, William. "The Baptism of Jesus: A Story Modeled on the Binding of Isaac." *Bible Review,* Fall 1985, pp. 36–46.

Suchocki, Marjorie Hewitt. *God-Christ-Church.* New York: The Crossroad Publishing Company, 1984.

Surin, Kenneth. *Theology and the Problem of Evil.* New York: Basil Blackwell Inc., 1986.

Terrien, Samuel. *The Elusive Presence.* San Francisco: Harper & Row, Publishers, 1978.

Tillich, Paul. *Systematic Theology,* Vols. II and III. Chicago: The University of Chicago Press, 1957 and 1963.

Torrance, Thomas. *Theology in Reconstruction.* Grand Rapids: Wm. B. Eerdmans Pub. Co., 1975.

Tracy, David. *The Analogical Imagination.* New York: The Crossroad Publishing Co., 1981.

———— *Plurality and Ambiguity.* San Francisco: Harper & Row, Publishers, 1987.

Urbach, Ephraim. *The Sages—Their Concepts and Beliefs.* Jerusalem: Magnes Press, The Hebrew University, 1979.

van Buren, Paul. *Christ in Context.* New York: The Seabury Press, 1987.

———— *A Christian Theology of the People Israel.* New York: The Seabury Press, 1983.

———— *Discerning the Way.* New York: The Seabury Press, 1980.

van Dusen, Henry P. *Spirit, Son and Father.* New York: Charles Scribner's Sons, 1958.

Welch, Claude. *The Trinity in Contemporary Theology.* London: SCM Press, 1953.

Westermann, Claus. *Isaiah 40–66* ("The Old Testament Library" series). Philadelphia: The Westminster Press, 1969.

Whitehead, Alfred North. *Religion in the Making.* New York: The New American Library, 1960.

Whitney, Barry. *Evil and the Process God.* New York and Toronto: The Edwin Mellen Press, 1985.

Wieman, Henry Nelson. *The Source of Human Good.* Carbondale, Ill.: Southern Illinois University Press, 1974.

Wiles, Maurice. "The Holy Spirit and the Incarnation." In Dow Kirkpatrick, ed., *The Holy Spirit* (Nashville: Tidings, 1974), pp. 90–104.

Williams, Daniel Day. *The Spirit and the Forms of Love.* New York: Harper & Row, Publishers, 1968.

Williamson, Clark. "Anti-Judaism in Process Christologies?" *Process Studies,* Vol. 10, Nos. 3–4 (Fall-Winter, 1980), pp. 73–92.

———— *Has God Rejected His People?* Nashville: Abingdon Press, 1982.

———— "Process Hermeneutics and Christianity's Post-Holocaust Reinterpretation of Itself." *Process Studies,* Vol. 12, No. 2 (Summer, 1982), pp. 77–93.

———— "Reversing the Reversal: Covenant and Election in Jewish and Process Theology." Unpublished manuscript, 1986.

———— "Things Do Go Wrong (and Right)." *Journal of Religion,* Vol. 63 (Jan. 1983), pp. 44–56.

Winquist, Charles. "Reconstruction in Process Theology." *Anglican Theological Review,* Vol. LV, No. 2 (April 1973), pp. 169–181.

Woodhouse, H. F. "Pneumatology and Process Theology." *Scottish Journal of Theology,* Vol. 25 (Nov. 1972), pp. 383–391.

Wynkoop, Mildred Bangs. *A Theology of Love: The Dynamic of Wesleyanism.* Beacon Hill Press of Kansas City, 1972.

Wyschogrod, Michael. *The Body of Faith: Judaism as Corporeal Election.* New York: The Seabury Press, 1983.

Index of Names and Subjects

232

Clemens Thoma and Michael Wyschogrod, editors, *Parable and Story in Judaism and Christianity* (A Stimulus Book, 1989).

Eugene J. Fisher and Leon Klenicki, editors, *In Our Time: The Flowering of Jewish–Catholic Dialogue* (A Stimulus Book, 1990).

Leon Klenicki, editor, *Toward a Theological Encounter* (A Stimulus Book, 1991).

David Burrell and Yehezkel Landau, editors, *Voices from Jerusalem* (A Stimulus Book, 1992).

John Rousmaniere, *A Bridge to Dialogue: The Story of Jewish-Christian Relations* (A Stimulus Book, 1991).

STIMULUS BOOKS are developed by Stimulus Foundation, a not-for-profit organization, and are published by Paulist Press. The Foundation wishes to further the publication of scholarly books on Jewish and Christian topics that are of importance to Judaism and Christianity.

Stimulus Foundation was established by an erstwhile refugee from Nazi Germany who intends to contribute with these publications to the improvement of communication between Jews and Christians.

Books for publication in this Series will be selected by a committee of the Foundation, and offers of manuscripts and works in progress should be addressed to:

Stimulus Foundation
785 West End Ave.
New York, N.Y. 10025